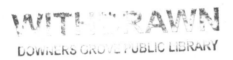

ULTIMATE X-MEN

Story
Mark Millar

Pencils
Chris Bachalo

Inks
Tim Townsend
with Andy Owens
and Aaron Sowd

Colors
Paul Mounts

Letters
Chris Eliopoulos

Cover
**Chris Bachalo &
Richard Isanove**

Assistant Editor
Stephanie Moore

Associate Editors
**C. B. Cebulski
Brian Smith**

Editor
Ralph Macchio

Editor in Chief
Joe Quesada

President
Bill Jemas

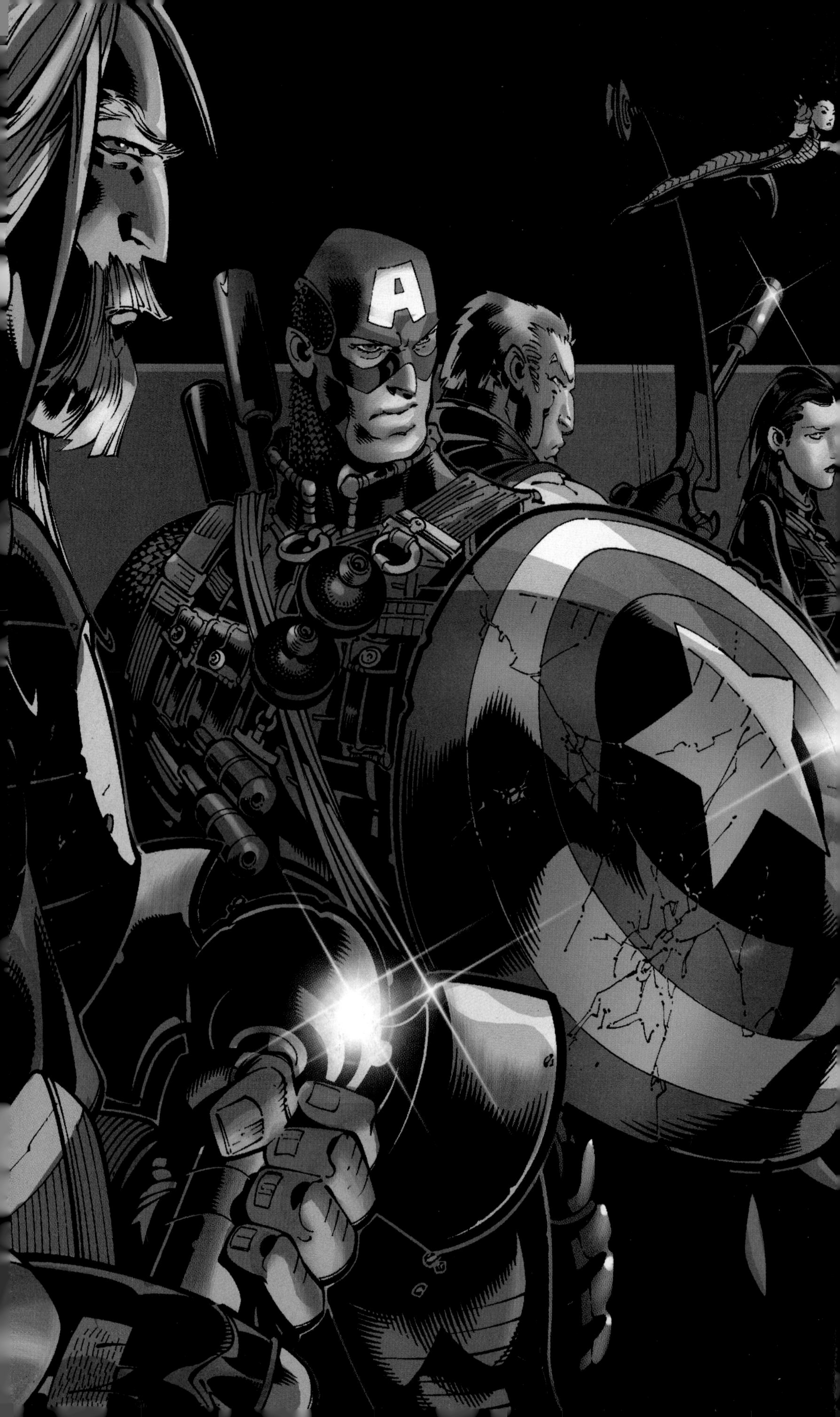

ULTIMATE X-MEN VOL. 5: ULTIMATE WAR. Contains material originally published in magazine form as ULTIMATE WAR #1-4. First printing 2003. ISBN# 0-7851-1129-8. Published by MARVEL COMICS, a division of MARVEL ENTERTAINMENT GROUP, INC. OFFICE OF PUBLICATION: 10 East 40th Street, New York, NY 10016. Copyright © 2003 Marvel Characters, Inc. All rights reserved. $10.99 per copy in the U.S. and $17.75 in Canada (GST #R127032852); Canadian Agreement #40668537. All characters featured in this issue and the distinctive names and likenesses thereof, and all related indicia are trademarks of Marvel Characters, Inc. No similarity between any of the names, characters, persons, and/or institutions in this magazine with those of any living or dead person or institution is intended, and any such similarity which may exist is purely coincidental. **Printed in Canada.** STAN LEE, Chairman Emeritus. For information regarding advertising in Marvel Comics or on Marvel.com, please contact Russell Brown, Executive Vice President,

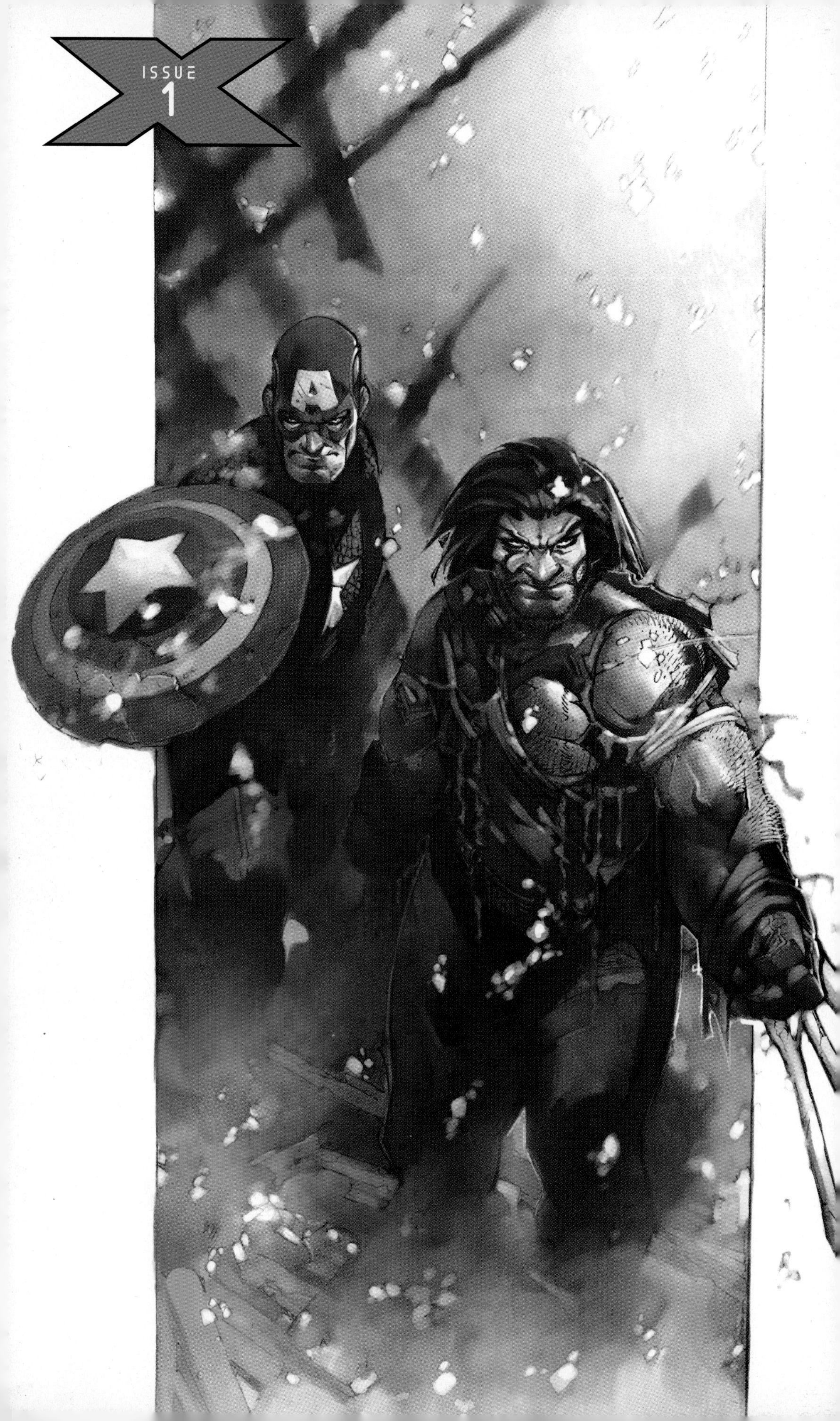
ISSUE
1

PREVIOUSLY IN ULTIMATE X-MEN:

ofessor Charles Xavier brought them together to bridge the gap between man and mutant: Cyclops. Marvel Girl. Storm. Iceman. st. Colossus. Wolverine. They are The X-Men, soldiers for Xavier's dream of peaceful coexistence. This dream is now slowly being forged into reality.

Iron Man. Giant-Man. Wasp. Hulk. Captain America. Thor. Hawkeye. Black Widow.
They are the Utlimates, a small but lethal army created to protect humanity from the newly rising threats to mankind.

Ouring his attack on Washington D.C., the mutant master of magnetism, Magneto, was apparently killed by Professor Xavier. lowever, in actuality, Xavier would never take the life of another living creature and secretly spared Magneto's life while still lowing the world at large to believe he had died. Xavier placed mental blocks in Magneto's mind and he has been living a simple existence as Erik Lensherr, completely unaware of his past life as a mutant terrorist.

uever, the new Brotherhood of Mutants has discovered that Magneto is indeed still alive. With the aid of their psychics, they are able to remove the mental blocks Xavier placed in his mind. Magneto has returned!

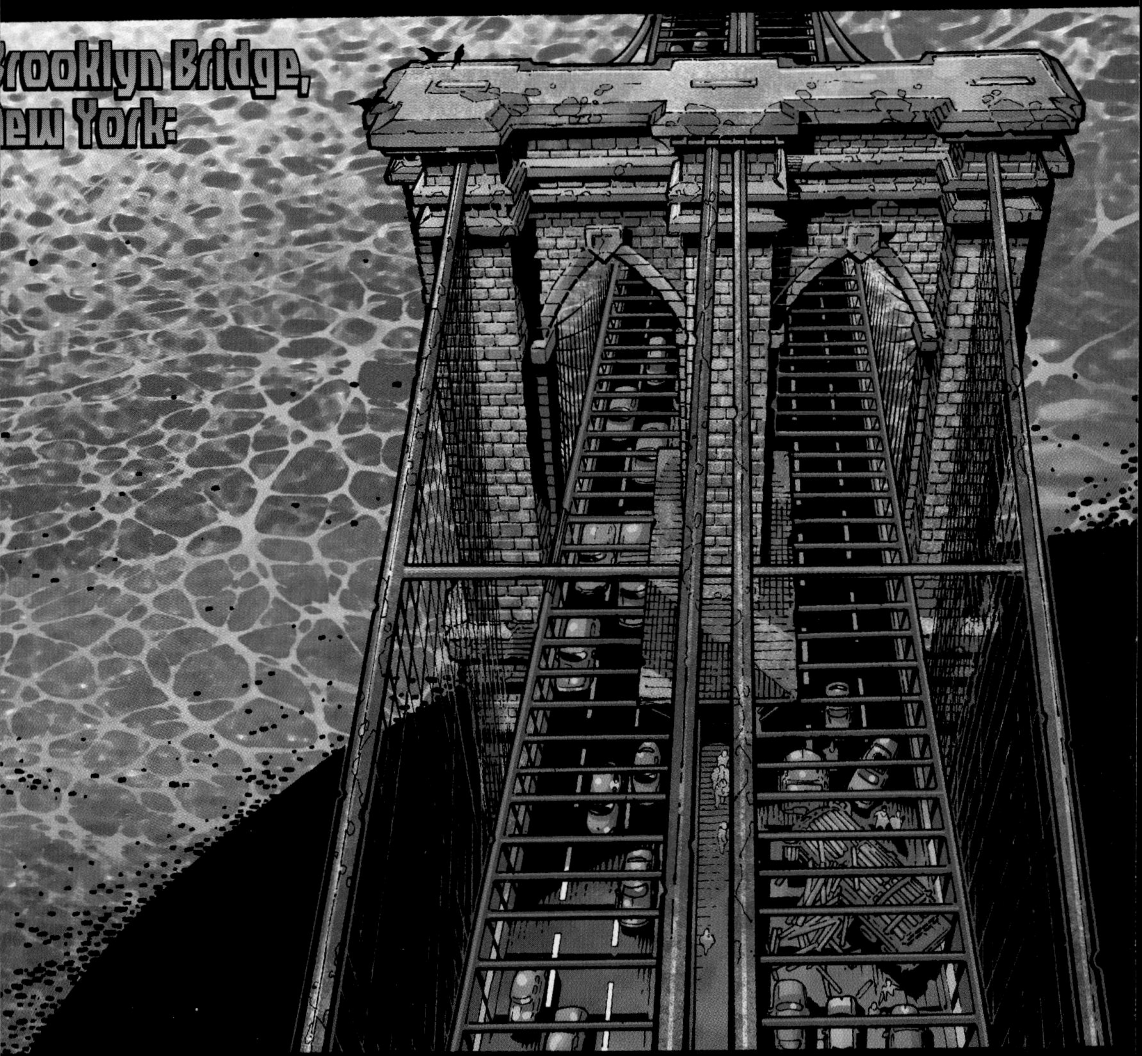
rooklyn Bridge,
ew York:

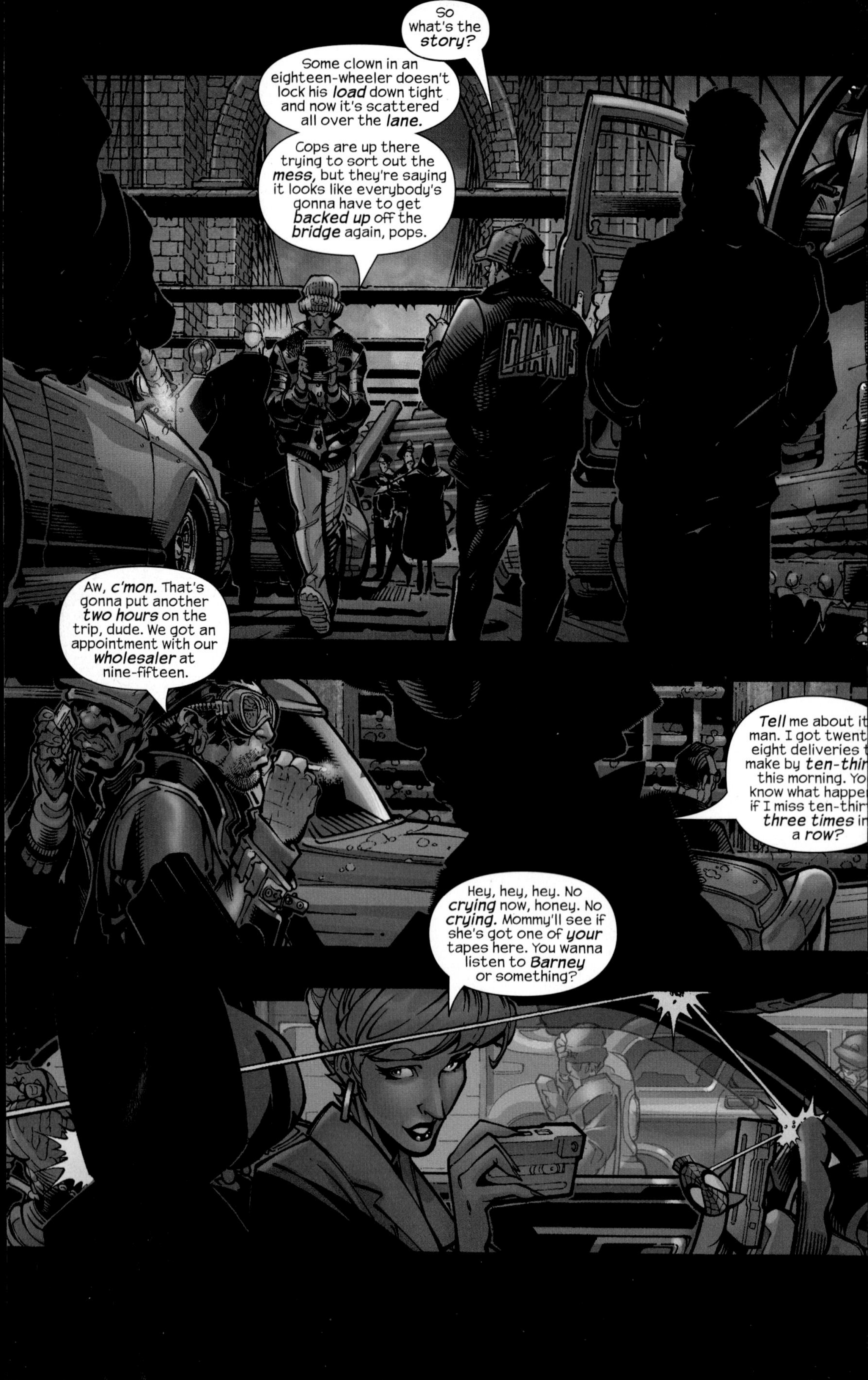
So what's the story?
Some clown in an eighteen-wheeler doesn't lock his load down tight and now it's scattered all over the lane.
Cops are up there trying to sort out the mess, but they're saying it looks like everybody's gonna have to get backed up off the bridge again, pops.
Aw, c'mon. That's gonna put another two hours on the trip, dude. We got an appointment with our wholesaler at nine-fifteen.
Tell me about i man. I got twent eight deliveries t make by ten-thir this morning. Yo know what happe if I miss ten-thir three times i a row?
Hey, hey, hey. No crying now, honey. No crying. Mommy'll see if she's got one of your tapes here. You wanna listen to Barney or something?

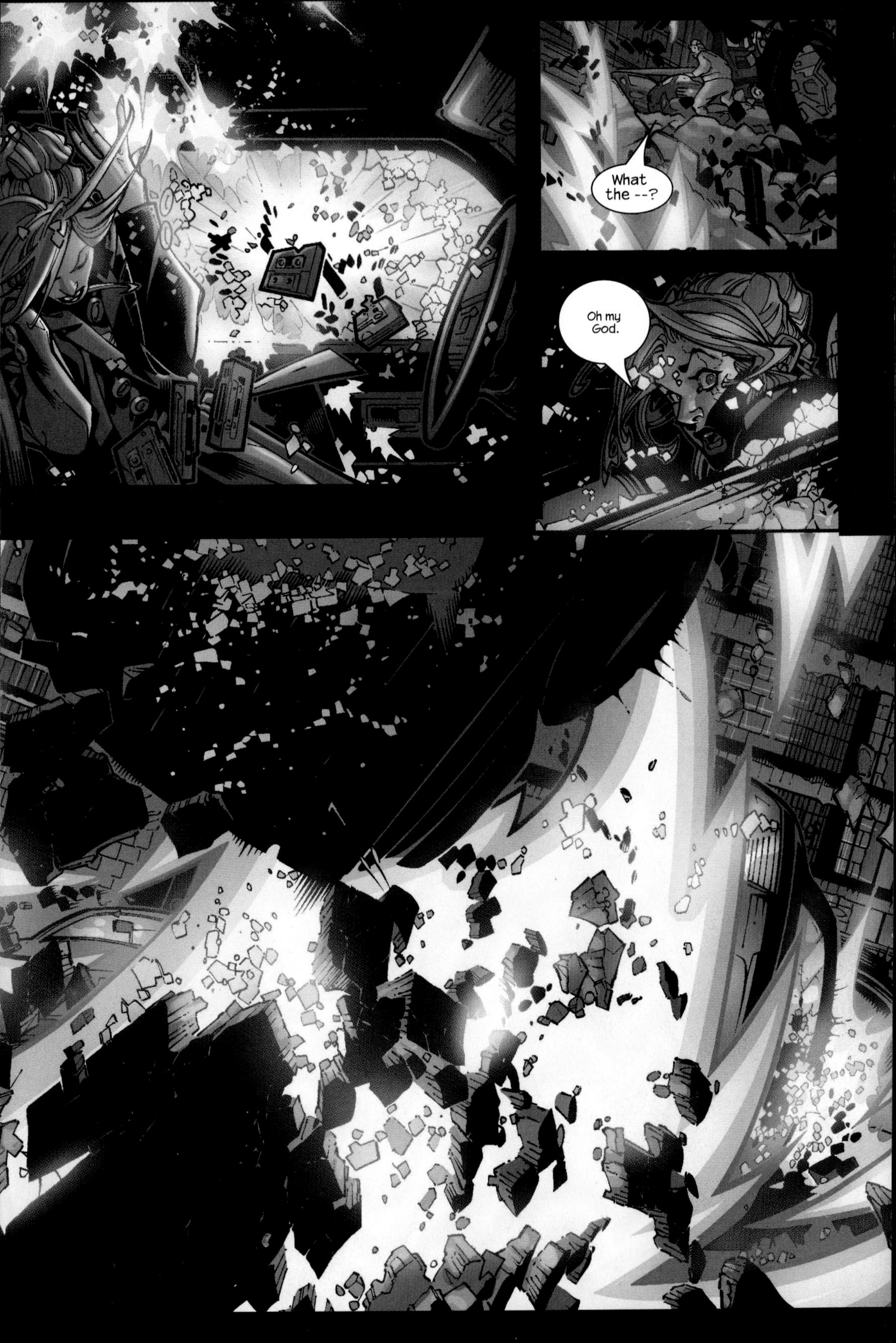
What the --?
Oh my God.

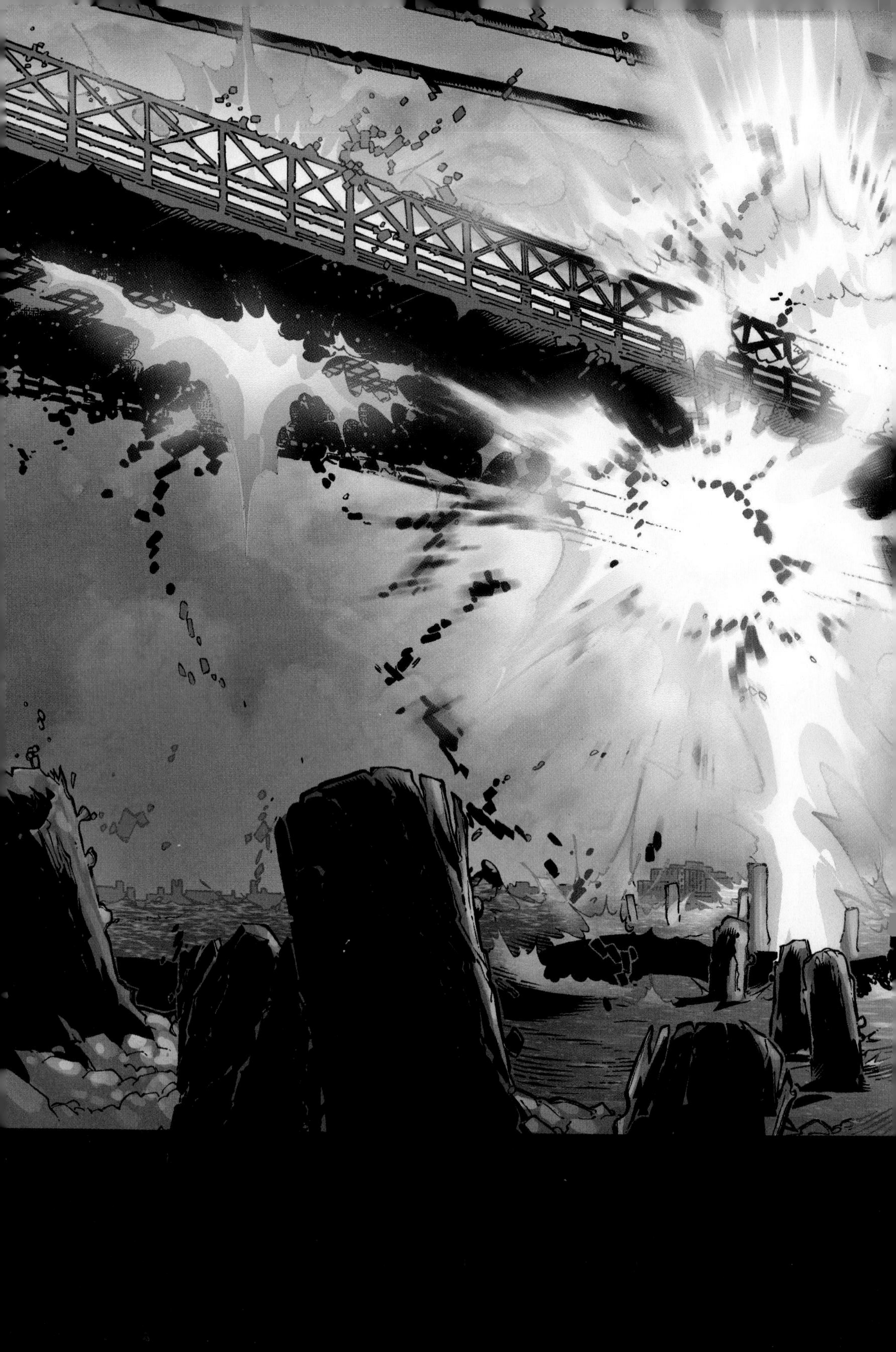

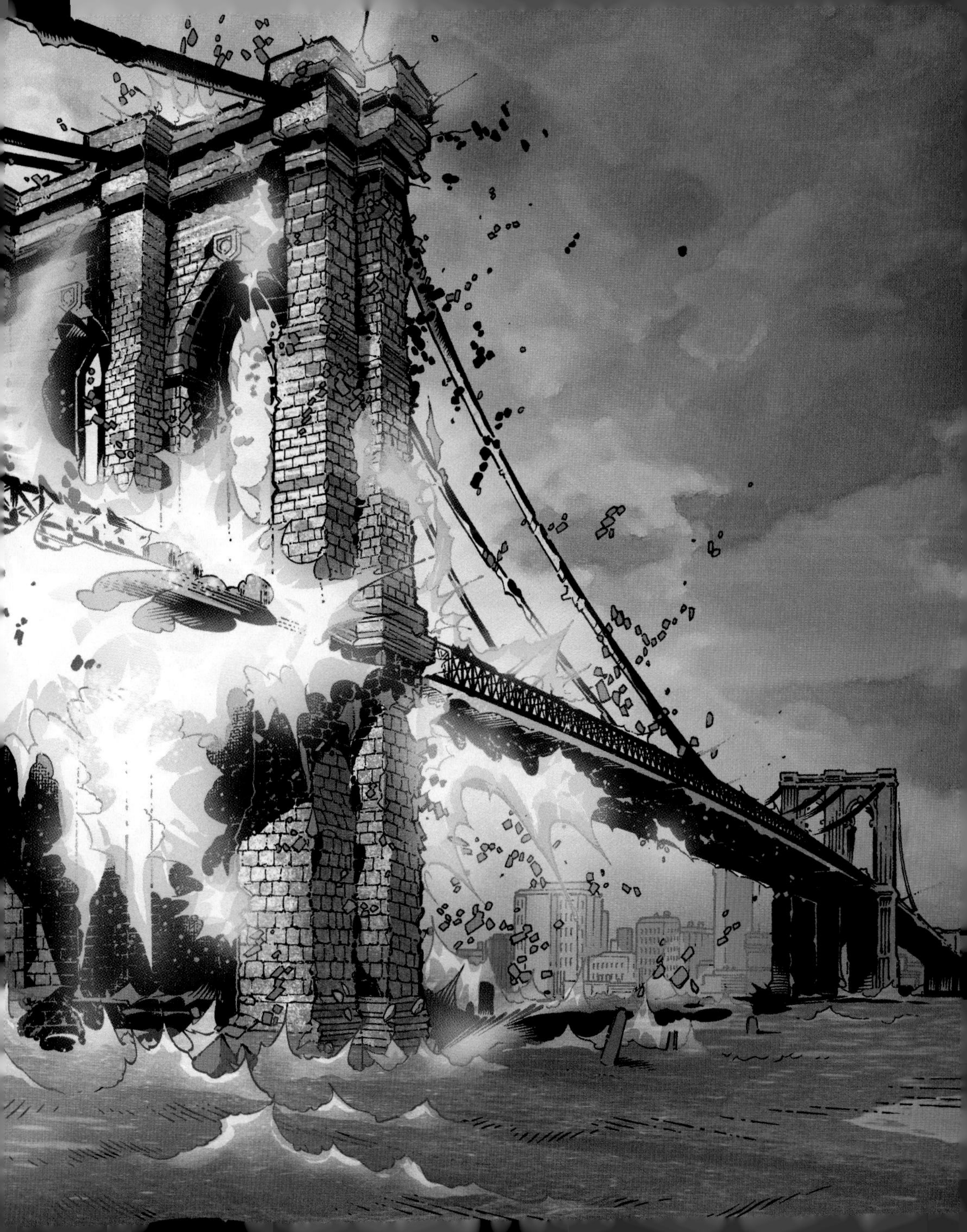

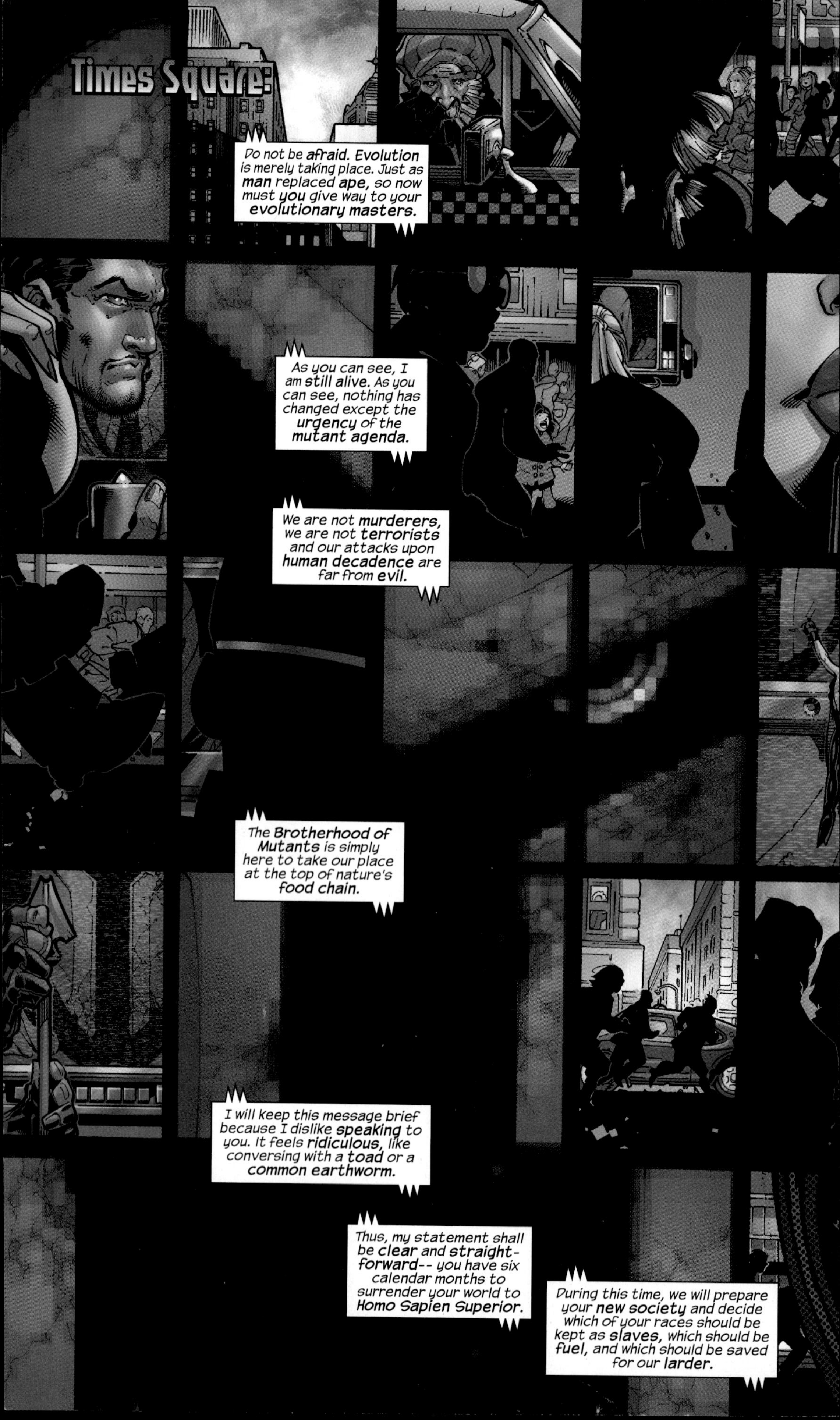
Times Square:
Do not be afraid. Evolution is merely taking place. Just as man replaced ape, so now must you give way to your evolutionary masters.
As you can see, I am still alive. As you can see, nothing has changed except the urgency of the mutant agenda.
We are not murderers, we are not terrorists and our attacks upon human decadence are far from evil.
The Brotherhood of Mutants is simply here to take our place at the top of nature's food chain.
I will keep this message brief because I dislike speaking to you. It feels ridiculous, like conversing with a toad or a common earthworm.
Thus, my statement shall be clear and straight-forward-- you have six calendar months to surrender your world to Homo Sapien Superior.
During this time, we will prepare your new society and decide which of your races should be kept as slaves, which should be fuel, and which should be saved for our larder.

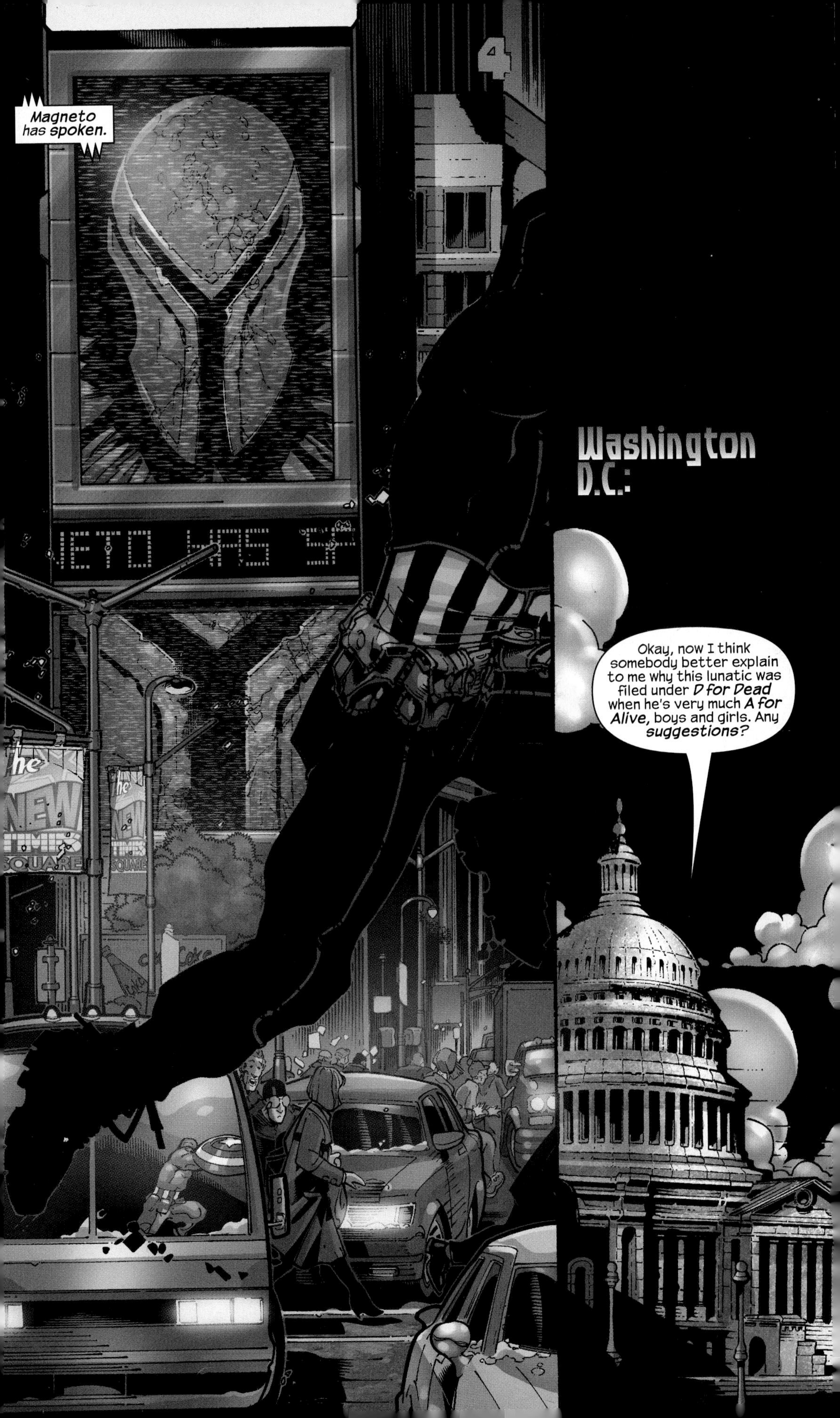

Magneto has spoken.
NETO HAS SP
Washington D.C.:
Okay, now I think somebody better explain to me why this lunatic was filed under *D for Dead* when he's very much *A for Alive,* boys and girls. Any *suggestions?*

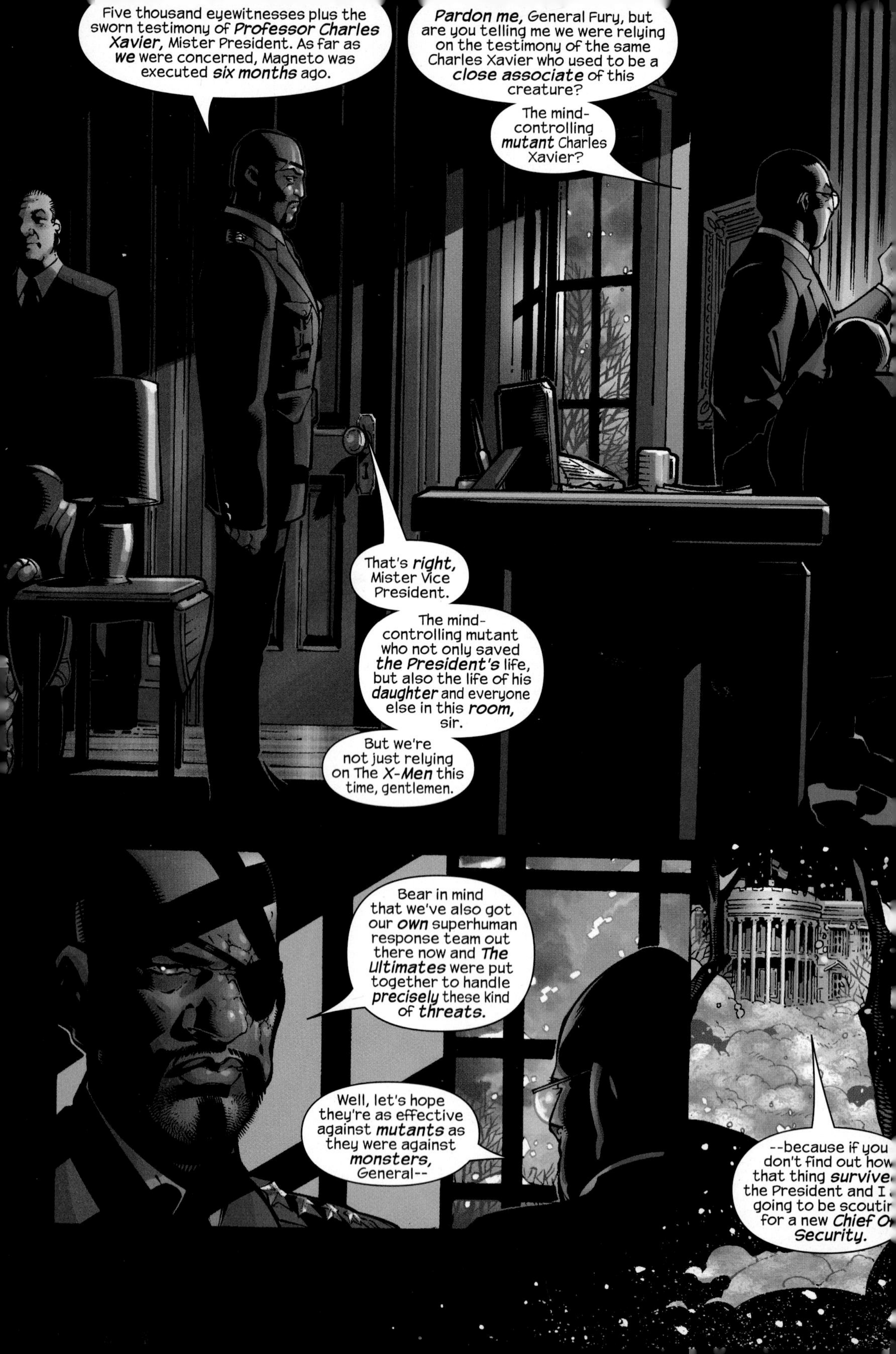
Five thousand eyewitnesses plus the sworn testimony of Professor Charles Xavier, Mister President. As far as we were concerned, Magneto was executed six months ago.
Pardon me, General Fury, but are you telling me we were relying on the testimony of the same Charles Xavier who used to be a close associate of this creature?
The mind-controlling mutant Charles Xavier?
That's right, Mister Vice President.
The mind-controlling mutant who not only saved the President's life, but also the life of his daughter and everyone else in this room, sir.
But we're not just relying on The X-Men this time, gentlemen.
Bear in mind that we've also got our own superhuman response team out there now and The Ultimates were put together to handle precisely these kind of threats.
Well, let's hope they're as effective against mutants as they were against monsters, General--
--because if you don't find out how that thing survive the President and I going to be scoutir for a new Chief O Security.

York:

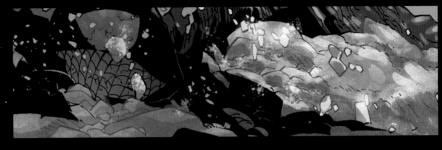

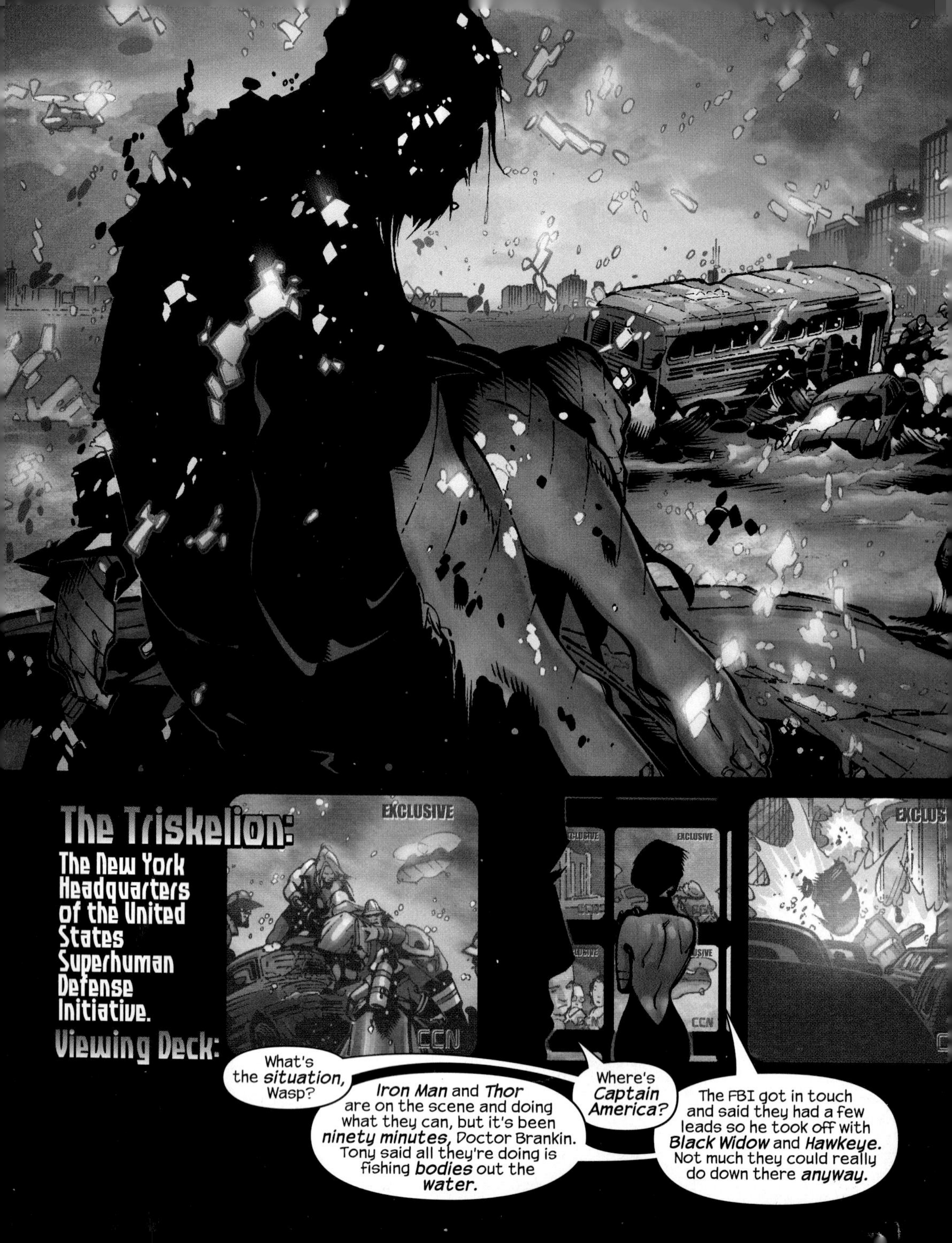

EXCLUSIVE
CCN
The Triskelion:
The New York Headquarters of the United States Superhuman Defense Initiative.
Viewing Deck:
What's the *situation,* Wasp?
Iron Man and *Thor* are on the scene and doing what they can, but it's been *ninety minutes,* Doctor Brankin. Tony said all they're doing is fishing *bodies* out the *water.*
Where's *Captain America?*
The FBI got in touch and said they had a few leads so he took off with *Black Widow* and *Hawkeye.* Not much they could really do down there *anyway.*

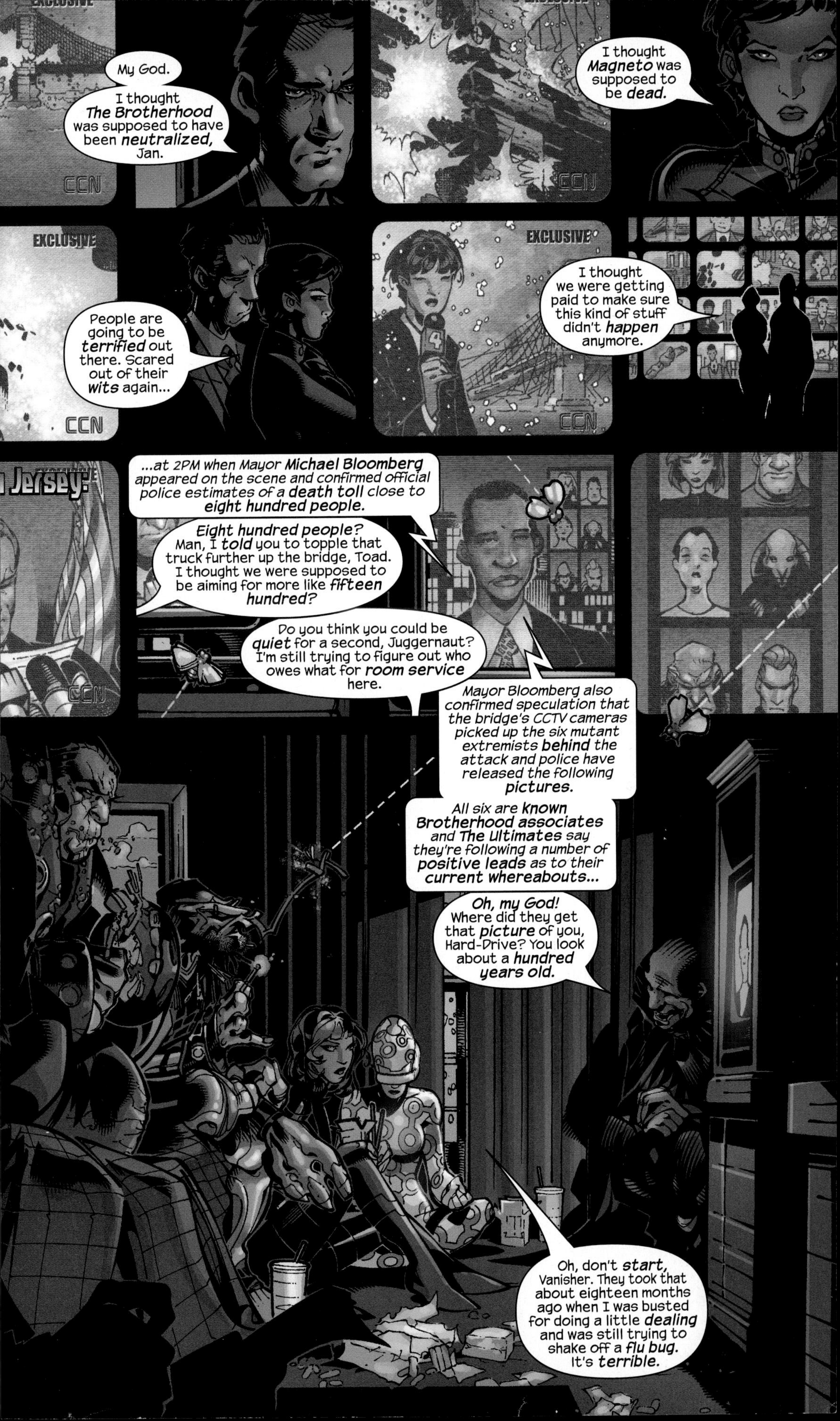

EXCLUSIVE
My God.
I thought The Brotherhood was supposed to have been neutralized, Jan.
CCN
CCN
I thought Magneto was supposed to be dead.
EXCLUSIVE
People are going to be terrified out there. Scared out of their wits again...
CCN
EXCLUSIVE
CCN
I thought we were getting paid to make sure this kind of stuff didn't happen anymore.
...at 2PM when Mayor Michael Bloomberg appeared on the scene and confirmed official police estimates of a death toll close to eight hundred people.
Eight hundred people? Man, I told you to topple that truck further up the bridge, Toad. I thought we were supposed to be aiming for more like fifteen hundred?
Do you think you could be quiet for a second, Juggernaut? I'm still trying to figure out who owes what for room service here.
Mayor Bloomberg also confirmed speculation that the bridge's CCTV cameras picked up the six mutant extremists behind the attack and police have released the following pictures.
All six are known Brotherhood associates and The Ultimates say they're following a number of positive leads as to their current whereabouts...
Oh, my God! Where did they get that picture of you, Hard-Drive? You look about a hundred years old.
Oh, don't start, Vanisher. They took that about eighteen months ago when I was busted for doing a little dealing and was still trying to shake off a flu bug. It's terrible.

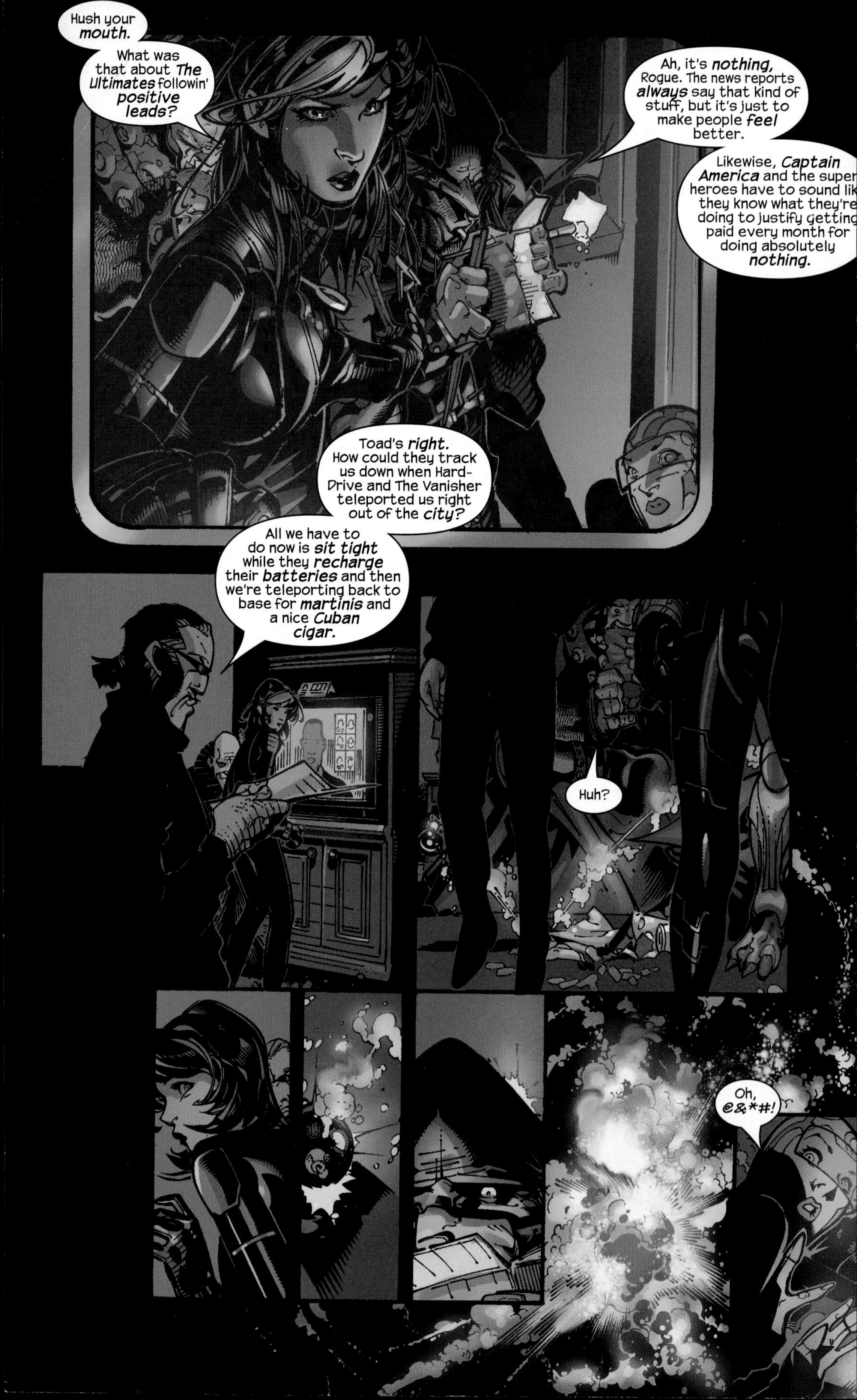
Hush your *mouth.*
What was that about *The Ultimates* followin' *positive leads?*
Ah, it's *nothing,* Rogue. The news reports *always* say that kind of stuff, but it's just to make people *feel* better.
Likewise, *Captain America* and the super heroes have to sound lik they know what they're doing to justify getting paid every month for doing absolutely *nothing.*
Toad's *right.* How could they track us down when Hard-Drive and The Vanisher teleported us right out of the *city?*
All we have to do now is *sit tight* while they *recharge* their *batteries* and then we're teleporting back to base for *martinis* and a nice *Cuban cigar.*
Huh?
Oh, @&*#!

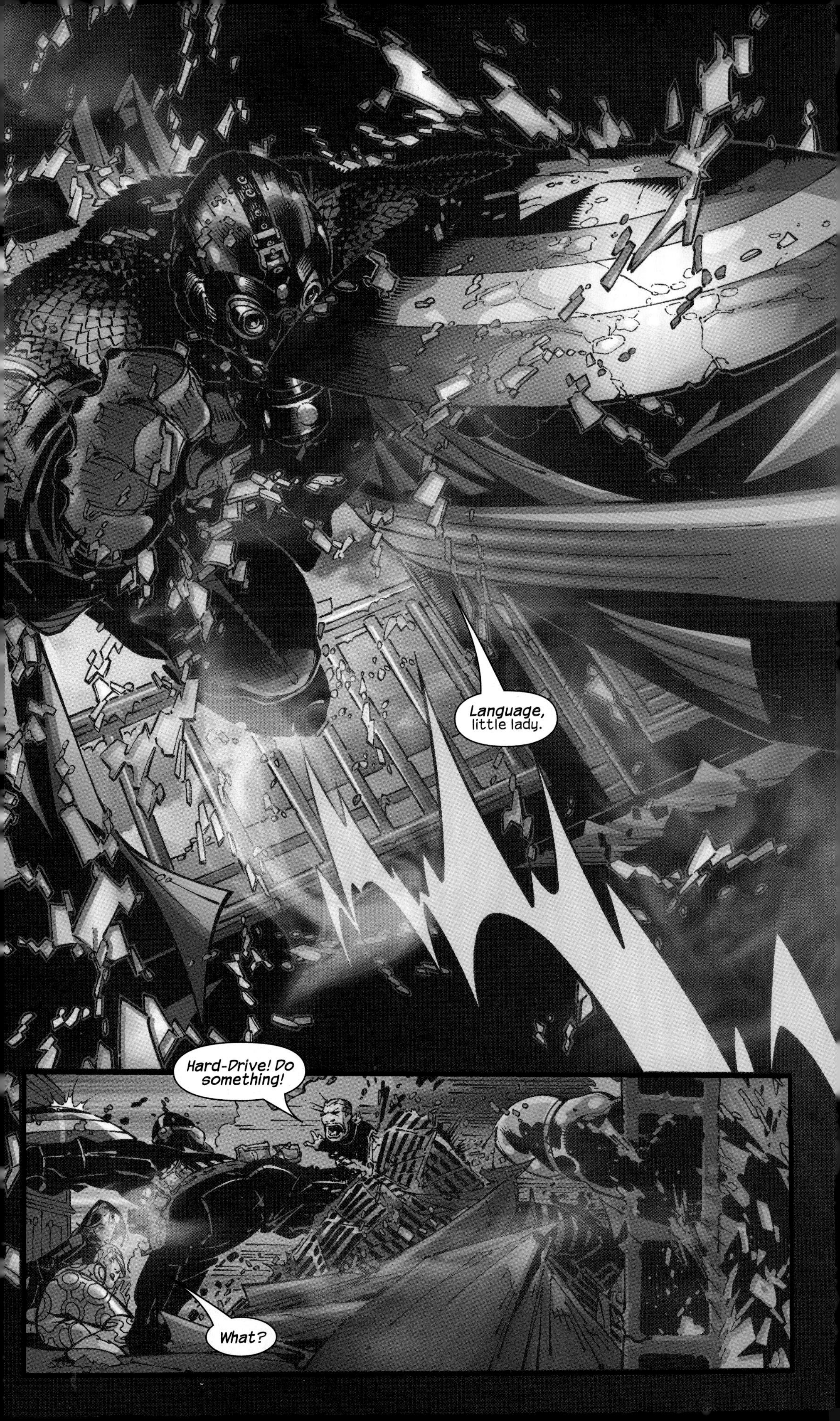
Language, little lady.
Hard-Drive! Do something!
What?

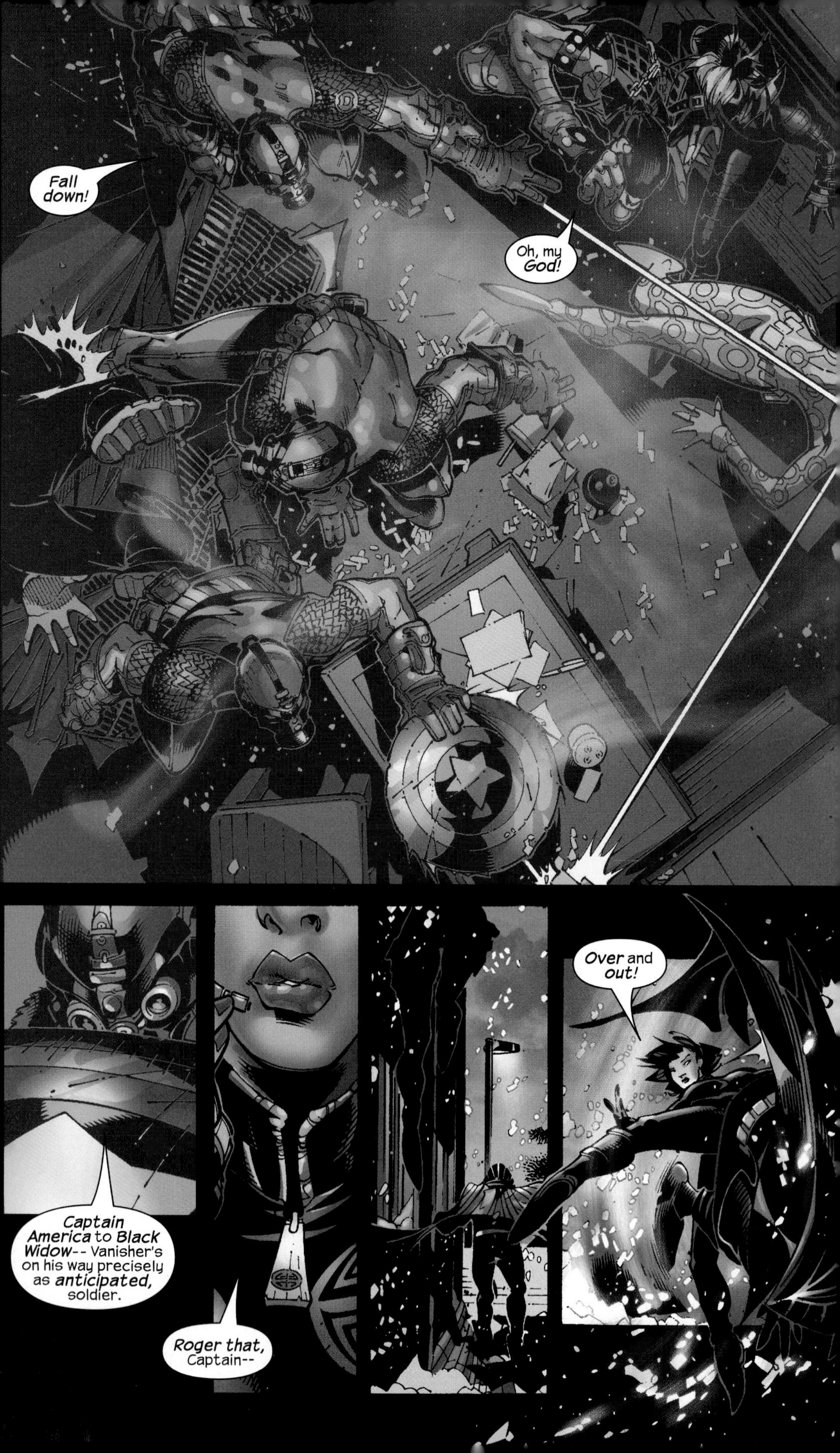
Fall down!
Oh, my God!
Captain America to Black Widow-- Vanisher's on his way precisely as anticipated, soldier.
Roger that, Captain--
Over and out!

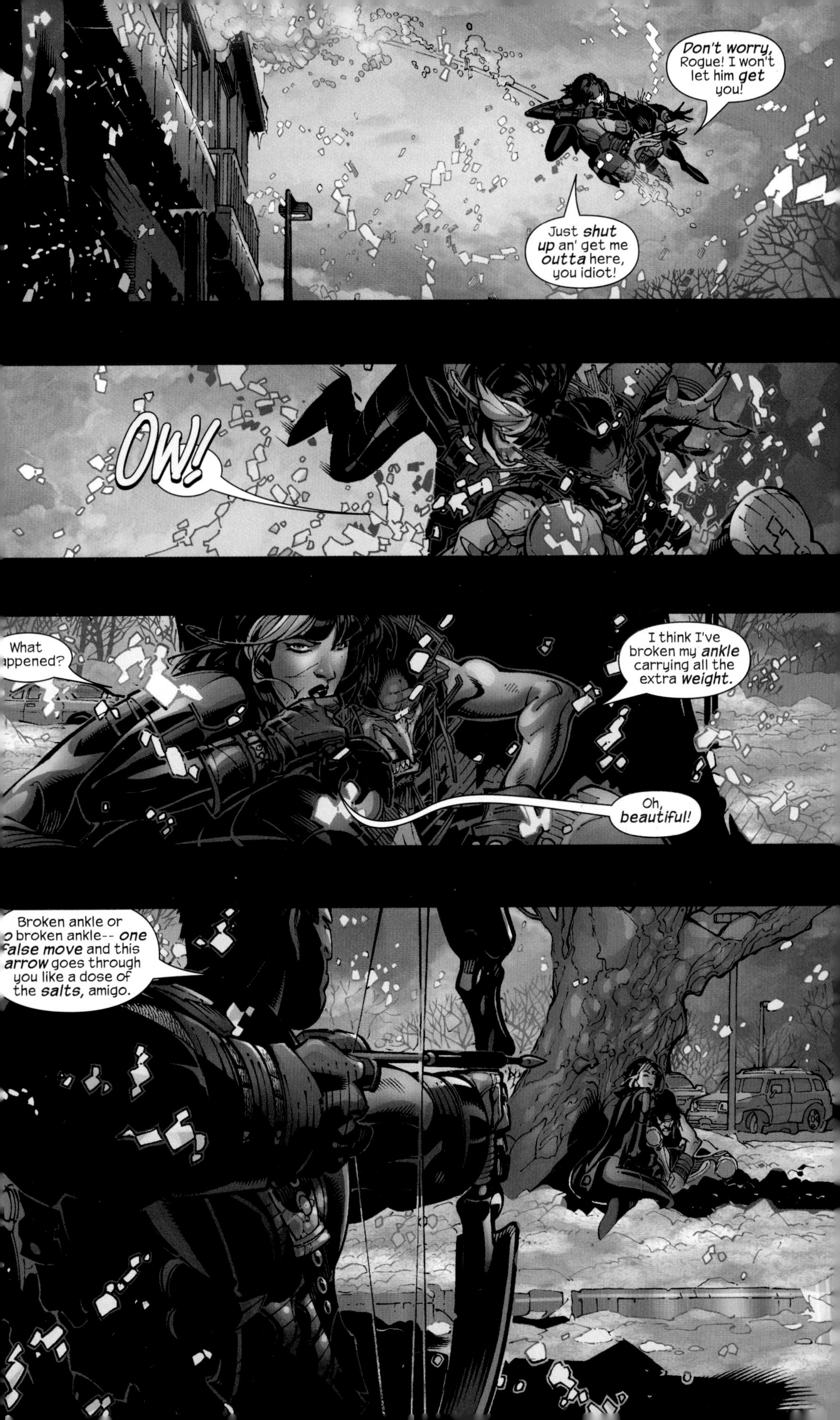

Don't worry, Rogue! I won't let him get you!
Just shut up an' get me outta here, you idiot!
OW!
What appened?
I think I've broken my ankle carrying all the extra weight.
Oh, beautiful!
Broken ankle or o broken ankle-- one false move and this arrow goes through you like a dose of the salts, amigo.

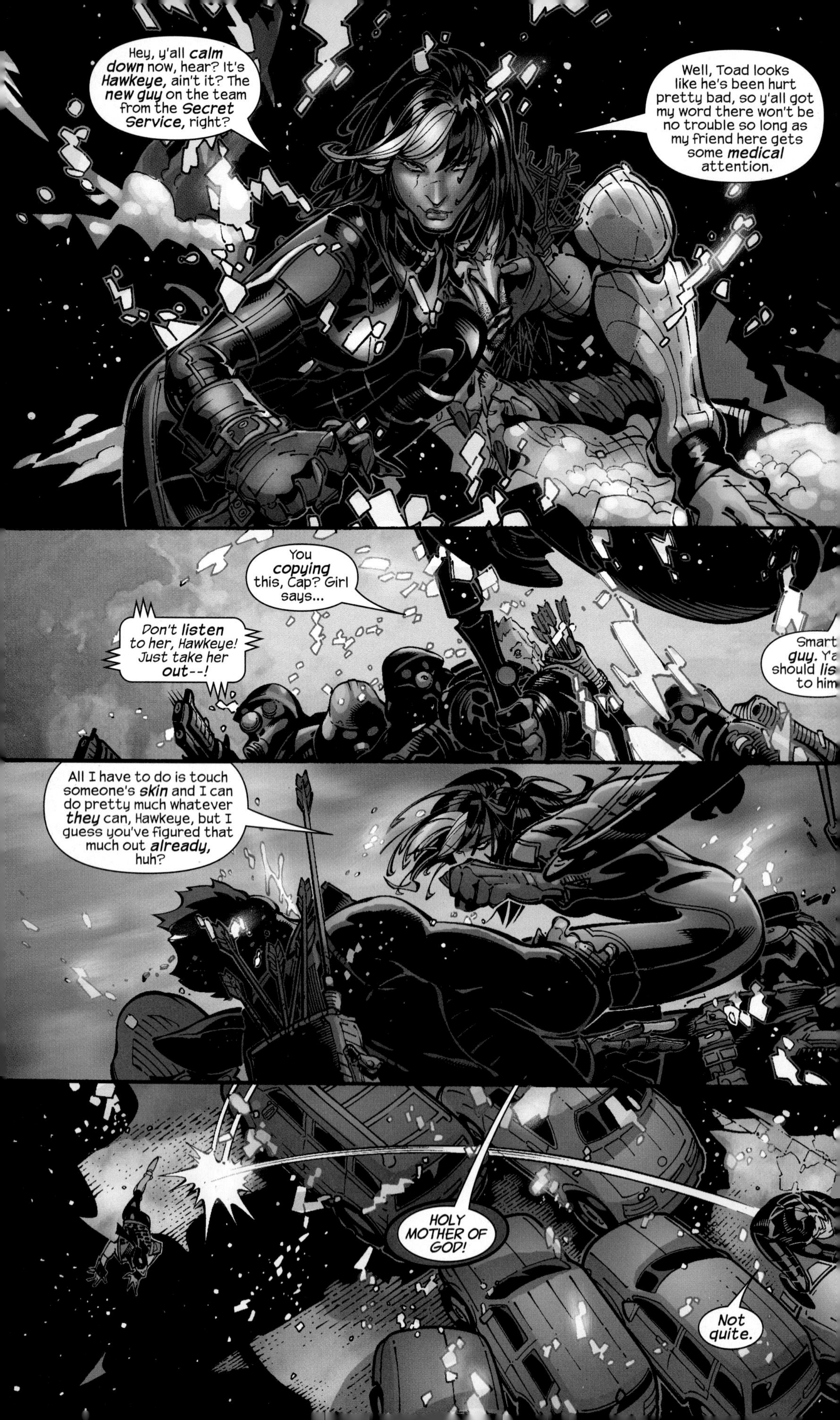
Hey, y'all calm down now, hear? It's Hawkeye, ain't it? The new guy on the team from the Secret Service, right?
Well, Toad looks like he's been hurt pretty bad, so y'all got my word there won't be no trouble so long as my friend here gets some medical attention.
You copying this, Cap? Girl says...
Don't listen to her, Hawkeye! Just take her out--!
Smart guy. Y'a should lis to him
All I have to do is touch someone's skin and I can do pretty much whatever they can, Hawkeye, but I guess you've figured that much out already, huh?
HOLY MOTHER OF GOD!
Not quite.

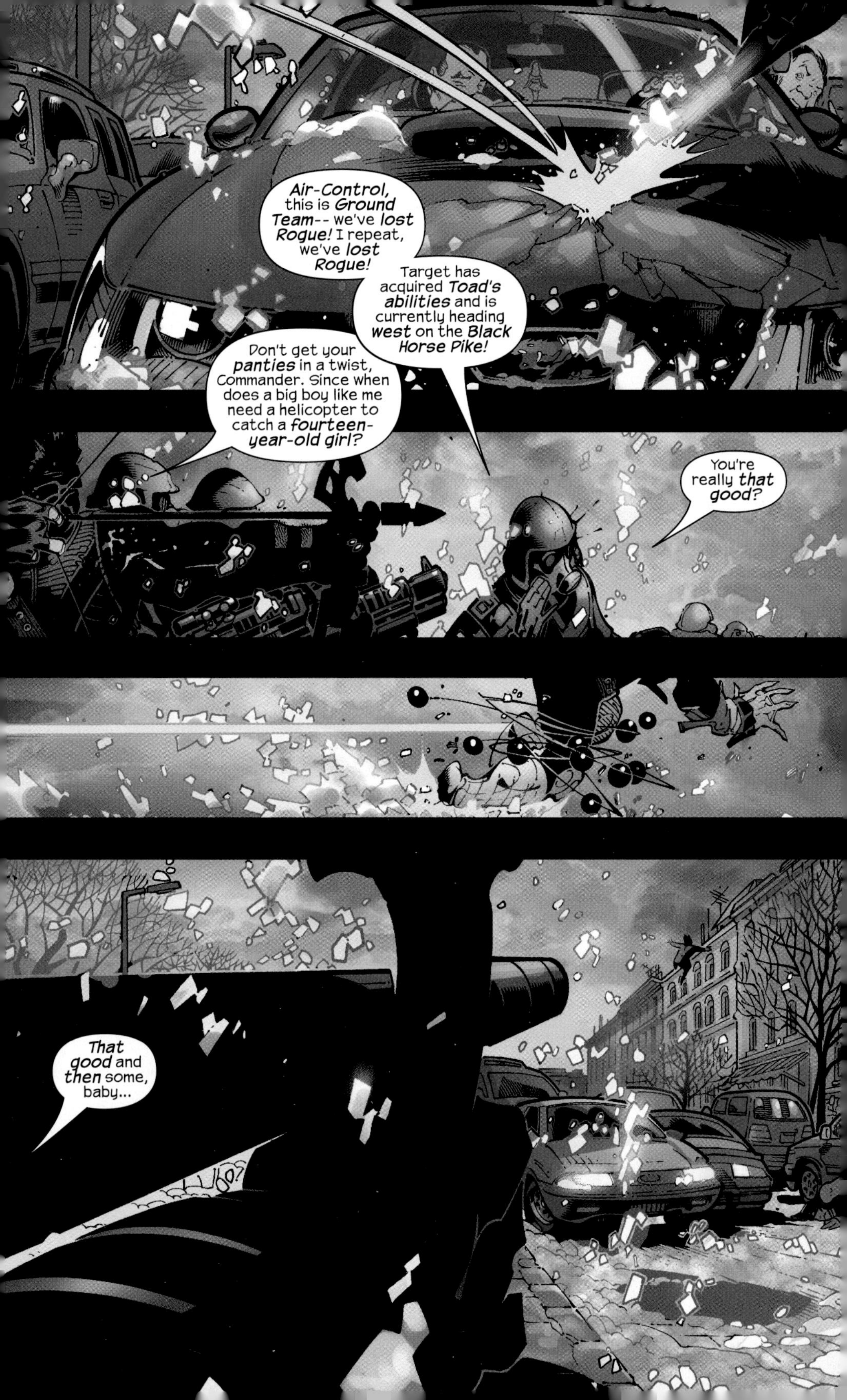
Air-Control, this is Ground Team-- we've lost Rogue! I repeat, we've lost Rogue!
Target has acquired Toad's abilities and is currently heading west on the Black Horse Pike!
Don't get your panties in a twist, Commander. Since when does a big boy like me need a helicopter to catch a fourteen-year-old girl?
You're really that good?
That good and then some, baby...

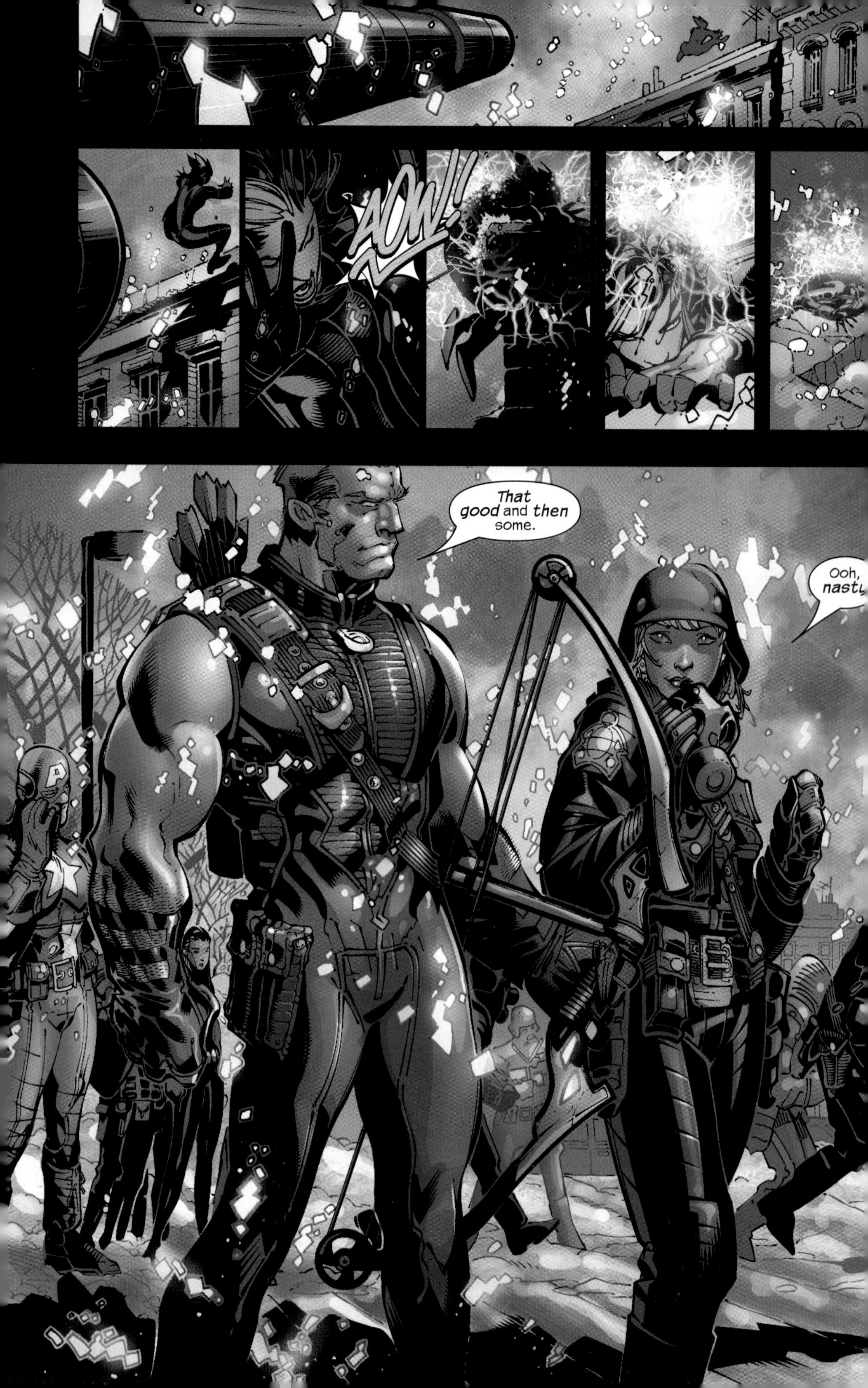
AOW!!
That good and then some.
Ooh, nast

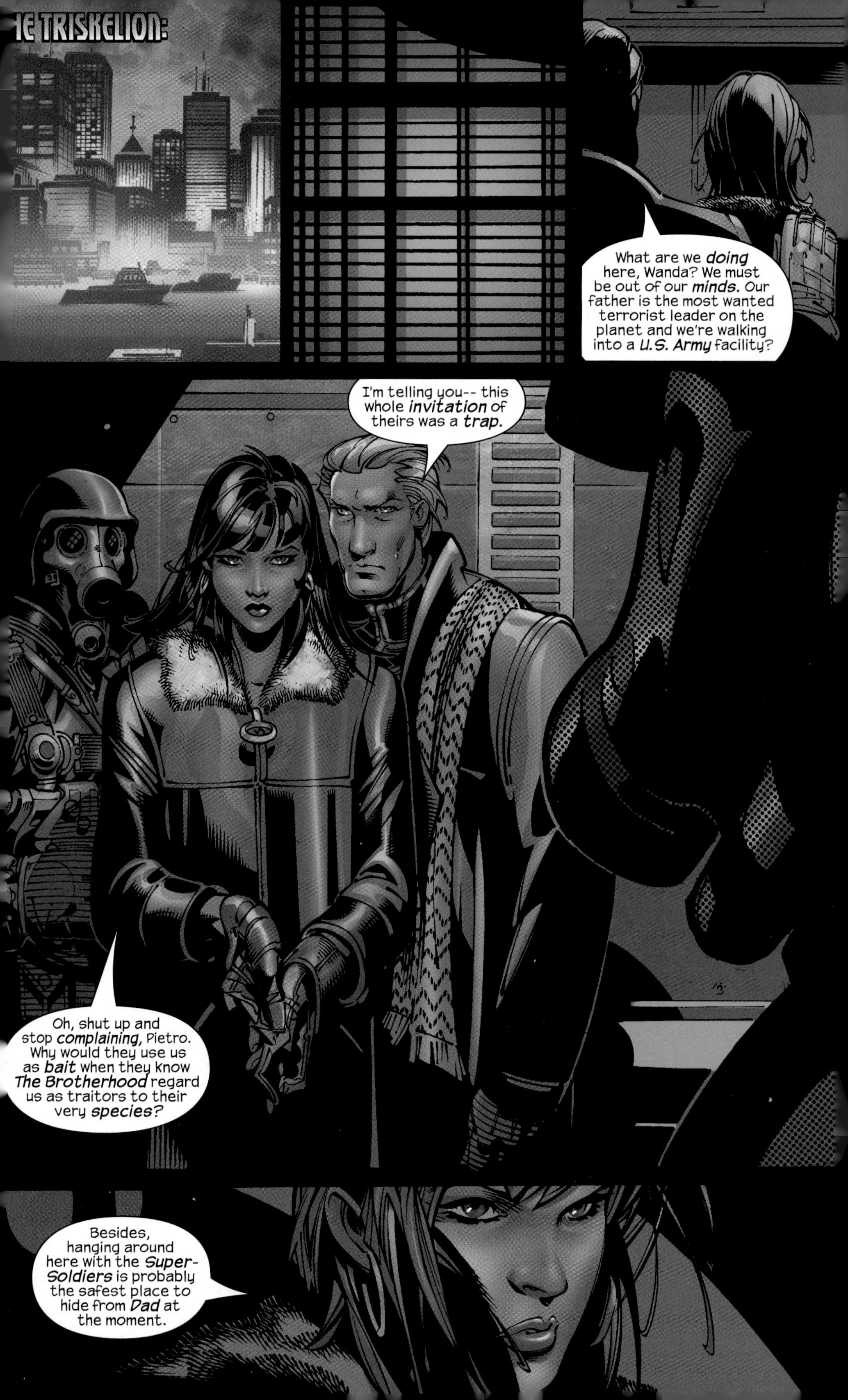
IE TRISKELION:
What are we doing here, Wanda? We must be out of our minds. Our father is the most wanted terrorist leader on the planet and we're walking into a U.S. Army facility?
I'm telling you-- this whole invitation of theirs was a trap.
Oh, shut up and stop complaining, Pietro. Why would they use us as bait when they know The Brotherhood regard us as traitors to their very species?
Besides, hanging around here with the Super-Soldiers is probably the safest place to hide from Dad at the moment.

Oh, *please.* Don't stop *gossiping* about us on *our* account, Captain. I'm sure it's nothing we haven't heard *before.*

Actually, I was just outlining the new anti-terrorist measures Secretary *Rumsfeld* and I drew up this morning, Quicksilver.

If you'd like to take a seat, I'm sure both you and Scarlet Witch could make a *valuable contribution* here.

Uh, to be *perfectly honest,* I'm really not sure that's such a *wonderful idea,* Comrade.

Excuse me?

I know S.H.I.E.L.D. *black-ops* is merging with the public team, but our two mutant *friends* here are former *leaders* of The Brotherhood, for God's sake.

Am I the only person in the room who thinks it might be a little *impractical* to have them around while we're plotting against their *father?*

What are you trying to *say* here?

Just what everyone else is *thinking,* darling. *No offense,* but you know what they say about *leopards* and *spots.*

Actually, I think Wanda and Pietro have proved themselves on a number of covert missions for the U.S. government. While toning down the activities of The Brotherhood, Natasha...

...and if we're exclud colleagues with *color pasts* at the momer does this *new rule* yours apply to forme KGB super-spies *too?*

Touché, Mister Rogers.

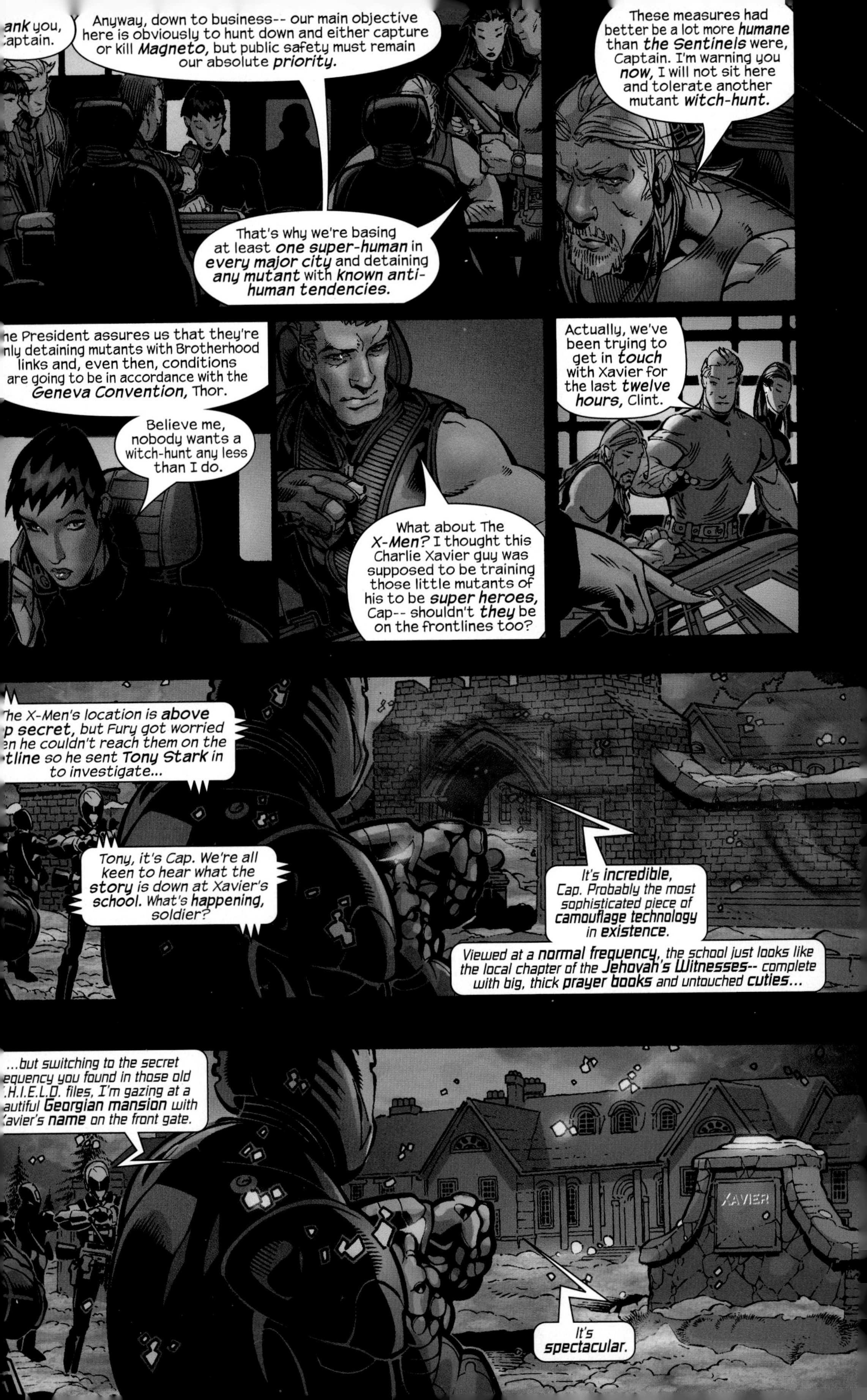
ank you, aptain.
Anyway, down to business-- our main objective here is obviously to hunt down and either capture or kill Magneto, but public safety must remain our absolute priority.
That's why we're basing at least one super-human in every major city and detaining any mutant with known anti-human tendencies.
These measures had better be a lot more humane than the Sentinels were, Captain. I'm warning you now, I will not sit here and tolerate another mutant witch-hunt.
he President assures us that they're nly detaining mutants with Brotherhood links and, even then, conditions are going to be in accordance with the Geneva Convention, Thor.
Believe me, nobody wants a witch-hunt any less than I do.
What about The X-Men? I thought this Charlie Xavier guy was supposed to be training those little mutants of his to be super heroes, Cap-- shouldn't they be on the frontlines too?
Actually, we've been trying to get in touch with Xavier for the last twelve hours, Clint.
he X-Men's location is above p secret, but Fury got worried en he couldn't reach them on the tline so he sent Tony Stark in to investigate...
Tony, it's Cap. We're all keen to hear what the story is down at Xavier's school. What's happening, soldier?
It's incredible, Cap. Probably the most sophisticated piece of camouflage technology in existence.
Viewed at a normal frequency, the school just looks like the local chapter of the Jehovah's Witnesses-- complete with big, thick prayer books and untouched cuties...
...but switching to the secret equency you found in those old .H.I.E.L.D. files, I'm gazing at a autiful Georgian mansion with avier's name on the front gate.
XAVIER
It's spectacular.

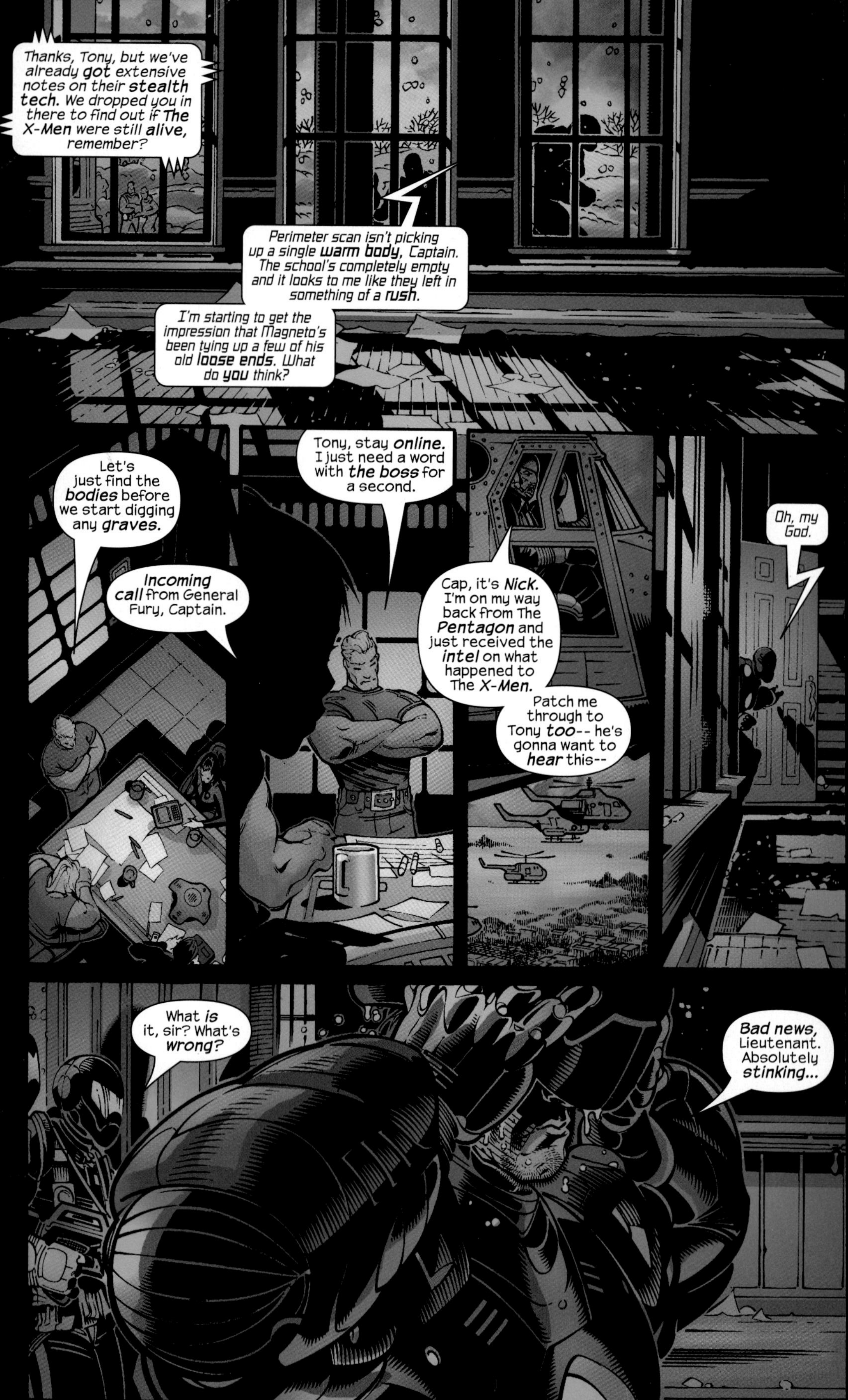
Thanks, Tony, but we've already got extensive notes on their stealth tech. We dropped you in there to find out if The X-Men were still alive, remember?
Perimeter scan isn't picking up a single warm body, Captain. The school's completely empty and it looks to me like they left in something of a rush.
I'm starting to get the impression that Magneto's been tying up a few of his old loose ends. What do you think?
Let's just find the bodies before we start digging any graves.
Incoming call from General Fury, Captain.
Tony, stay online. I just need a word with the boss for a second.
Cap, it's Nick. I'm on my way back from The Pentagon and just received the intel on what happened to The X-Men.
Patch me through to Tony too-- he's gonna want to hear this--
Oh, my God.
What is it, sir? What's wrong?
Bad news, Lieutenant. Absolutely stinking...

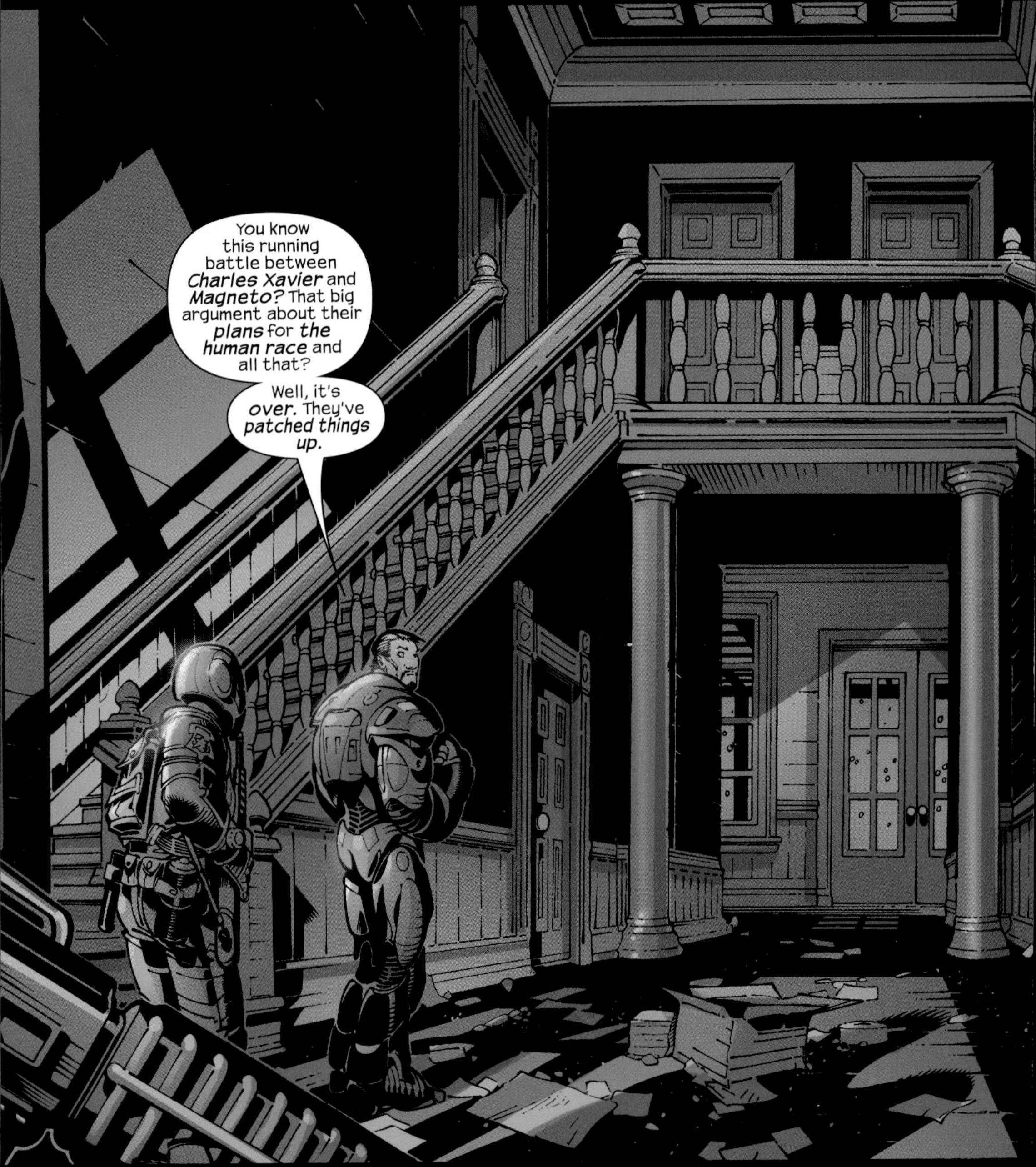
You know this running battle between Charles Xavier and Magneto? That big argument about their plans for the human race and all that?
Well, it's over. They've patched things up.

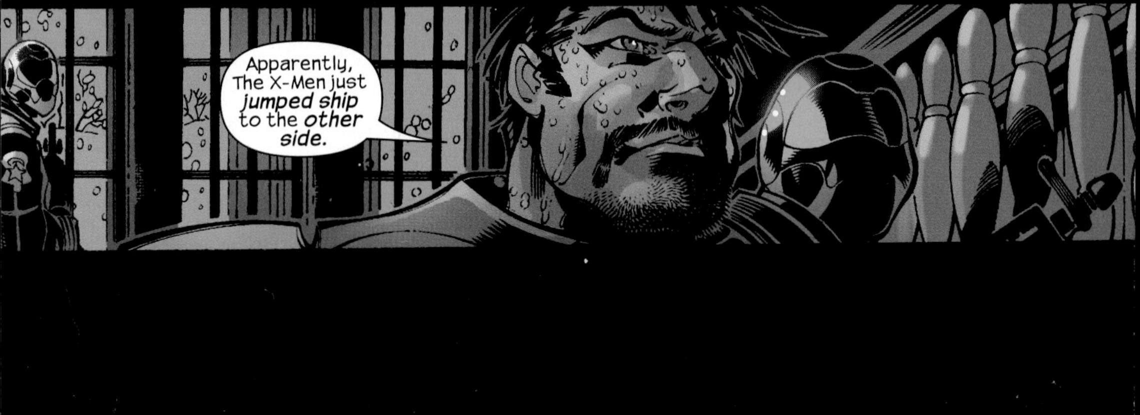
Apparently, The X-Men just jumped ship to the other side.

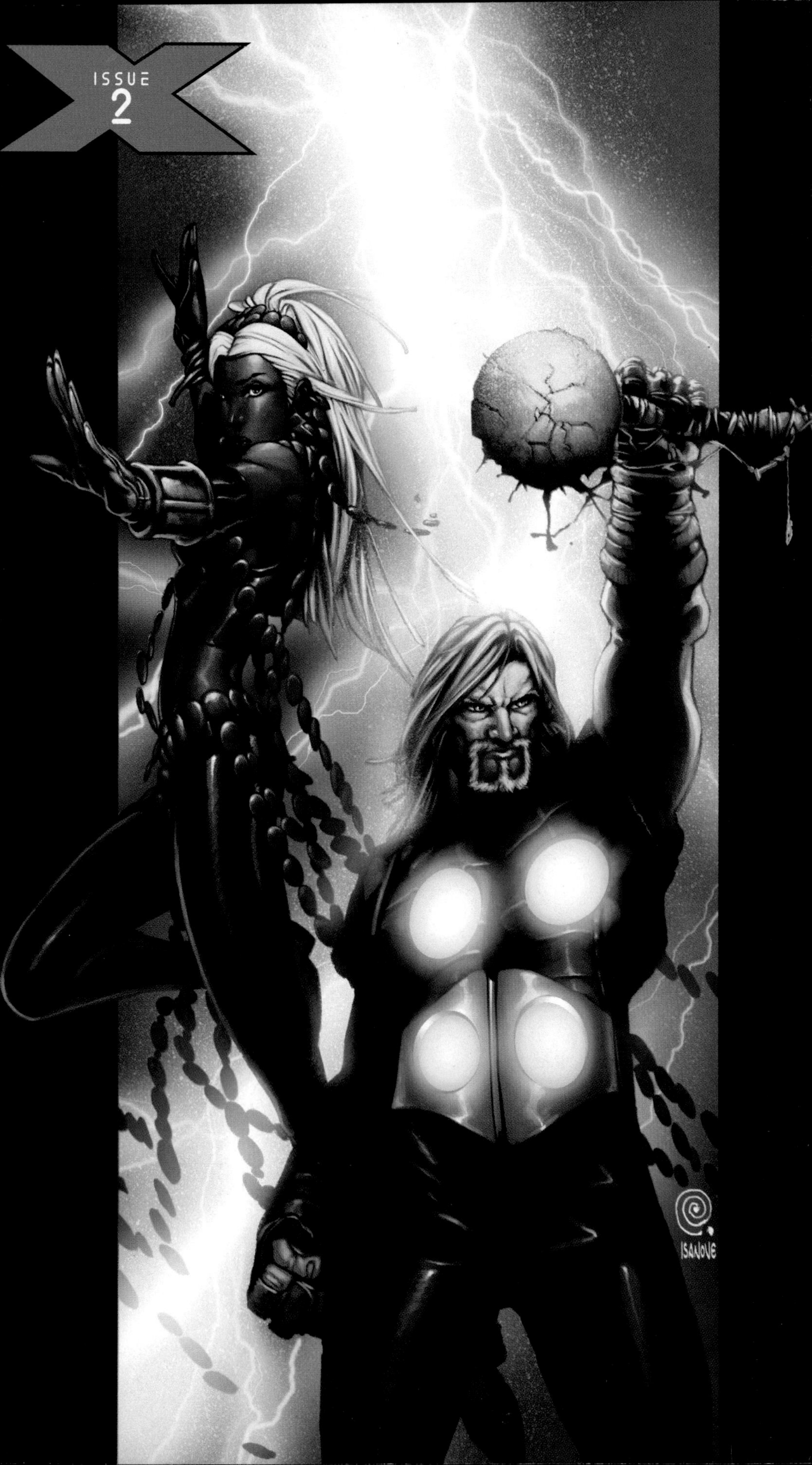
ISSUE
2
ISANOVE

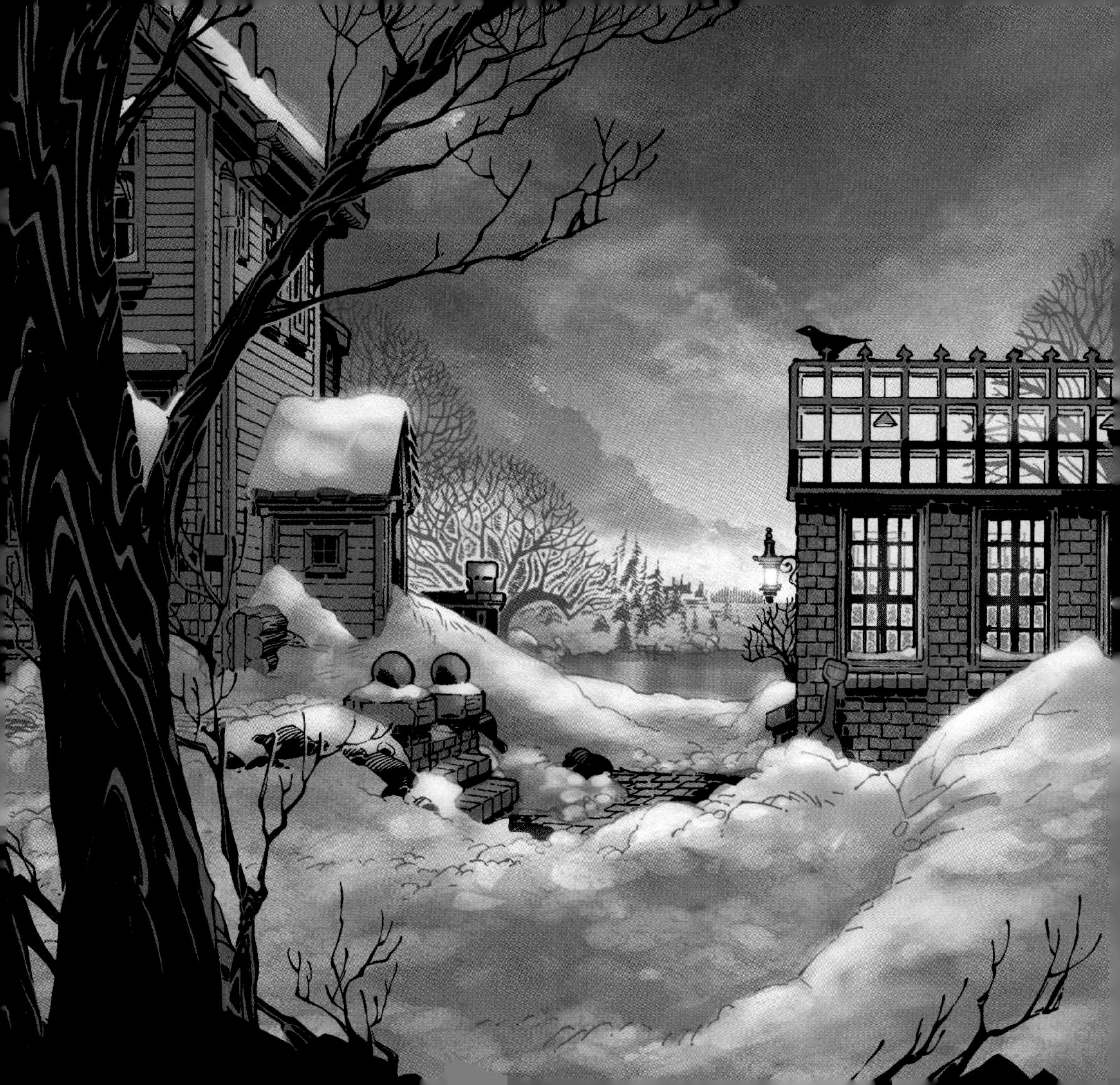

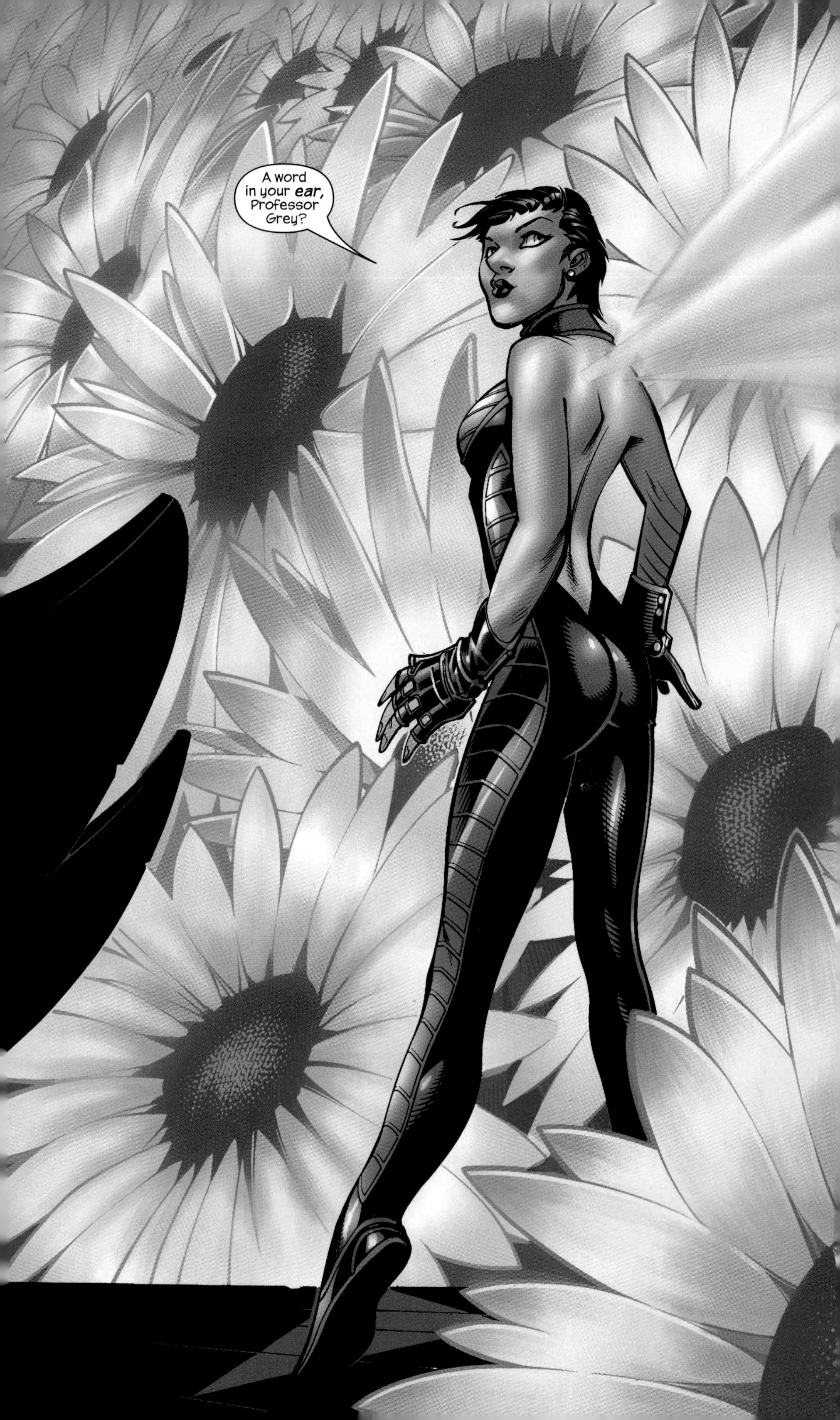
A word in your ear, Professor Grey?

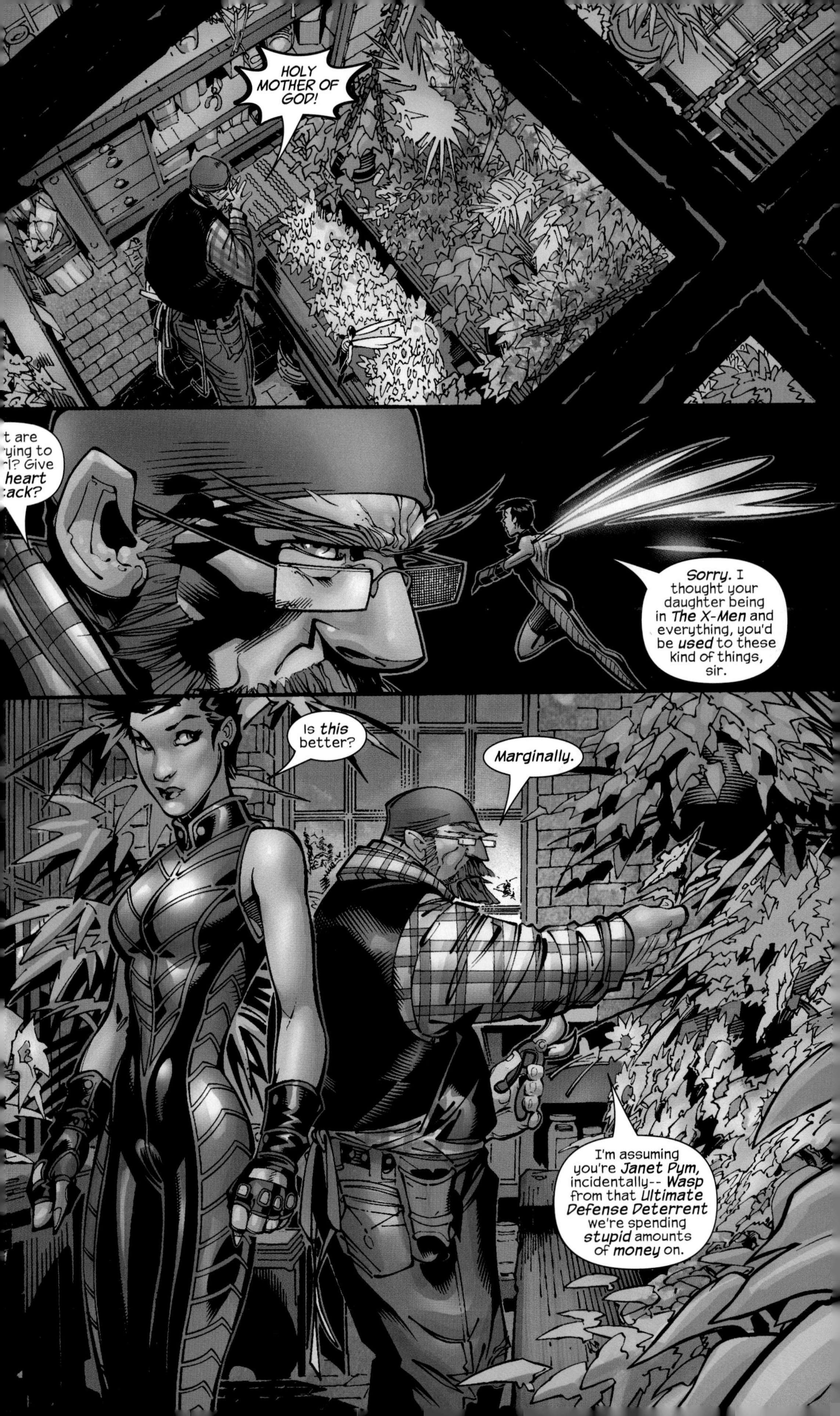
HOLY MOTHER OF GOD!
Sorry. I thought your daughter being in *The X-Men* and everything, you'd be ***used*** to these kind of things, sir.
Is *this* better?
Marginally.
I'm assuming you're *Janet Pym,* incidentally-- *Wasp* from that *Ultimate Defense Deterrent* we're spending ***stupid*** amounts of ***money*** on.

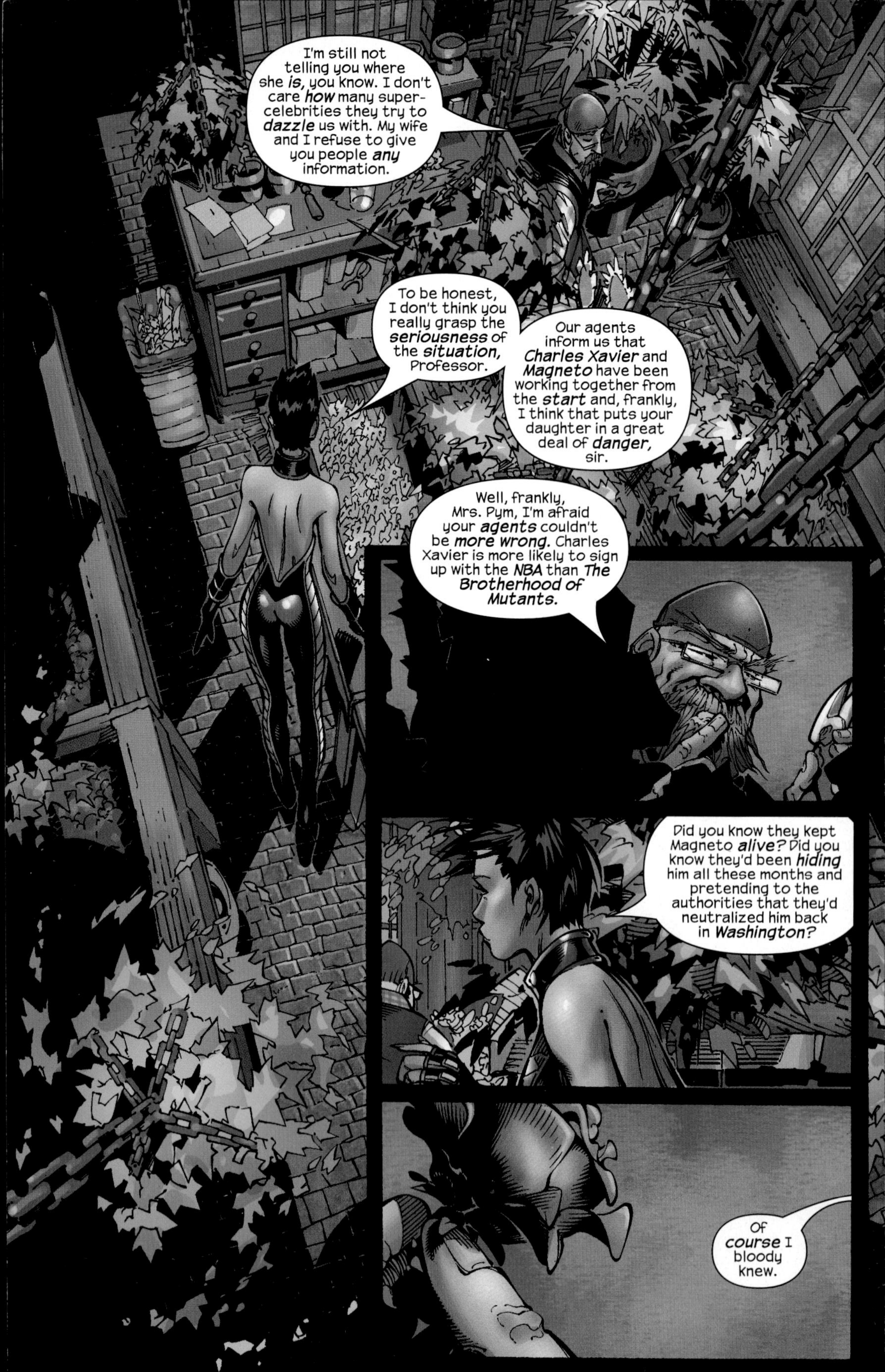
I'm still not telling you where she is, you know. I don't care how many super-celebrities they try to dazzle us with. My wife and I refuse to give you people any information.
To be honest, I don't think you really grasp the seriousness of the situation, Professor.
Our agents inform us that Charles Xavier and Magneto have been working together from the start and, frankly, I think that puts your daughter in a great deal of danger, sir.
Well, frankly, Mrs. Pym, I'm afraid your agents couldn't be more wrong. Charles Xavier is more likely to sign up with the NBA than The Brotherhood of Mutants.
Did you know they kept Magneto alive? Did you know they'd been hiding him all these months and pretending to the authorities that they'd neutralized him back in Washington?
Of course I bloody knew.

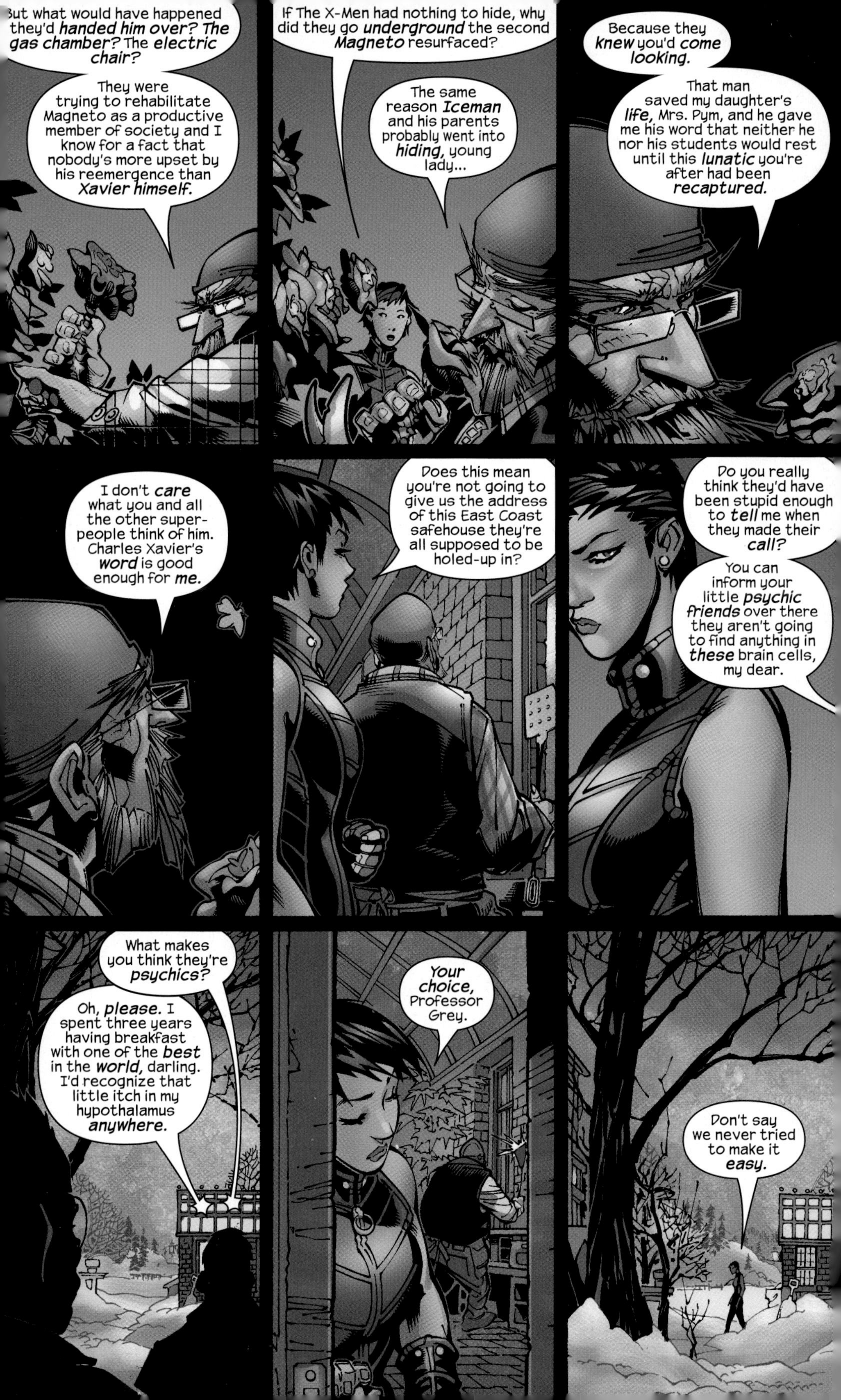
But what would have happened if they'd handed him over? The gas chamber? The electric chair?
They were trying to rehabilitate Magneto as a productive member of society and I know for a fact that nobody's more upset by his reemergence than Xavier himself.
If The X-Men had nothing to hide, why did they go underground the second Magneto resurfaced?
The same reason Iceman and his parents probably went into hiding, young lady...
Because they knew you'd come looking.
That man saved my daughter's life, Mrs. Pym, and he gave me his word that neither he nor his students would rest until this lunatic you're after had been recaptured.
I don't care what you and all the other super-people think of him. Charles Xavier's word is good enough for me.
Does this mean you're not going to give us the address of this East Coast safehouse they're all supposed to be holed-up in?
Do you really think they'd have been stupid enough to tell me when they made their call?
You can inform your little psychic friends over there they aren't going to find anything in these brain cells, my dear.
What makes you think they're psychics?
Oh, please. I spent three years having breakfast with one of the best in the world, darling. I'd recognize that little itch in my hypothalamus anywhere.
Your choice, Professor Grey.
Don't say we never tried to make it easy.

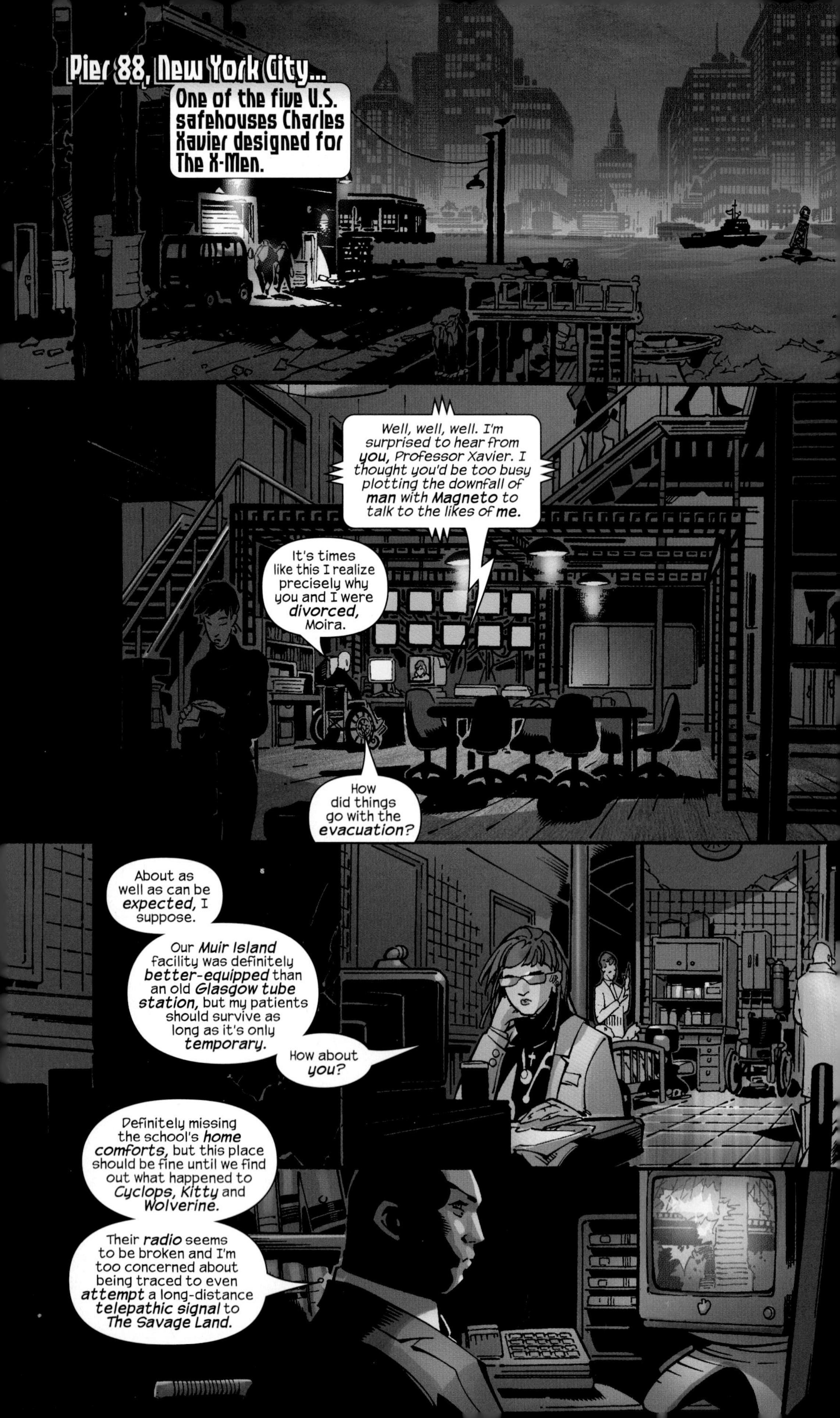

Pier 88, New York City...
One of the five U.S. safehouses Charles Xavier designed for The X-Men.
Well, well, well. I'm surprised to hear from you, Professor Xavier. I thought you'd be too busy plotting the downfall of man with Magneto to talk to the likes of me.
It's times like this I realize precisely why you and I were divorced, Moira.
How did things go with the evacuation?
About as well as can be expected, I suppose.
Our Muir Island facility was definitely better-equipped than an old Glasgow tube station, but my patients should survive as long as it's only temporary.
How about you?
Definitely missing the school's home comforts, but this place should be fine until we find out what happened to Cyclops, Kitty and Wolverine.
Their radio seems to be broken and I'm too concerned about being traced to even attempt a long-distance telepathic signal to The Savage Land.

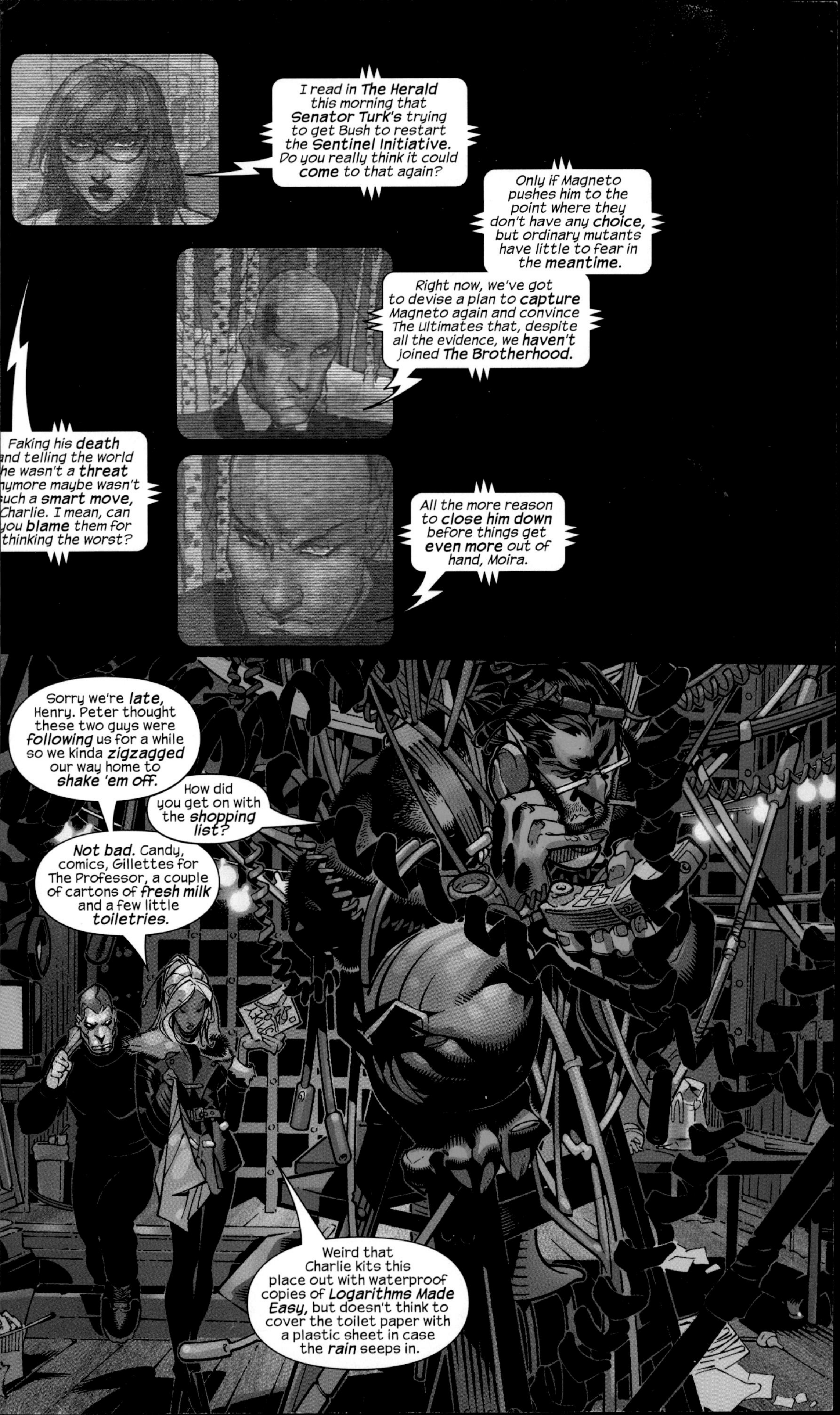

I read in The Herald this morning that Senator Turk's trying to get Bush to restart the Sentinel Initiative. Do you really think it could come to that again?
Only if Magneto pushes him to the point where they don't have any choice, but ordinary mutants have little to fear in the meantime.
Right now, we've got to devise a plan to capture Magneto again and convince The Ultimates that, despite all the evidence, we haven't joined The Brotherhood.
Faking his death and telling the world he wasn't a threat anymore maybe wasn't such a smart move, Charlie. I mean, can you blame them for thinking the worst?
All the more reason to close him down before things get even more out of hand, Moira.
Sorry we're late, Henry. Peter thought these two guys were following us for a while so we kinda zigzagged our way home to shake 'em off.
How did you get on with the shopping list?
Not bad. Candy, comics, Gillettes for The Professor, a couple of cartons of fresh milk and a few little toiletries.
Weird that Charlie kits this place out with waterproof copies of Logarithms Made Easy, but doesn't think to cover the toilet paper with a plastic sheet in case the rain seeps in.

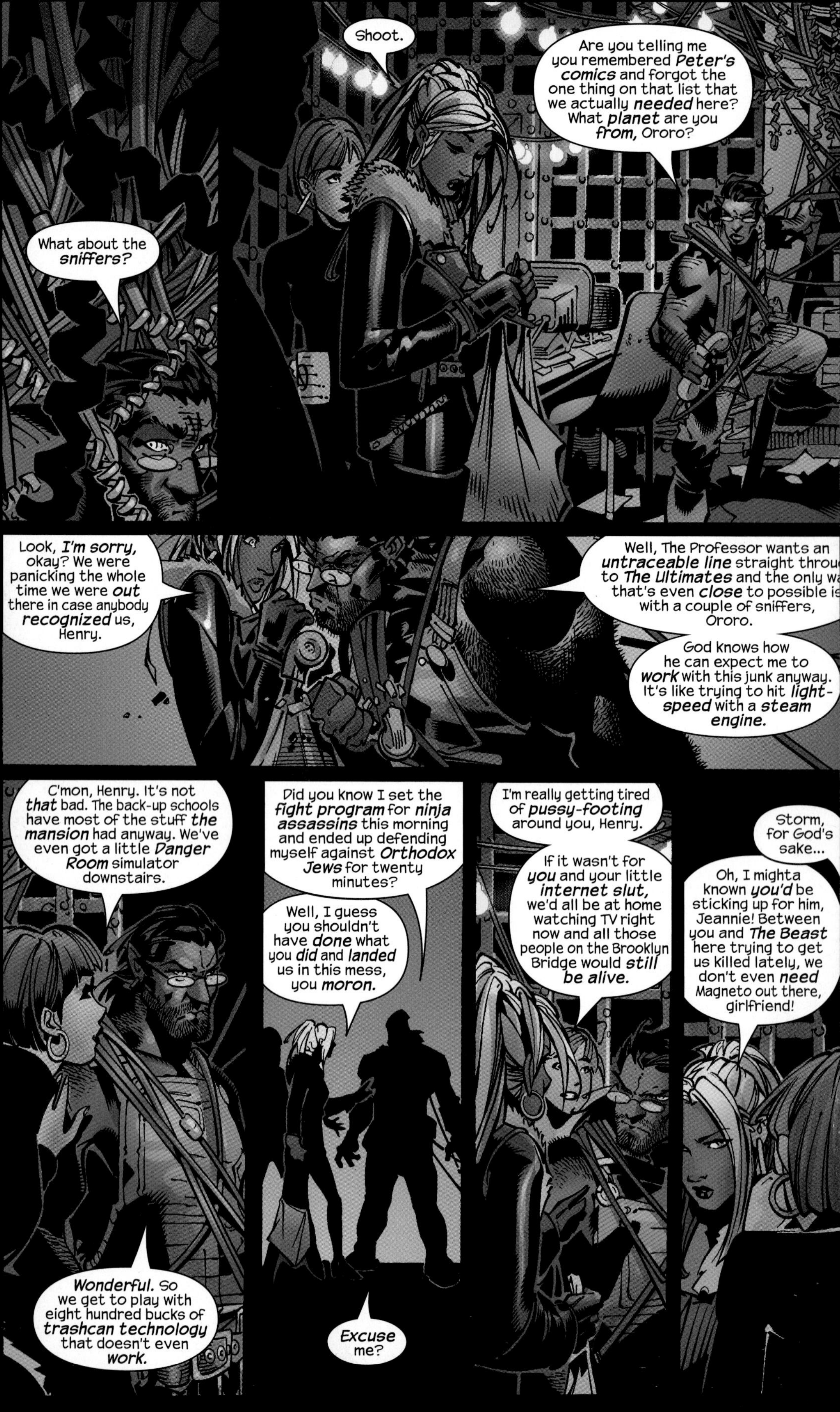
Shoot.
Are you telling me you remembered Peter's comics and forgot the one thing on that list that we actually needed here? What planet are you from, Ororo?
What about the sniffers?
Look, I'm sorry, okay? We were panicking the whole time we were out there in case anybody recognized us, Henry.
Well, The Professor wants an untraceable line straight throu to The Ultimates and the only wa that's even close to possible is with a couple of sniffers, Ororo.
God knows how he can expect me to work with this junk anyway. It's like trying to hit light-speed with a steam engine.
C'mon, Henry. It's not that bad. The back-up schools have most of the stuff the mansion had anyway. We've even got a little Danger Room simulator downstairs.
Wonderful. So we get to play with eight hundred bucks of trashcan technology that doesn't even work.
Did you know I set the fight program for ninja assassins this morning and ended up defending myself against Orthodox Jews for twenty minutes?
Well, I guess you shouldn't have done what you did and landed us in this mess, you moron.
Excuse me?
I'm really getting tired of pussy-footing around you, Henry.
If it wasn't for you and your little internet slut, we'd all be at home watching TV right now and all those people on the Brooklyn Bridge would still be alive.
Storm, for God's sake...
Oh, I mighta known you'd be sticking up for him, Jeannie! Between you and The Beast here trying to get us killed lately, we don't even need Magneto out there, girlfriend!

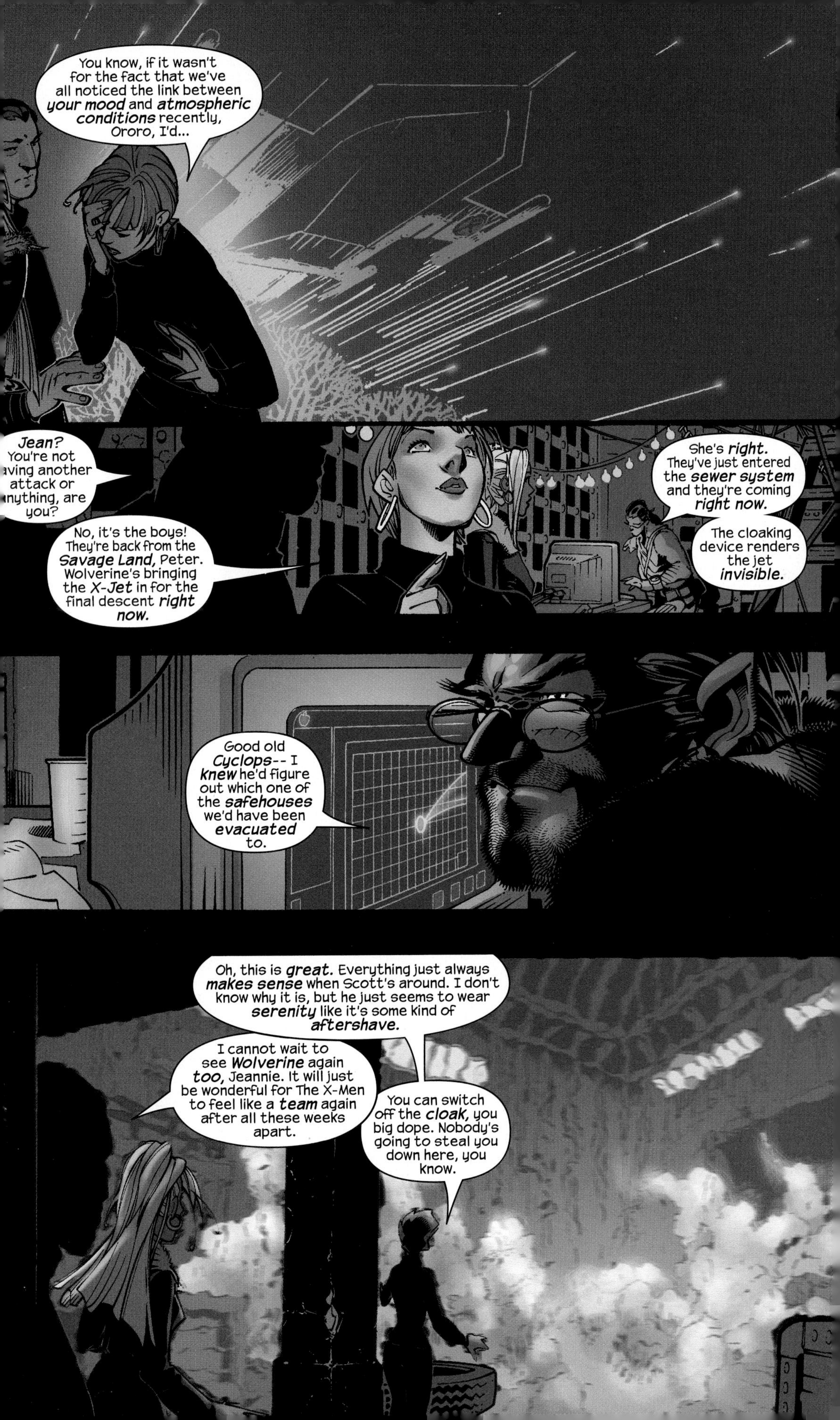

You know, if it wasn't for the fact that we've all noticed the link between your mood and atmospheric conditions recently, Ororo, I'd...
Jean? You're not aving another attack or nything, are you?
No, it's the boys! They're back from the Savage Land, Peter. Wolverine's bringing the X-Jet in for the final descent right now.
She's right. They've just entered the sewer system and they're coming right now.
The cloaking device renders the jet invisible.
Good old Cyclops-- I knew he'd figure out which one of the safehouses we'd have been evacuated to.
Oh, this is great. Everything just always makes sense when Scott's around. I don't know why it is, but he just seems to wear serenity like it's some kind of aftershave.
I cannot wait to see Wolverine again too, Jeannie. It will just be wonderful for The X-Men to feel like a team again after all these weeks apart.
You can switch off the cloak, you big dope. Nobody's going to steal you down here, you know.

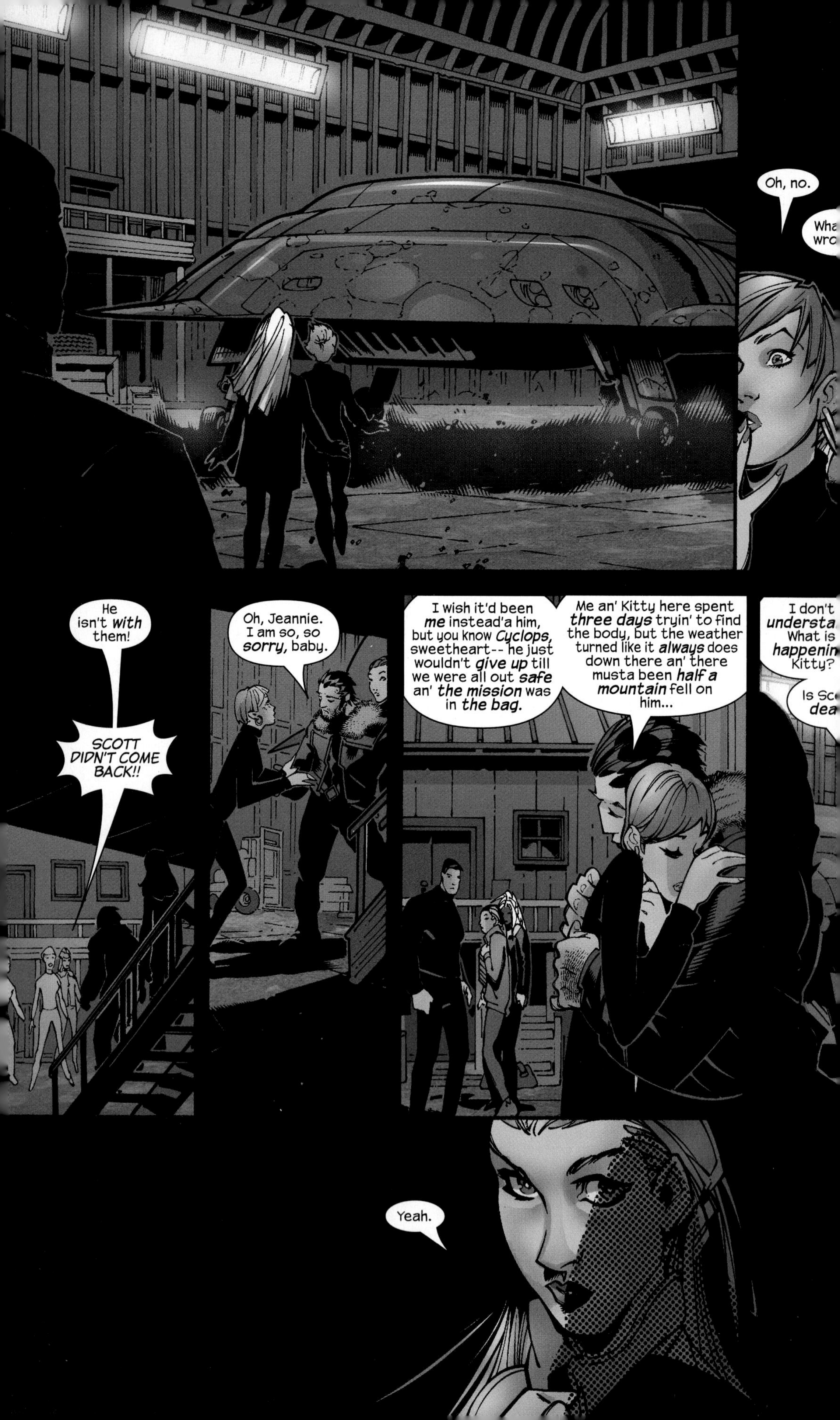
Oh, no.
He isn't *with* them!
SCOTT DIDN'T COME BACK!!
Oh, Jeannie. I am so, so *sorry,* baby.
I wish it'd been *me* instead'a him, but you know *Cyclops,* sweetheart-- he just wouldn't *give up* till we were all out *safe* an' *the mission* was in *the bag.*
Me an' Kitty here spent *three days* tryin' to find the body, but the weather turned like it *always* does down there an' there musta been *half a mountain* fell on him...
Yeah.

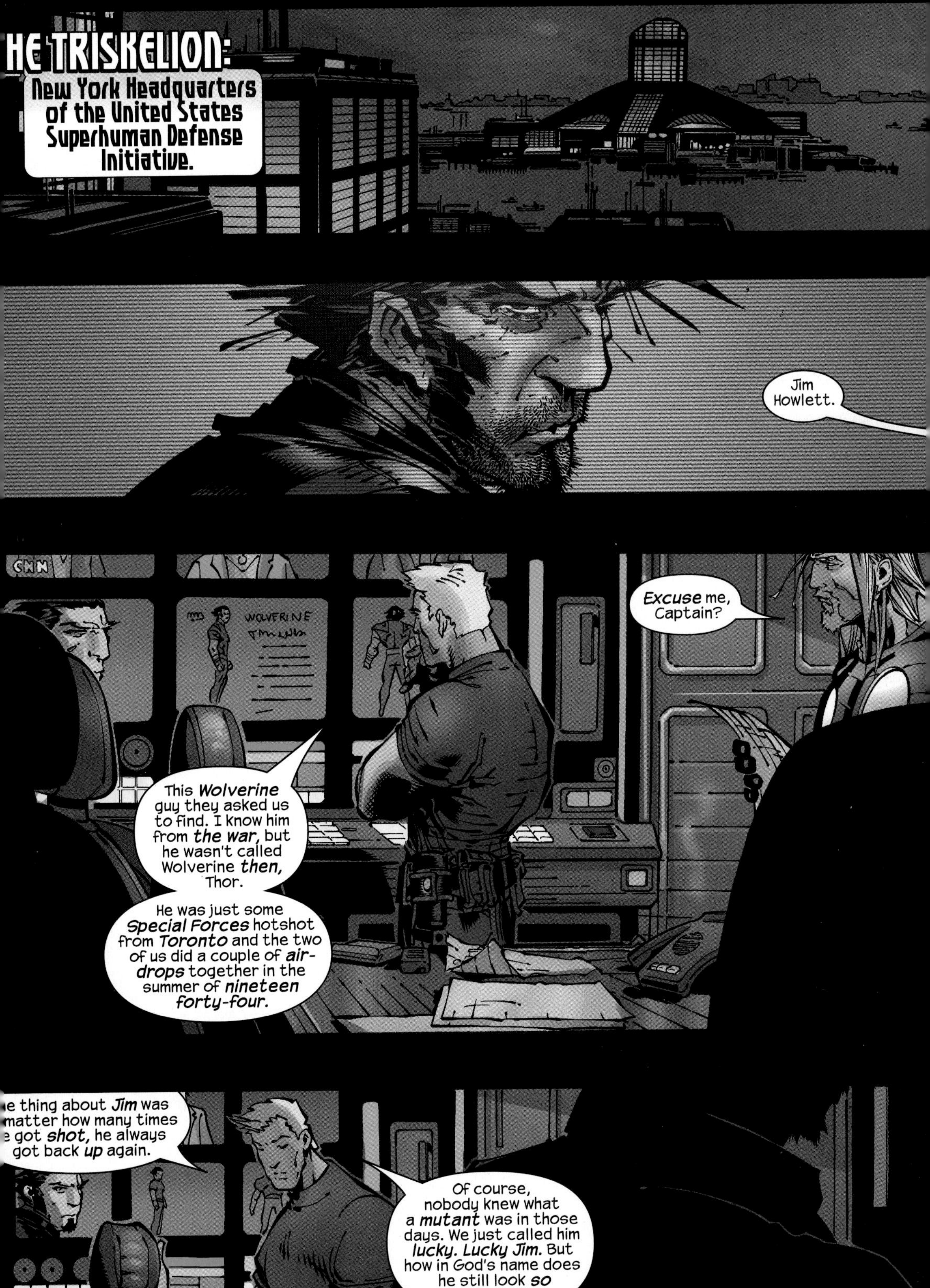
HE TRISKELION:
New York Headquarters of the United States Superhuman Defense Initiative.
Jim Howlett.
CNN
WOLVERINE
Excuse me, Captain?
This Wolverine guy they asked us to find. I know him from the war, but he wasn't called Wolverine then, Thor.
He was just some Special Forces hotshot from Toronto and the two of us did a couple of air-drops together in the summer of nineteen forty-four.
e thing about Jim was matter how many times e got shot, he always got back up again.
Of course, nobody knew what a mutant was in those days. We just called him lucky. Lucky Jim. But how in God's name does he still look so young?

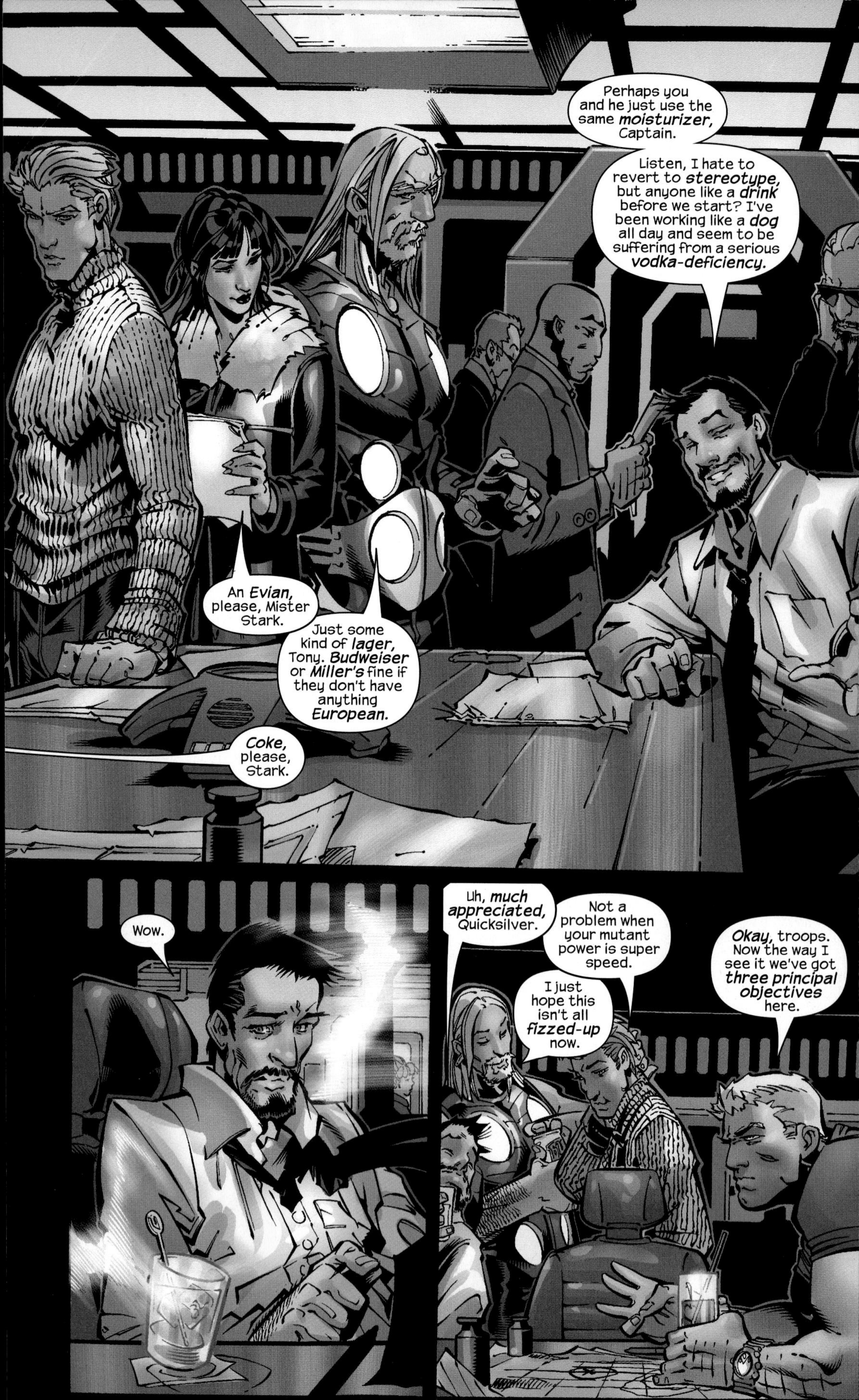

Perhaps you and he just use the same moisturizer, Captain.
Listen, I hate to revert to stereotype, but anyone like a drink before we start? I've been working like a dog all day and seem to be suffering from a serious vodka-deficiency.
An Evian, please, Mister Stark.
Just some kind of lager, Tony. Budweiser or Miller's fine if they don't have anything European.
Coke, please, Stark.
Wow.
Uh, much appreciated, Quicksilver.
Not a problem when your mutant power is super speed.
I just hope this isn't all fizzed-up now.
Okay, troops. Now the way I see it we've got three principal objectives here.

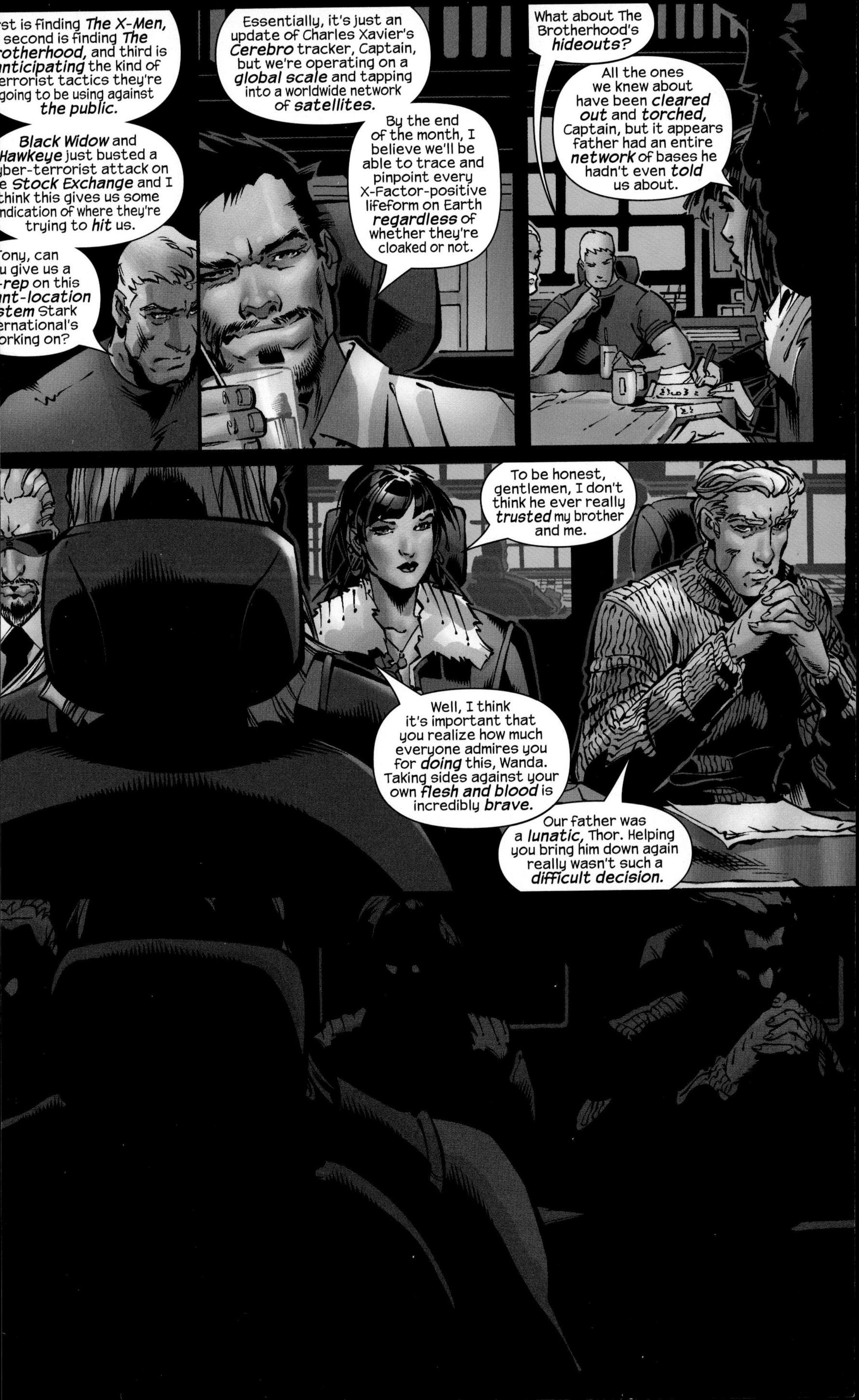
rst is finding The X-Men, second is finding The rotherhood, and third is nticipating the kind of errorist tactics they're going to be using against the public.
Black Widow and Hawkeye just busted a yber-terrorist attack on e Stock Exchange and I think this gives us some ndication of where they're trying to hit us.
Tony, can u give us a -rep on this nt-location stem Stark ernational's orking on?
Essentially, it's just an update of Charles Xavier's Cerebro tracker, Captain, but we're operating on a global scale and tapping into a worldwide network of satellites.
By the end of the month, I believe we'll be able to trace and pinpoint every X-Factor-positive lifeform on Earth regardless of whether they're cloaked or not.
What about The Brotherhood's hideouts?
All the ones we knew about have been cleared out and torched, Captain, but it appears father had an entire network of bases he hadn't even told us about.
To be honest, gentlemen, I don't think he ever really trusted my brother and me.
Well, I think it's important that you realize how much everyone admires you for doing this, Wanda. Taking sides against your own flesh and blood is incredibly brave.
Our father was a lunatic, Thor. Helping you bring him down again really wasn't such a difficult decision.

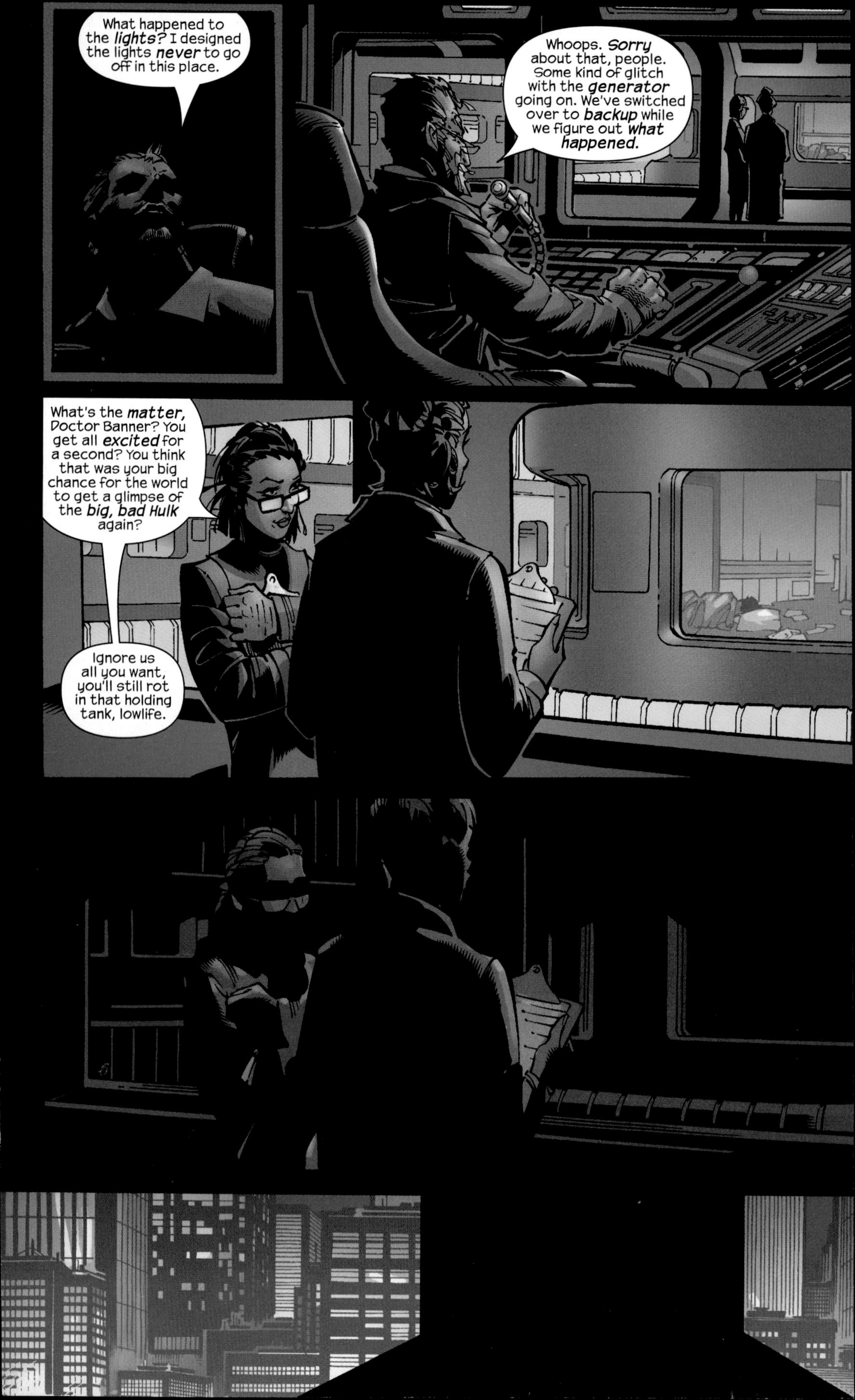

What happened to the *lights?* I designed the lights *never* to go off in this place.
Whoops. *Sorry* about that, people. Some kind of glitch with the *generator* going on. We've switched over to *backup* while we figure out *what happened.*
What's the *matter,* Doctor Banner? You get all *excited* for a second? You think that was your big chance for the world to get a glimpse of the *big, bad Hulk* again?
Ignore us all you want, you'll still rot in that holding tank, lowlife.

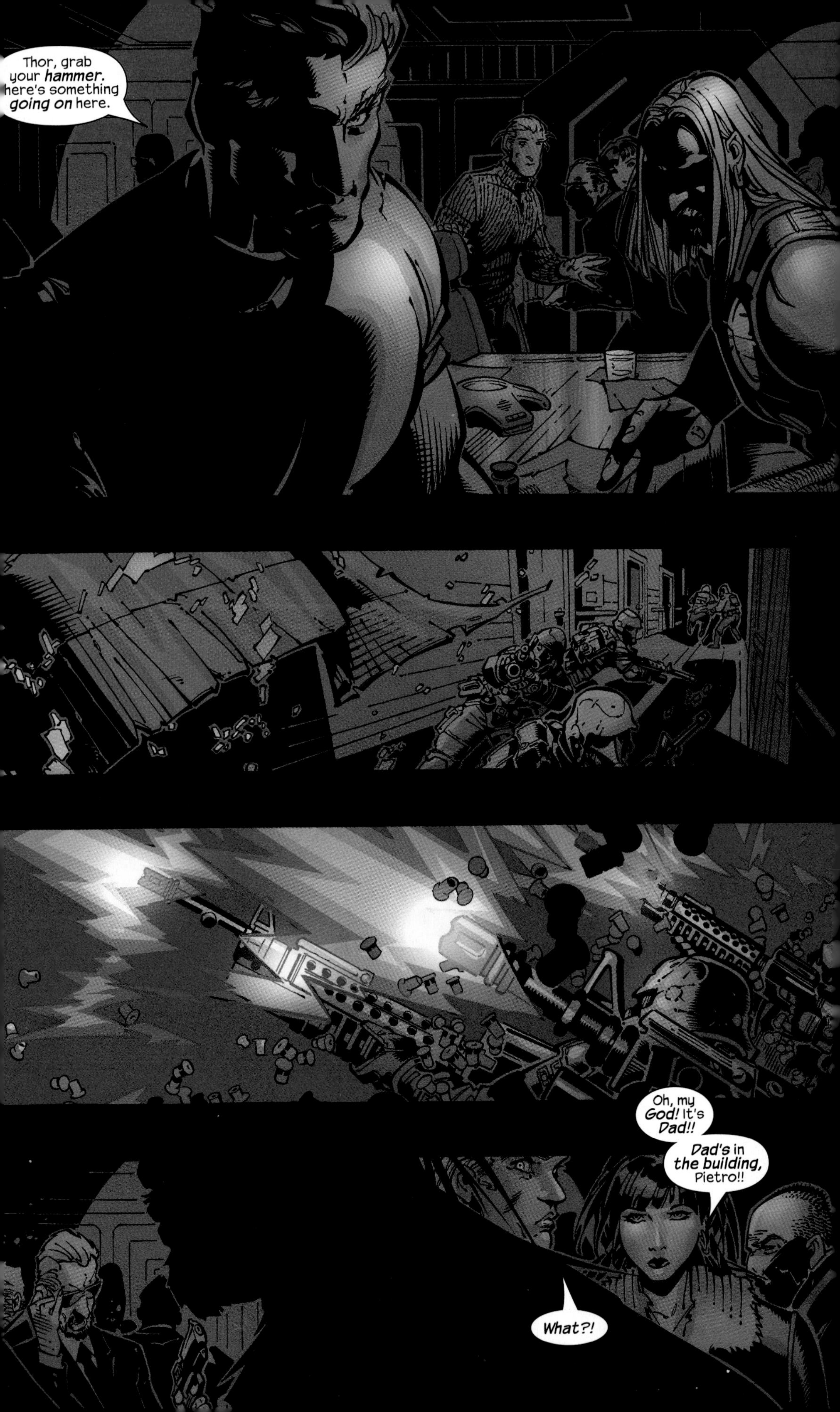
Thor, grab your **hammer.** here's something ***going on*** here.
Oh, my ***God!*** It's ***Dad!!***
Dad's in ***the building,*** Pietro!!
What?!

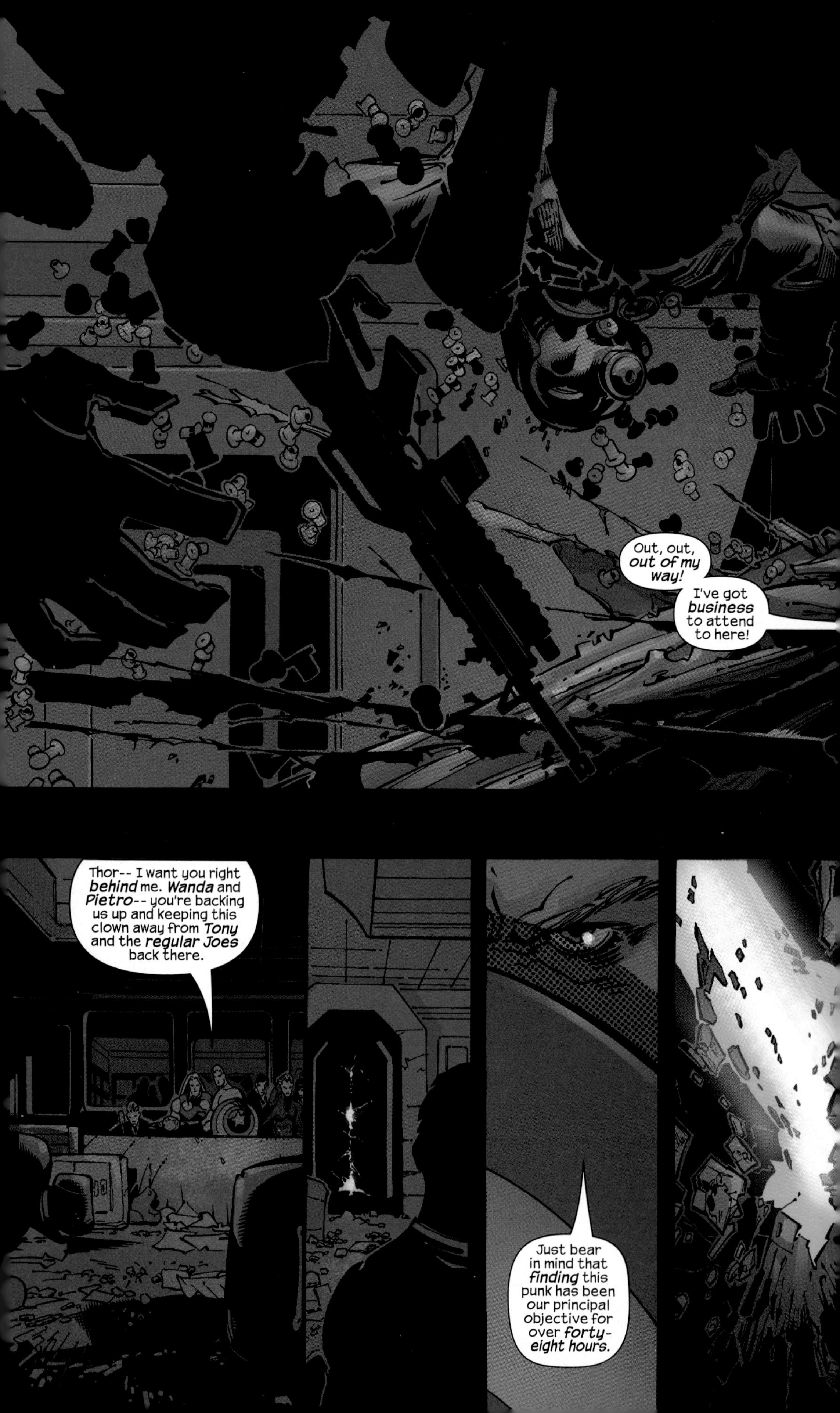

Out, out, out of my way!
I've got business to attend to here!
Thor-- I want you right behind me. Wanda and Pietro-- you're backing us up and keeping this clown away from Tony and the regular Joes back there.
Just bear in mind that finding this punk has been our principal objective for over forty-eight hours.

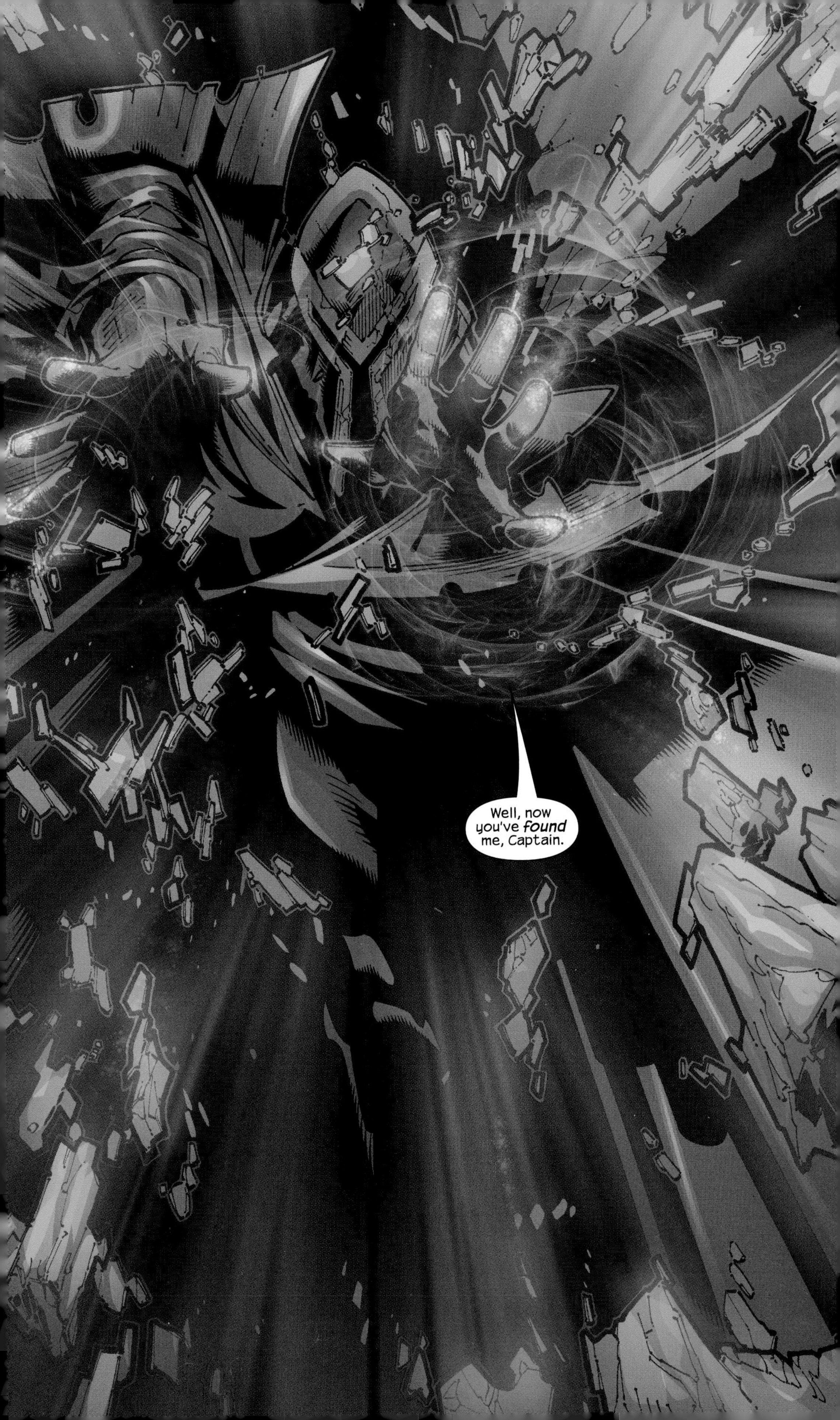
Well, now you've *found* me, Captain.

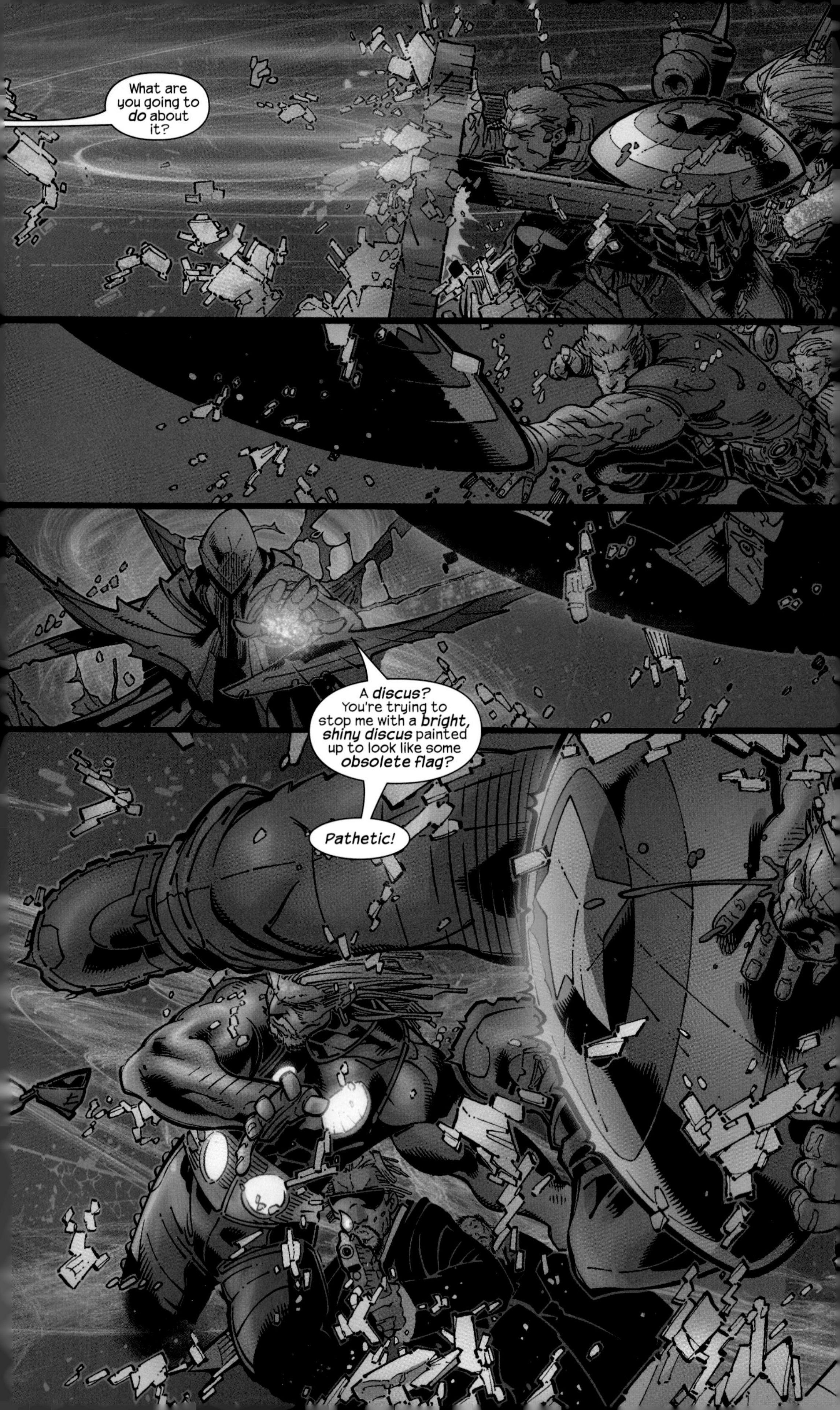
What are you going to *do* about it?
A *discus?* You're trying to stop me with a *bright, shiny discus* painted up to look like some *obsolete flag?*
Pathetic!

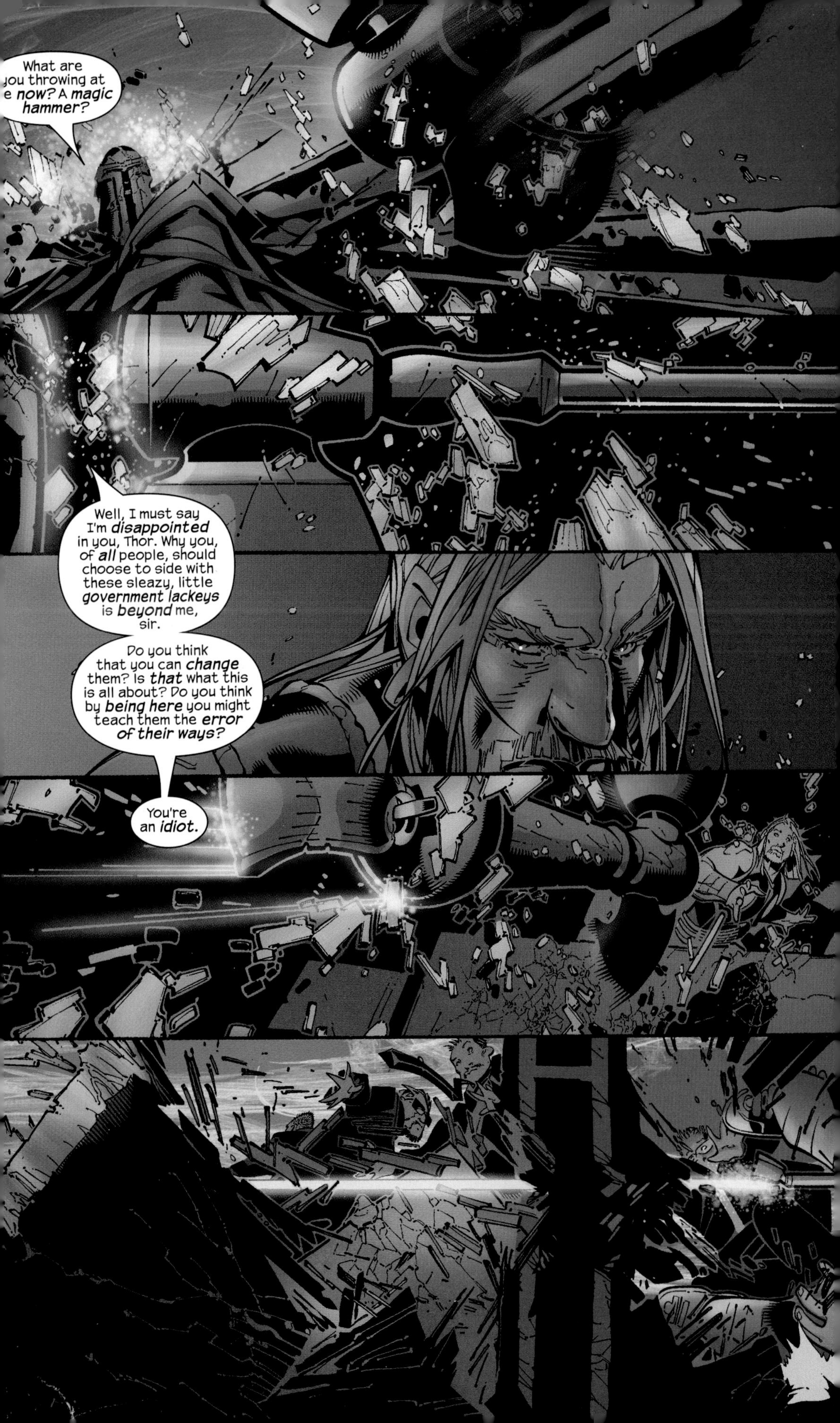
What are you throwing at e now? A magic hammer?
Well, I must say I'm disappointed in you, Thor. Why you, of all people, should choose to side with these sleazy, little government lackeys is beyond me, sir.
Do you think that you can change them? Is that what this is all about? Do you think by being here you might teach them the error of their ways?
You're an idiot.

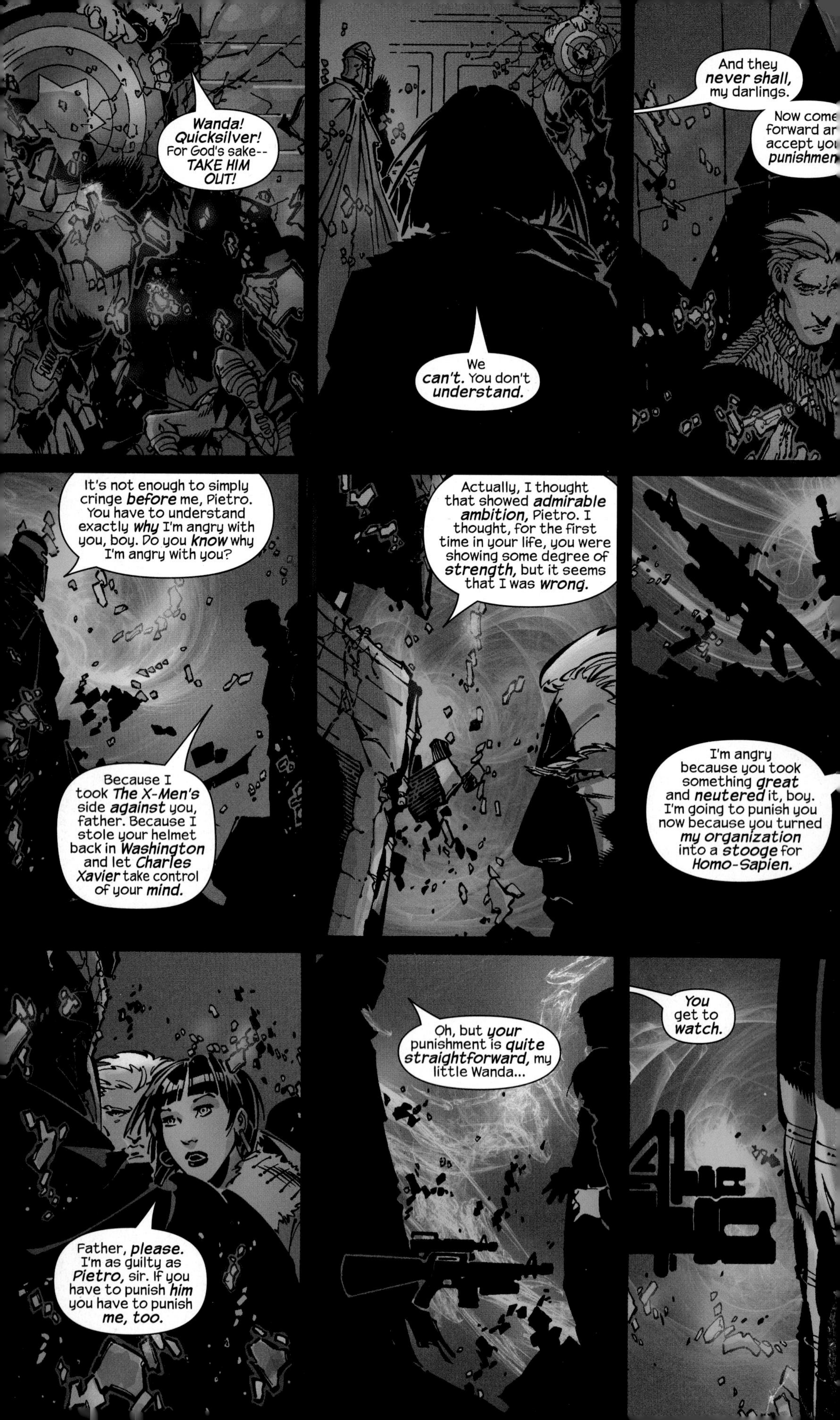
Wanda! Quicksilver! For God's sake-- TAKE HIM OUT!
We can't. You don't understand.
And they never shall, my darlings.
Now come forward ar accept you punishmen
It's not enough to simply cringe before me, Pietro. You have to understand exactly why I'm angry with you, boy. Do you know why I'm angry with you?
Because I took The X-Men's side against you, father. Because I stole your helmet back in Washington and let Charles Xavier take control of your mind.
Actually, I thought that showed admirable ambition, Pietro. I thought, for the first time in your life, you were showing some degree of strength, but it seems that I was wrong.
I'm angry because you took something great and neutered it, boy. I'm going to punish you now because you turned my organization into a stooge for Homo-Sapien.
Father, please. I'm as guilty as Pietro, sir. If you have to punish him you have to punish me, too.
Oh, but your punishment is quite straightforward, my little Wanda...
You get to watch.

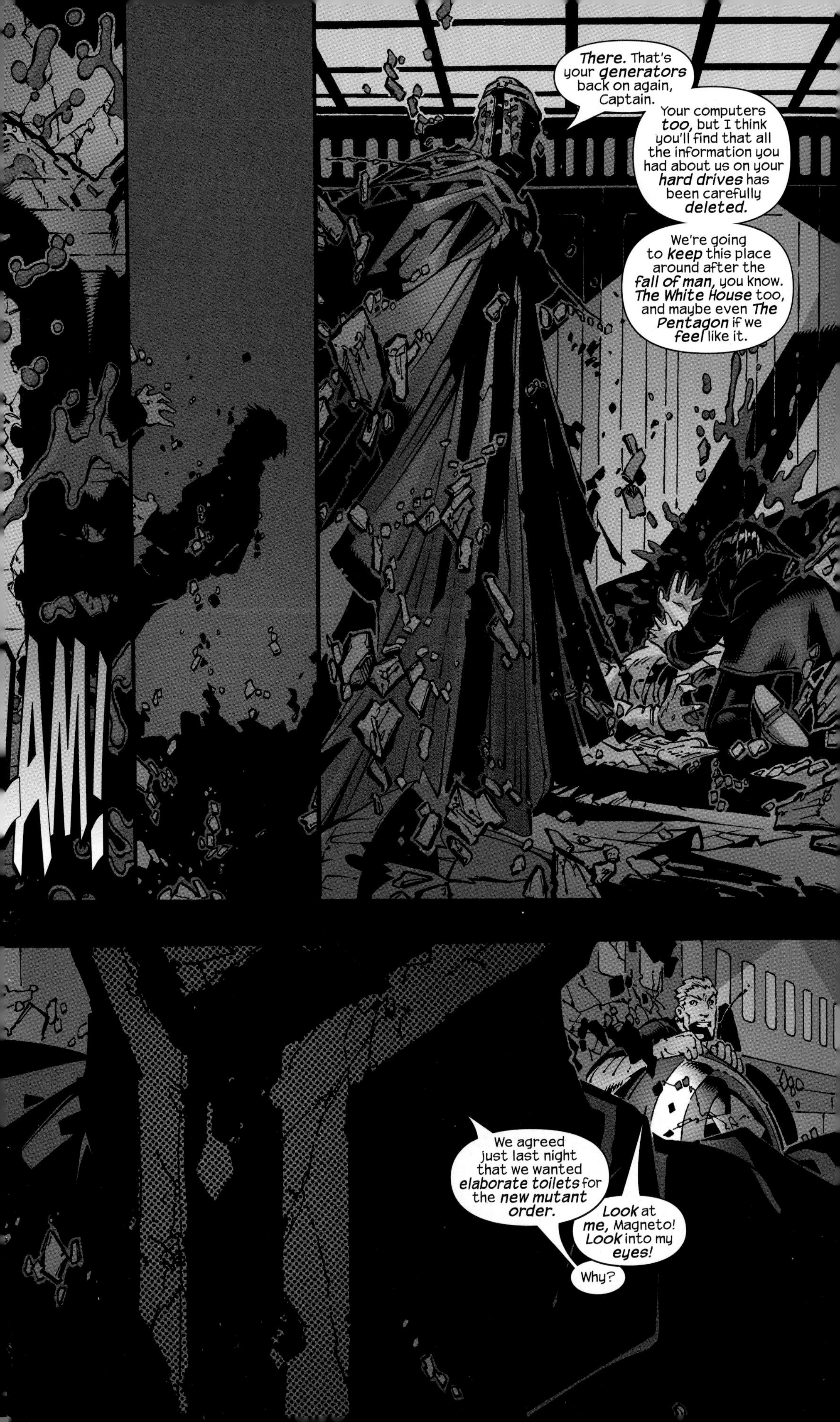
There. That's your generators back on again, Captain.
Your computers too, but I think you'll find that all the information you had about us on your hard drives has been carefully deleted.
We're going to keep this place around after the fall of man, you know. The White House too, and maybe even The Pentagon if we feel like it.
We agreed just last night that we wanted elaborate toilets for the new mutant order.
Look at me, Magneto! Look into my eyes!
Why?

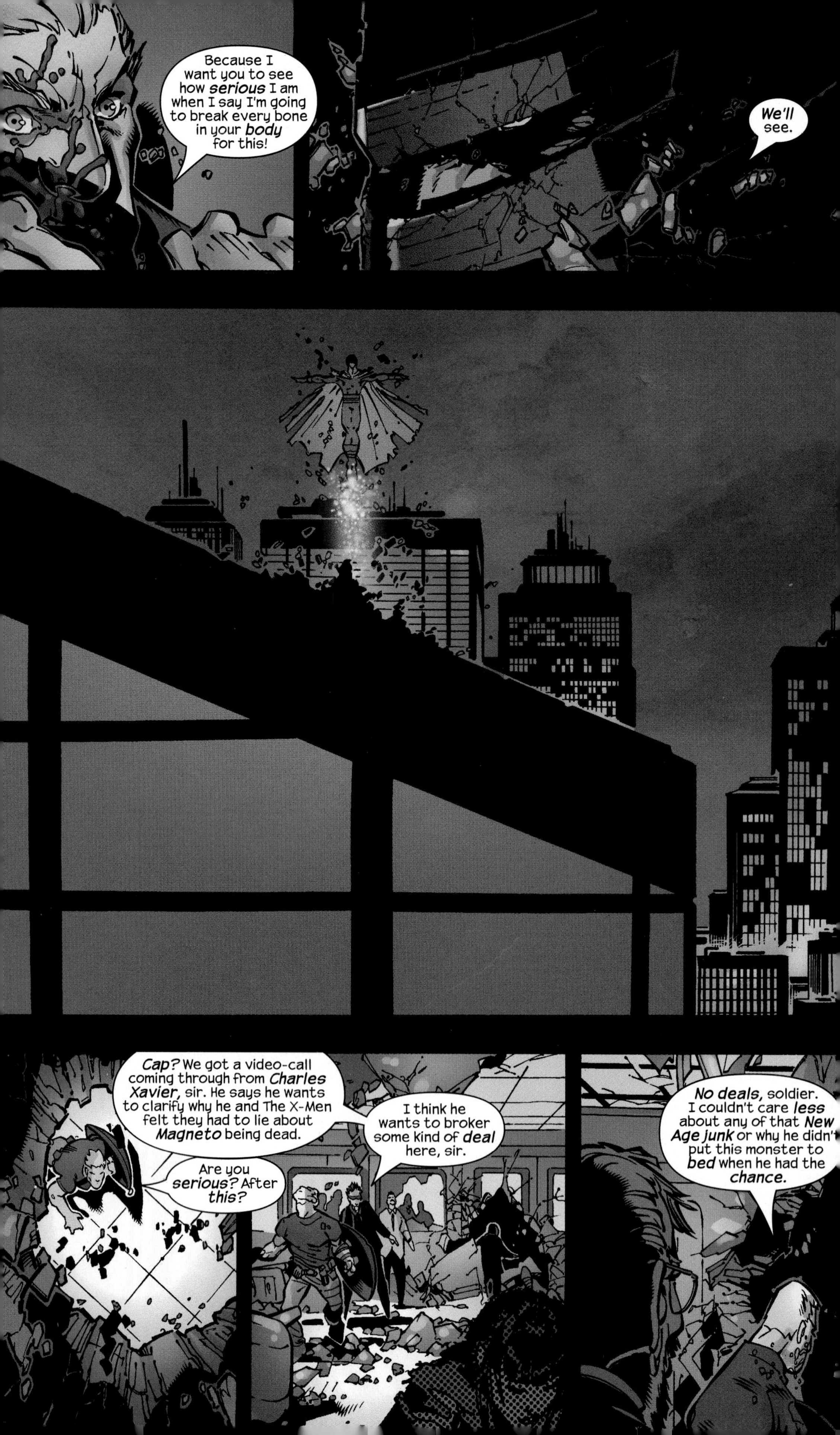
Because I want you to see how *serious* I am when I say I'm going to break every bone in your *body* for this!
We'll see.
Cap? We got a video-call coming through from *Charles Xavier,* sir. He says he wants to clarify why he and The X-Men felt they had to lie about *Magneto* being dead.
Are you *serious? After this?*
I think he wants to broker some kind of *deal* here, sir.
No deals, soldier. I couldn't care *less* about any of that *New Age junk* or why he didn't put this monster to *bed* when he had the *chance.*

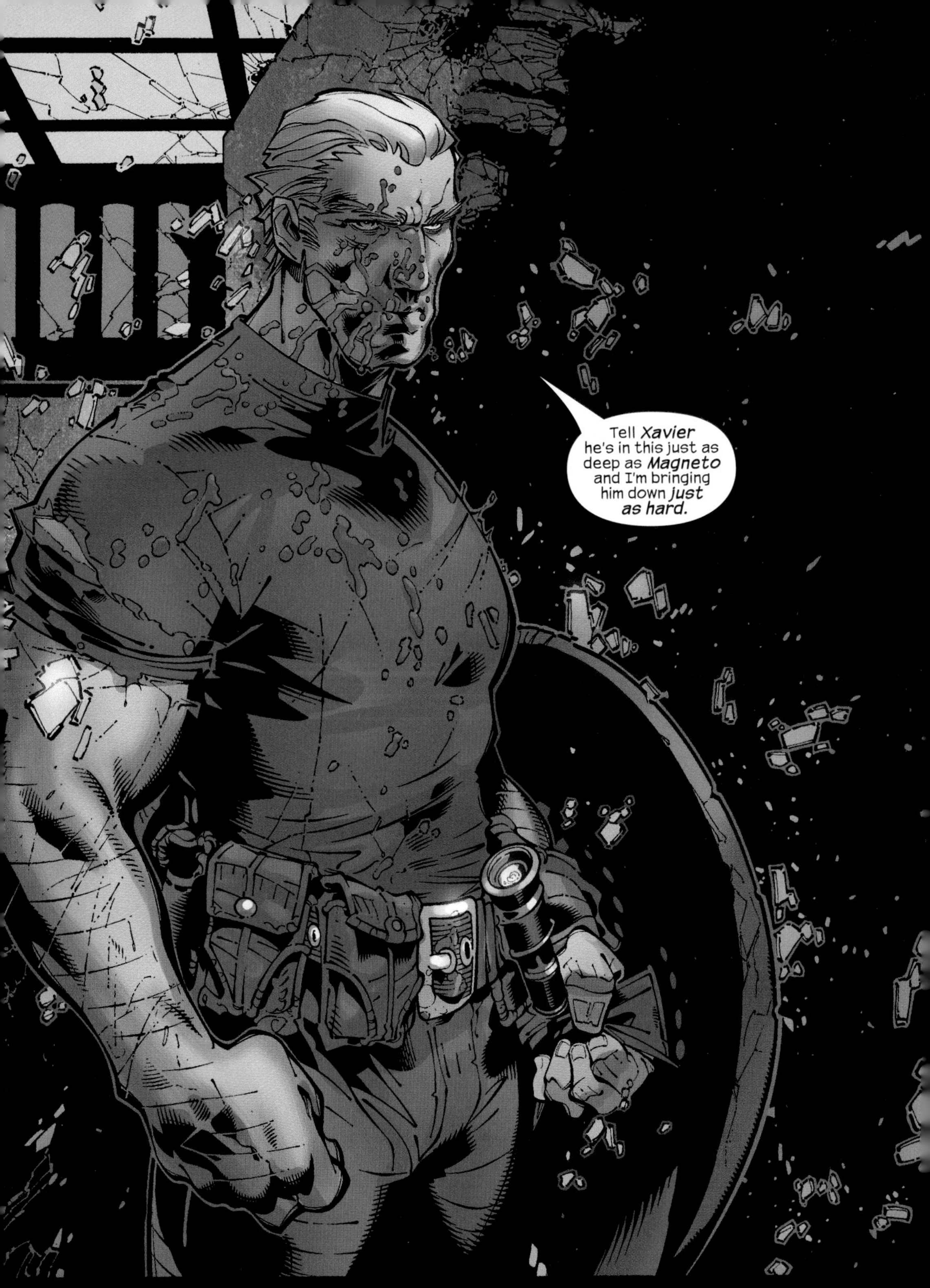
Tell *Xavier* he's in this just as deep as *Magneto* and I'm bringing him down *just as hard.*

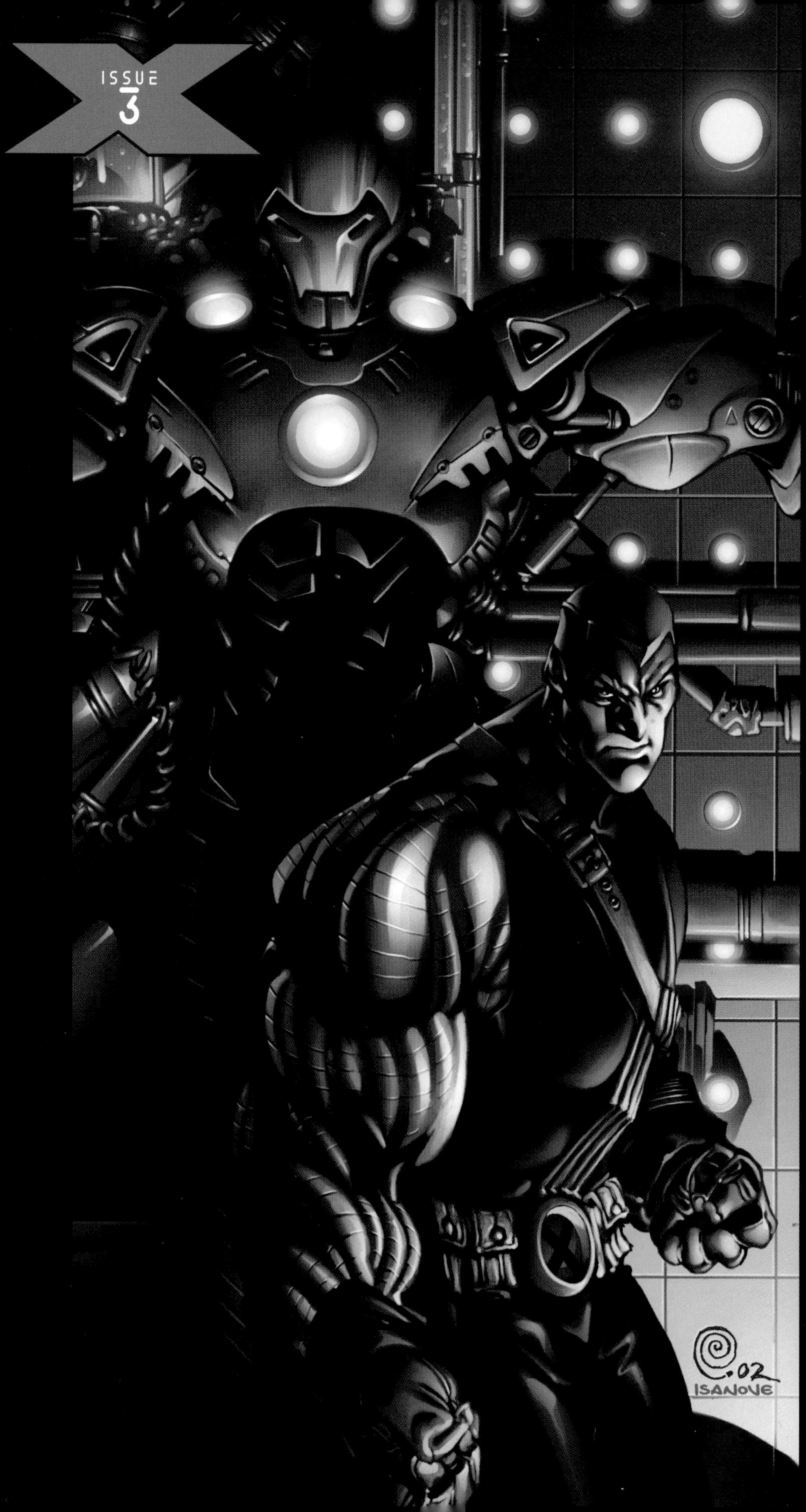
ISSUE
3
©.02
ISANOVE

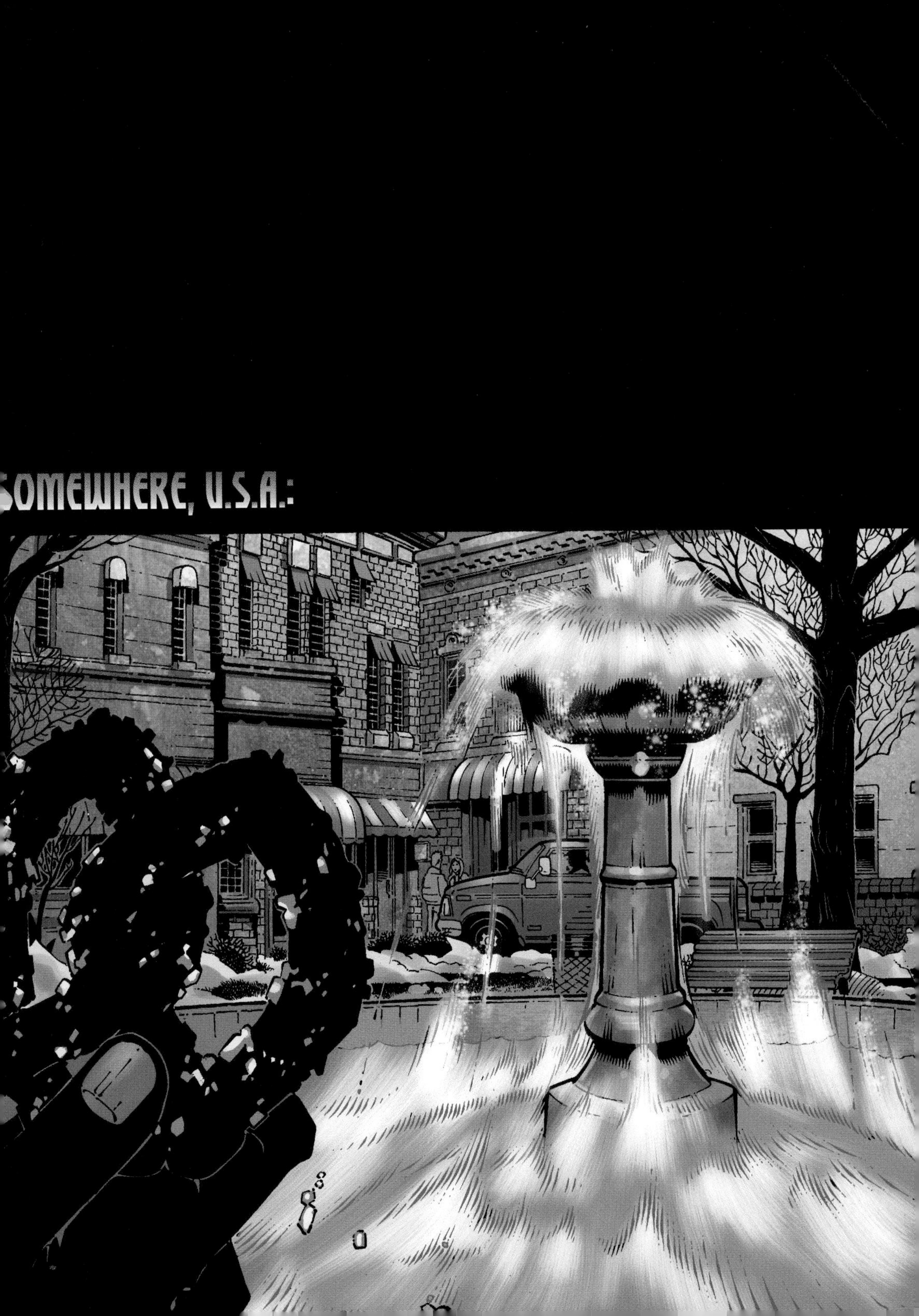
SOMEWHERE, U.S.A.:

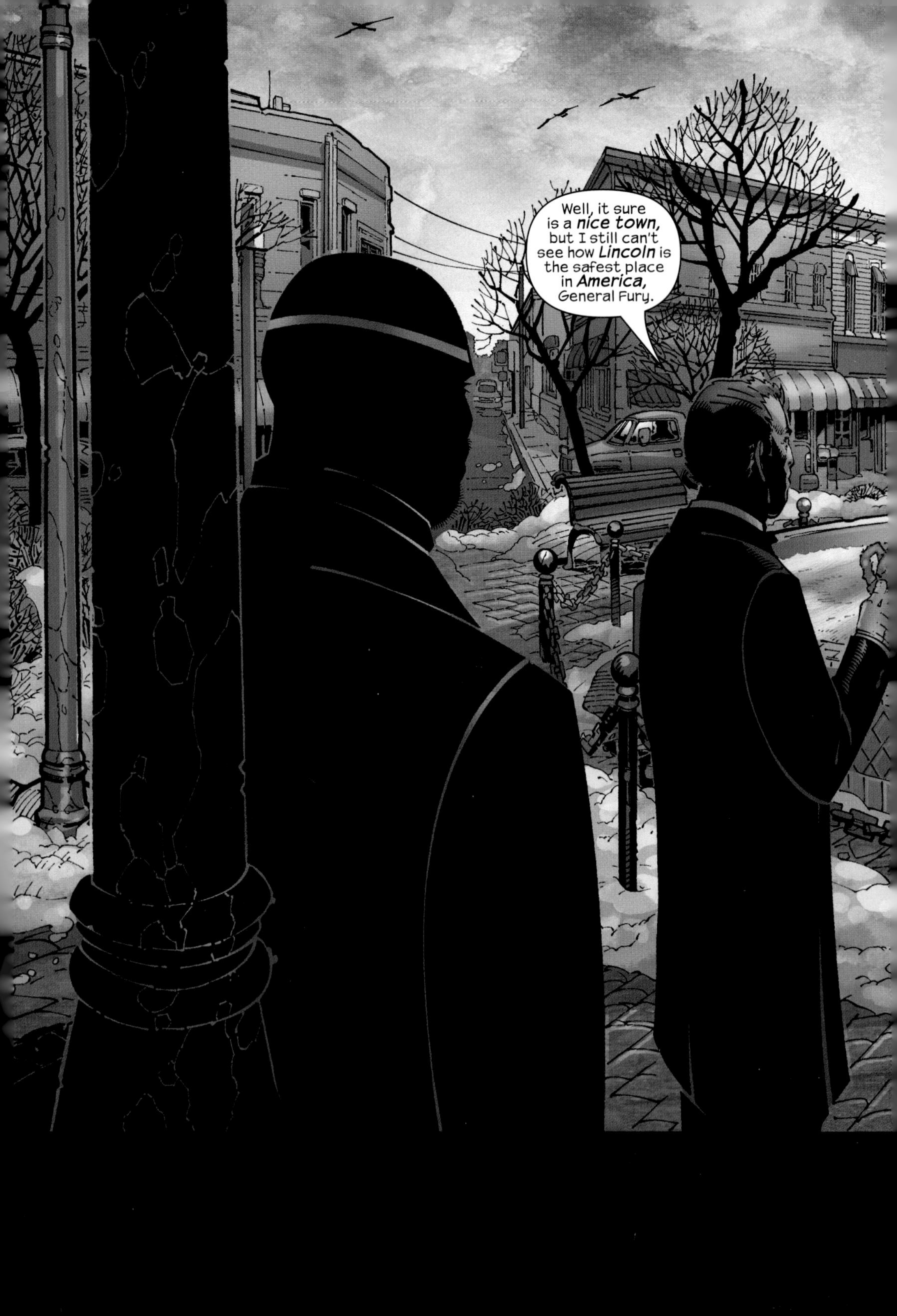
Well, it sure is a *nice town,* but I still can't see how *Lincoln* is the safest place in *America,* General Fury.

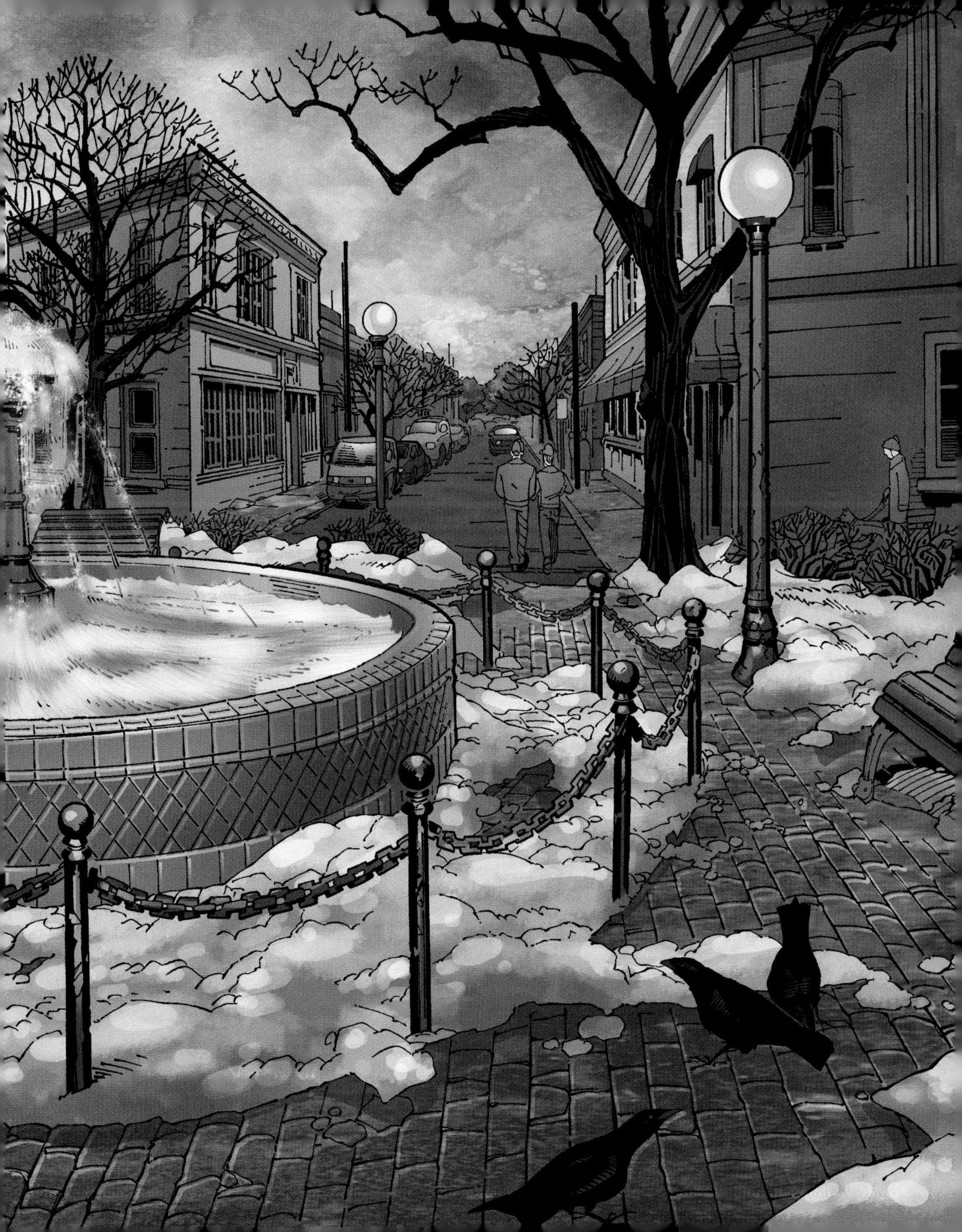

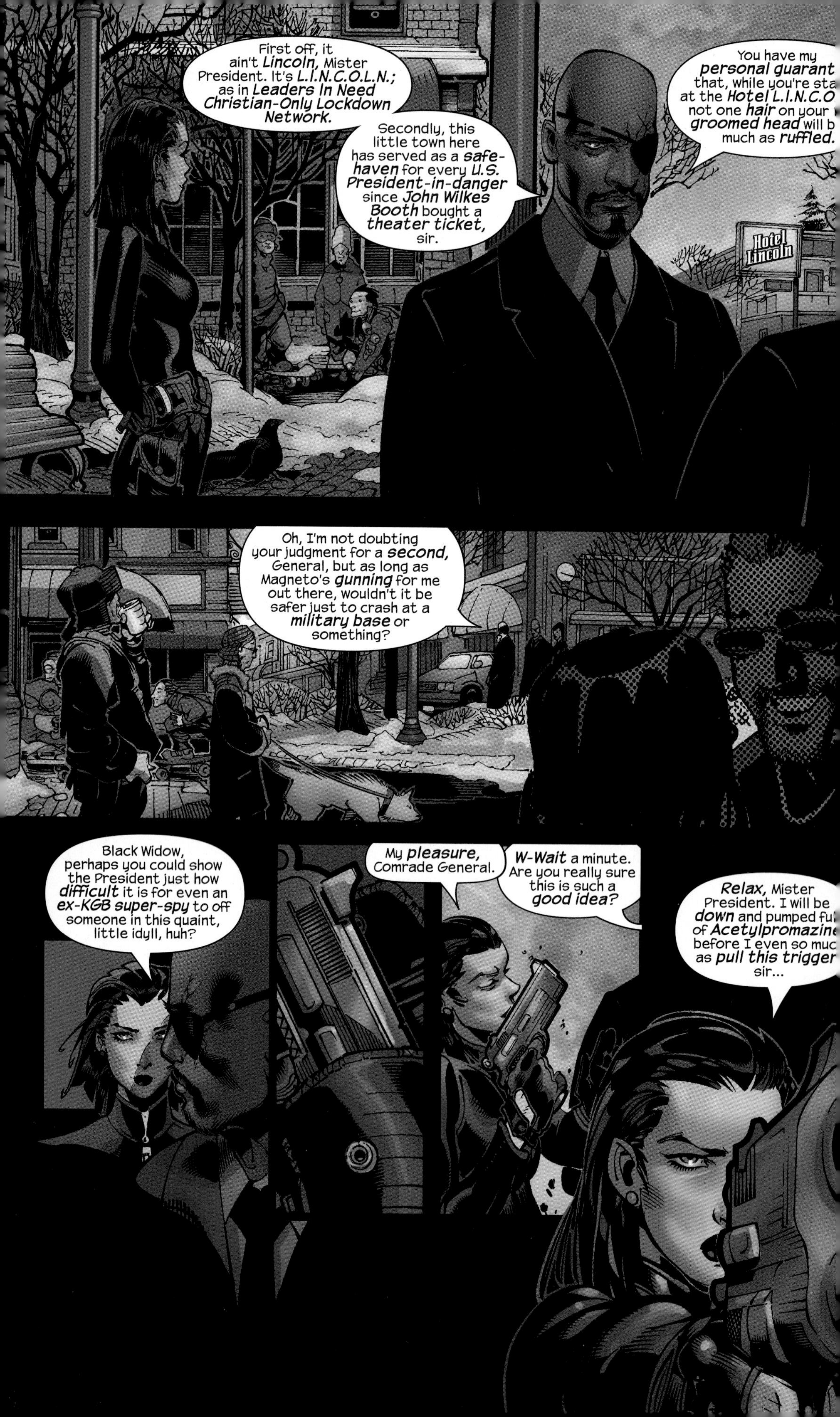

First off, it ain't Lincoln, Mister President. It's L.I.N.C.O.L.N.; as in Leaders In Need Christian-Only Lockdown Network.
Secondly, this little town here has served as a safe-haven for every U.S. President-in-danger since John Wilkes Booth bought a theater ticket, sir.
You have my personal guarant that, while you're sta at the Hotel L.I.N.C.O not one hair on your groomed head will b much as ruffled.
Hotel Lincoln
Oh, I'm not doubting your judgment for a second, General, but as long as Magneto's gunning for me out there, wouldn't it be safer just to crash at a military base or something?
Black Widow, perhaps you could show the President just how difficult it is for even an ex-KGB super-spy to off someone in this quaint, little idyll, huh?
My pleasure, Comrade General.
W-Wait a minute. Are you really sure this is such a good idea?
Relax, Mister President. I will be down and pumped fu of Acetylpromazine before I even so muc as pull this trigger sir...

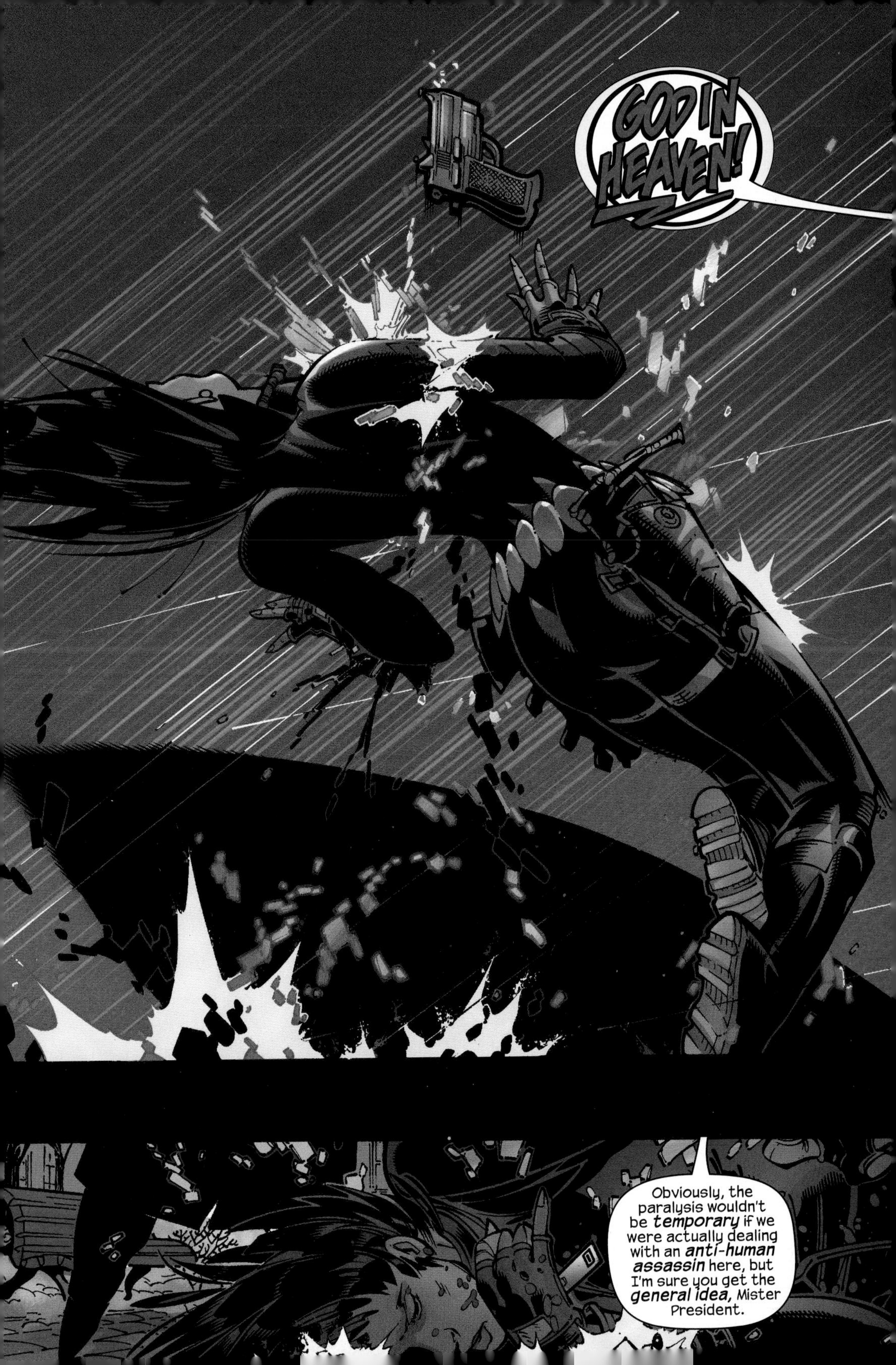
GOD IN HEAVEN!
Obviously, the paralysis wouldn't be temporary if we were actually dealing with an anti-human assassin here, but I'm sure you get the general idea, Mister President.

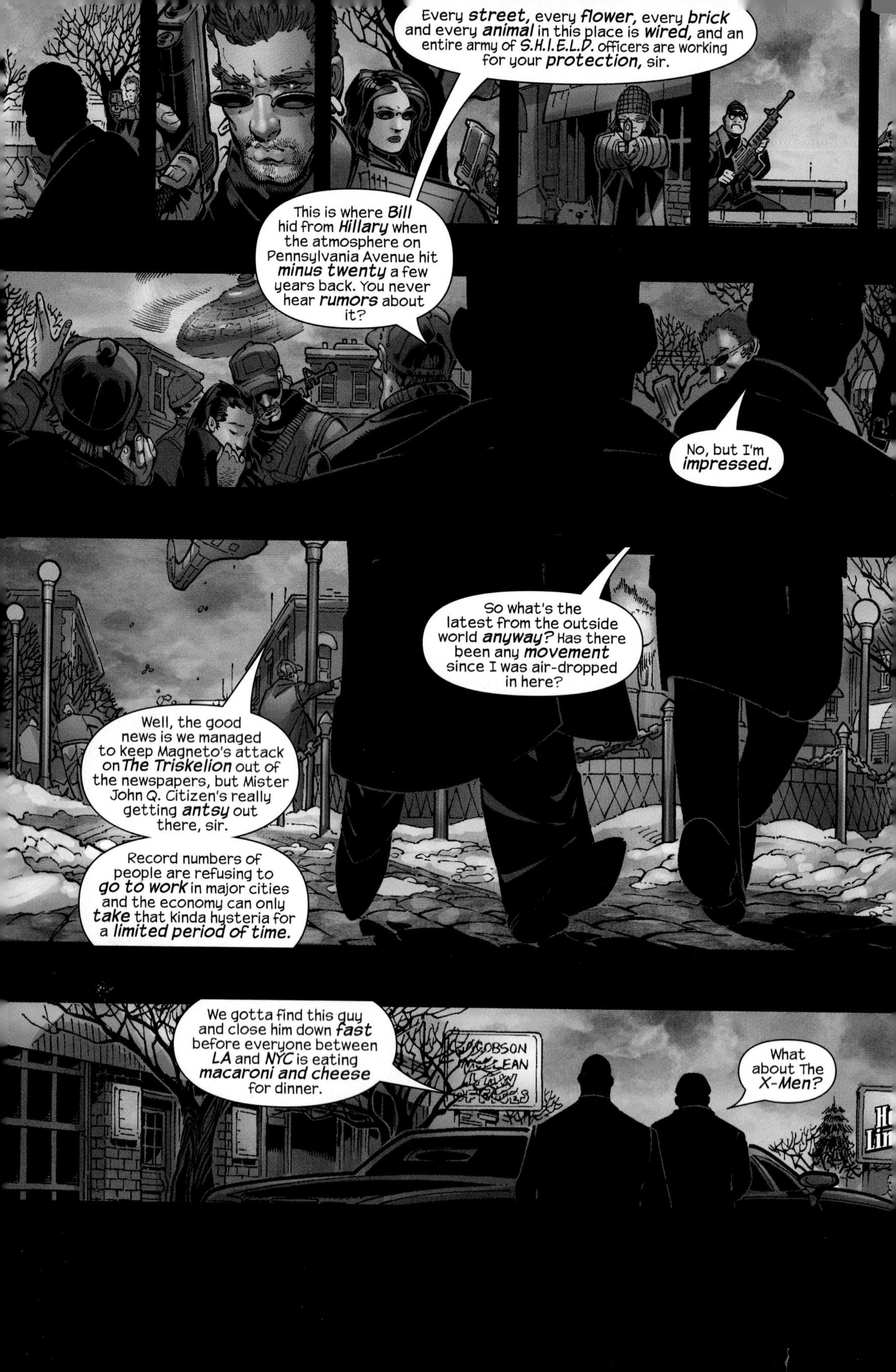

Every street, every flower, every brick and every animal in this place is wired, and an entire army of S.H.I.E.L.D. officers are working for your protection, sir.
This is where Bill hid from Hillary when the atmosphere on Pennsylvania Avenue hit minus twenty a few years back. You never hear rumors about it?
No, but I'm impressed.
So what's the latest from the outside world anyway? Has there been any movement since I was air-dropped in here?
Well, the good news is we managed to keep Magneto's attack on The Triskelion out of the newspapers, but Mister John Q. Citizen's really getting antsy out there, sir.
Record numbers of people are refusing to go to work in major cities and the economy can only take that kinda hysteria for a limited period of time.
We gotta find this guy and close him down fast before everyone between LA and NYC is eating macaroni and cheese for dinner.
What about The X-Men?

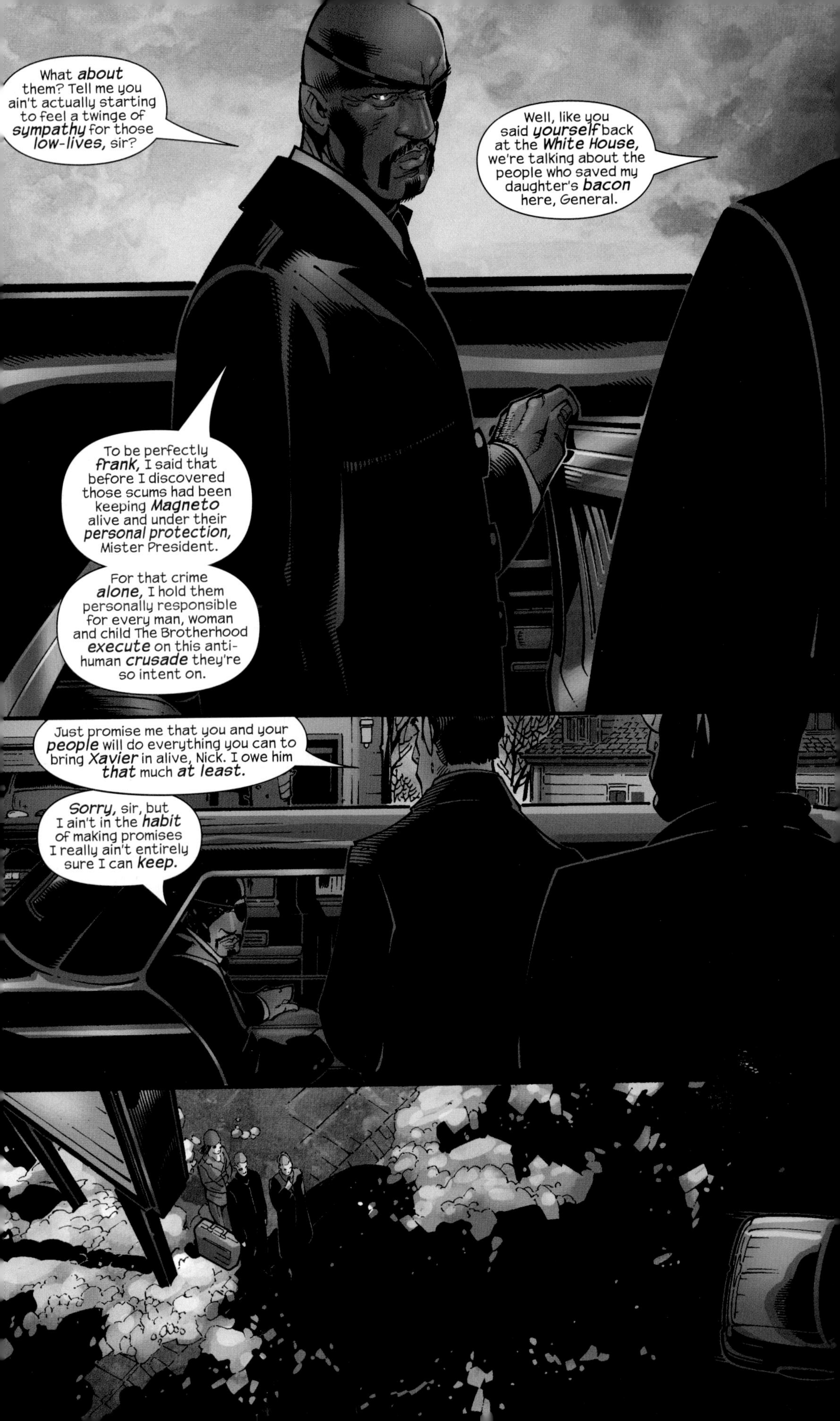
What about them? Tell me you ain't actually starting to feel a twinge of sympathy for those low-lives, sir?
Well, like you said yourself back at the White House, we're talking about the people who saved my daughter's bacon here, General.
To be perfectly frank, I said that before I discovered those scums had been keeping Magneto alive and under their personal protection, Mister President.
For that crime alone, I hold them personally responsible for every man, woman and child The Brotherhood execute on this anti-human crusade they're so intent on.
Just promise me that you and your people will do everything you can to bring Xavier in alive, Nick. I owe him that much at least.
Sorry, sir, but I ain't in the habit of making promises I really ain't entirely sure I can keep.

THE TRISKELION:
Upper-bay Manhattan headquarters of America's post-nuclear defense initiative, currently on high alert.

What the heck happened *here*?

Banner turned into The Hulk and escaped from the *holding bay* when Magneto switched the *power* off, Steve.

It was only a couple of minutes before the back-up generator kicked in and the *gas* knocked him out, but that was all he needed to break loose and eat the *nursing staff*.

He *ate* them?

All *six* of them. Every one of these people had *kids* and our resident *vegetarian* here downed them in *seconds*.

I don't usually *get* freaked out in a crisis. I'm usually really *good* with this stuff, but this whole *Brotherhood* thing has me *sick* to my *stomach* this time.

Jan, can I *talk* to you for a second?

Sure, you want me to take another look at *Quicksilver* and those poor, shot *kneecaps* of his? I told Nick I'd head along after my *coffee break*.

No, I know why this case is getting you so *upset*, Jan. We *all* do, and I want you to know that none of this *DNA stuff* matters to *anyone else* on the team.

What? What the hell are you *talking* about, Steve?

You don't have t pretend anymore, We know you're a *mu* and we know you we *born* with these powers.

Fury's know about it since day you *signe* honey. Appare it's one of the things they *sc* for at the *medical*.

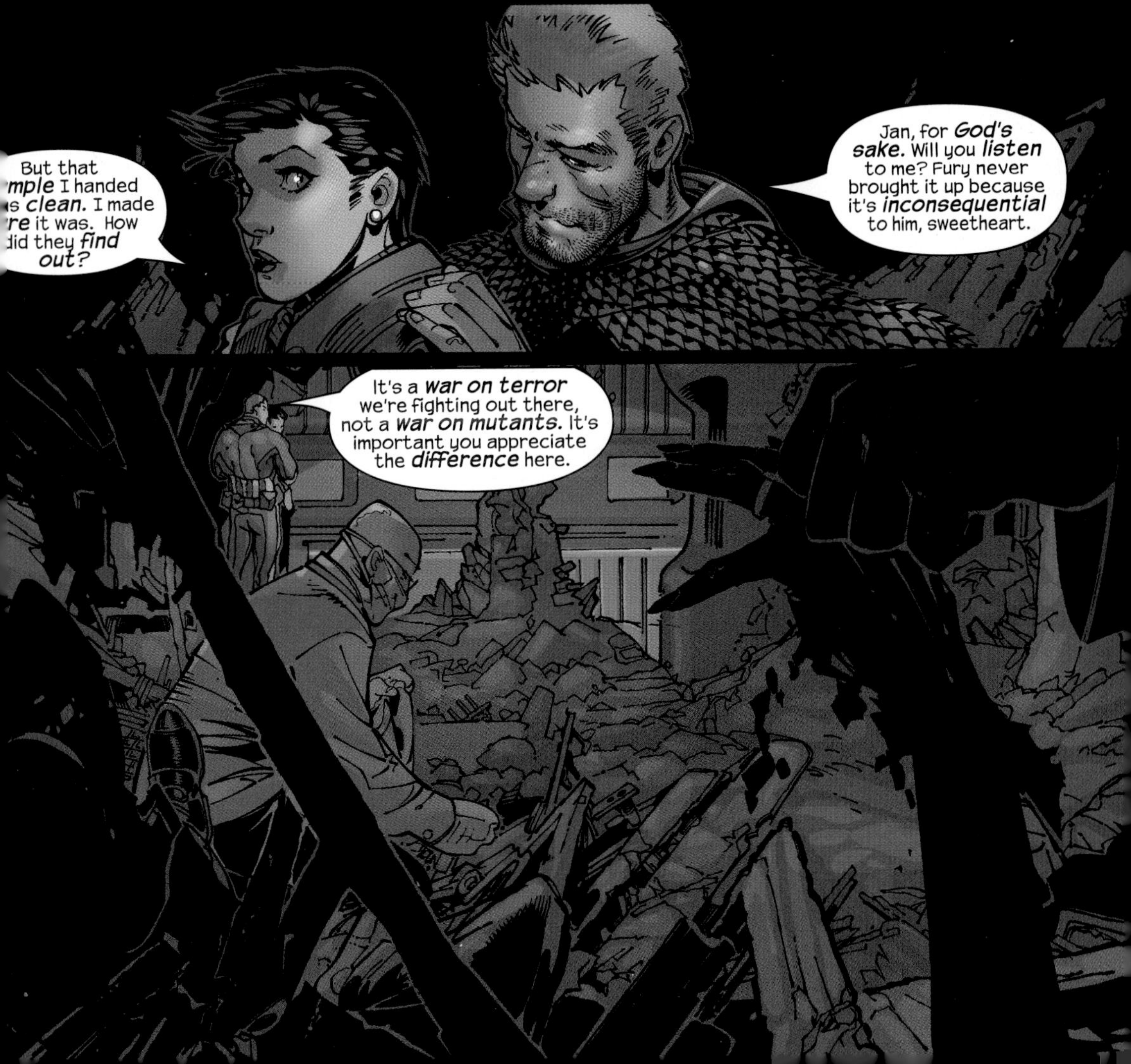
But that mple I handed s clean. I made re it was. How did they find out?
Jan, for God's sake. Will you listen to me? Fury never brought it up because it's inconsequential to him, sweetheart.
It's a war on terror we're fighting out there, not a war on mutants. It's important you appreciate the difference here.

CLEVELAND, OHIO:

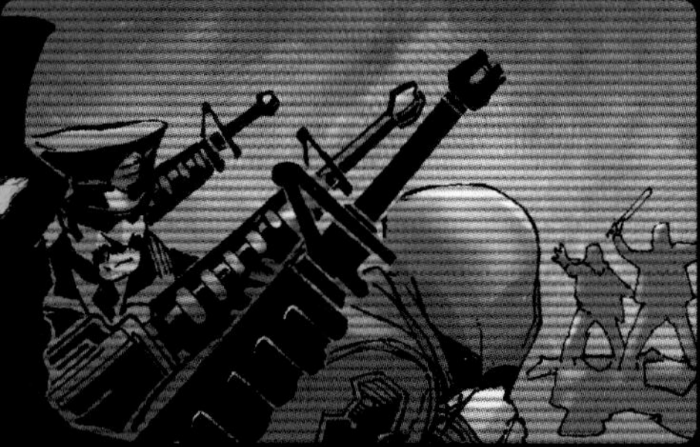

...in **Paris** last night as three known associates of The Brotherhood of Mutants were arrested after police foile a plot to destroy the famous **Champs Élysees.**

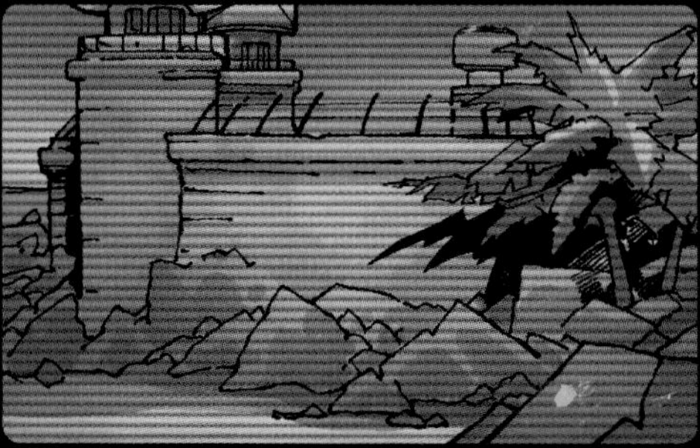

The suspects were flown to **Cuba** this morning where the being held in the controversial **Camp X-Factor,** much to dismay of both church leaders and human rights campaign

Camp conditions have been described as **inhumane,** but House spokesmen say they refuse to make compromises i wake of Magneto's attack on the **Brooklyn Bridge.**

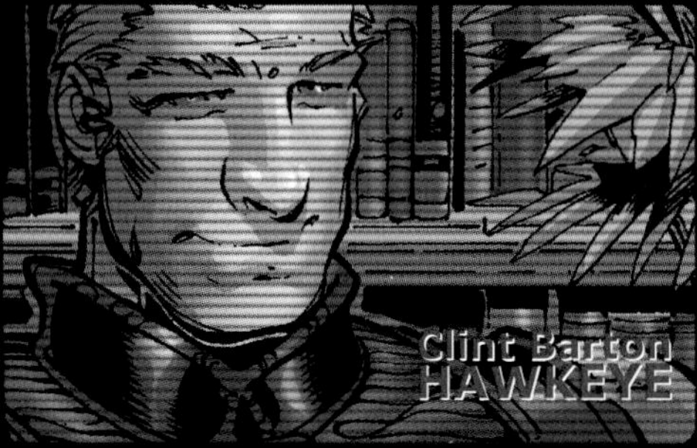
Clint Barton
HAWKEYE

For God's sake, how many times do we have to **say** this before it **sinks in,** honey-- no, this **isn't** a purge of every teenager with an **X-gene** in their system.

These arrests are just being localized to The **X-Men** and **Brotherhood** and nobody else has anything to fear, pro they're **registered** with **the authorities.**

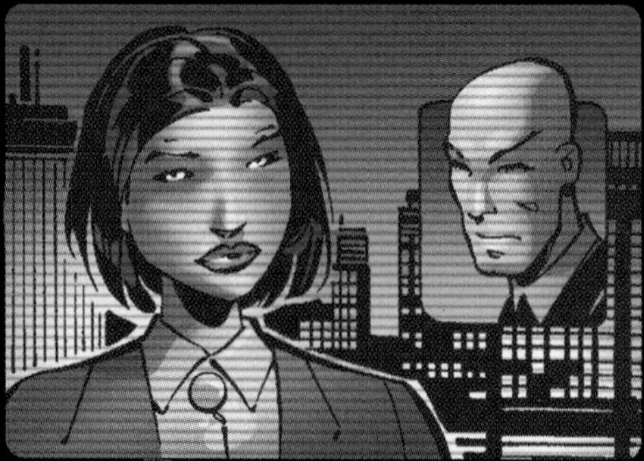

Professor Charles Xavier of The X-Men also reiterated th although he **did** hide Magneto from the security services i the past, he has now made a pledge to **catch** him for us.

White House spokesperson **Condoleezza Rice,** however, **dismissed** this latest plea for amnesty and stressed tha Charles Xavier could simply **no longer** be **trusted.**

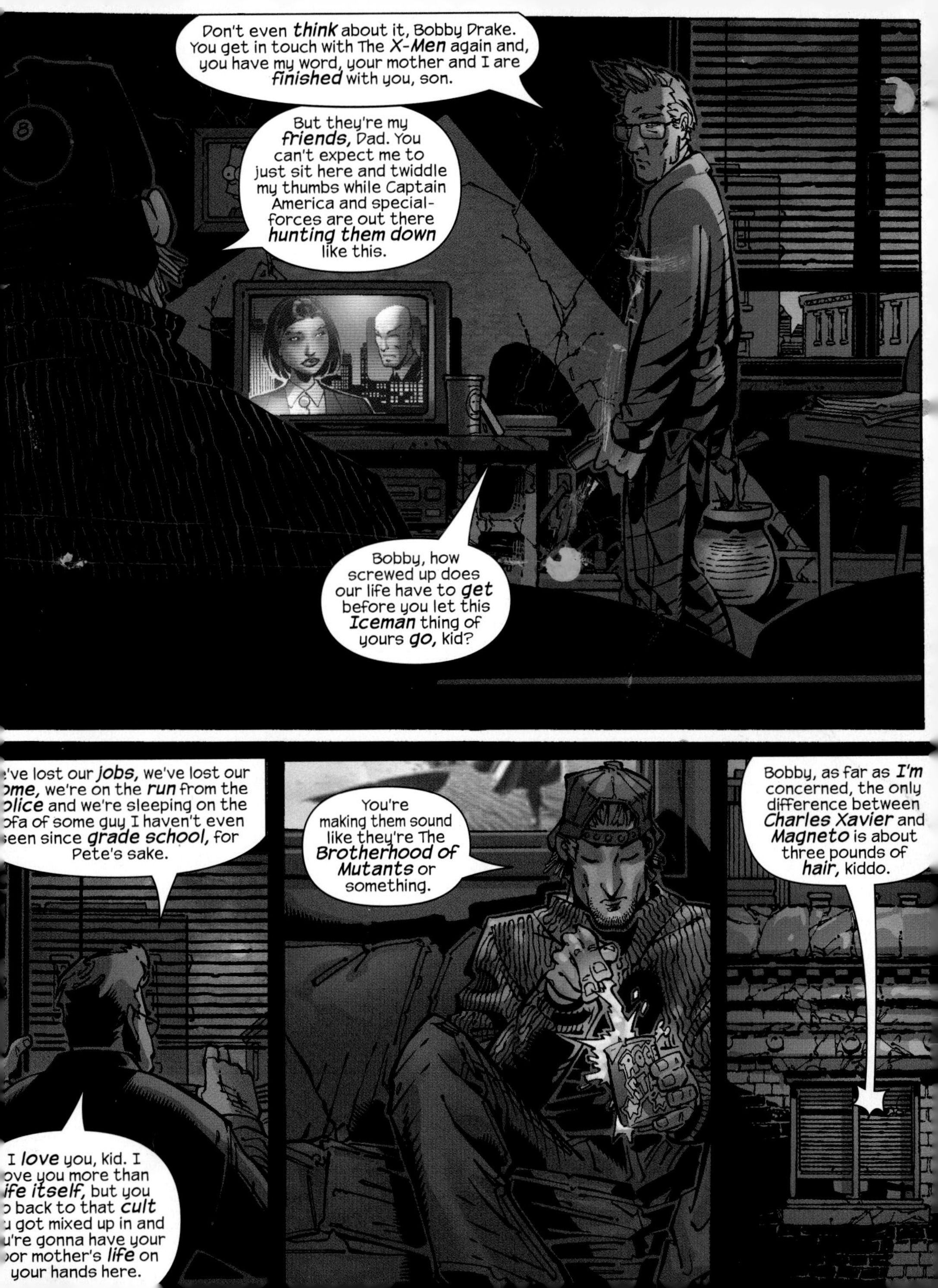

Don't even *think* about it, Bobby Drake. You get in touch with The *X-Men* again and, you have my word, your mother and I are *finished* with you, son.
But they're my *friends,* Dad. You can't expect me to just sit here and twiddle my thumbs while Captain America and special-forces are out there *hunting them down* like this.
Bobby, how screwed up does our life have to *get* before you let this *Iceman* thing of yours *go,* kid?
e've lost our *jobs,* we've lost our ome, we're on the *run* from the olice and we're sleeping on the ofa of some guy I haven't even seen since *grade school,* for Pete's sake.
You're making them sound like they're The *Brotherhood of Mutants* or something.
Bobby, as far as *I'm* concerned, the only difference between *Charles Xavier* and *Magneto* is about three pounds of *hair,* kiddo.
I *love* you, kid. I ove you more than ife itself, but you o back to that *cult* u got mixed up in and u're gonna have your oor mother's *life* on your hands here.

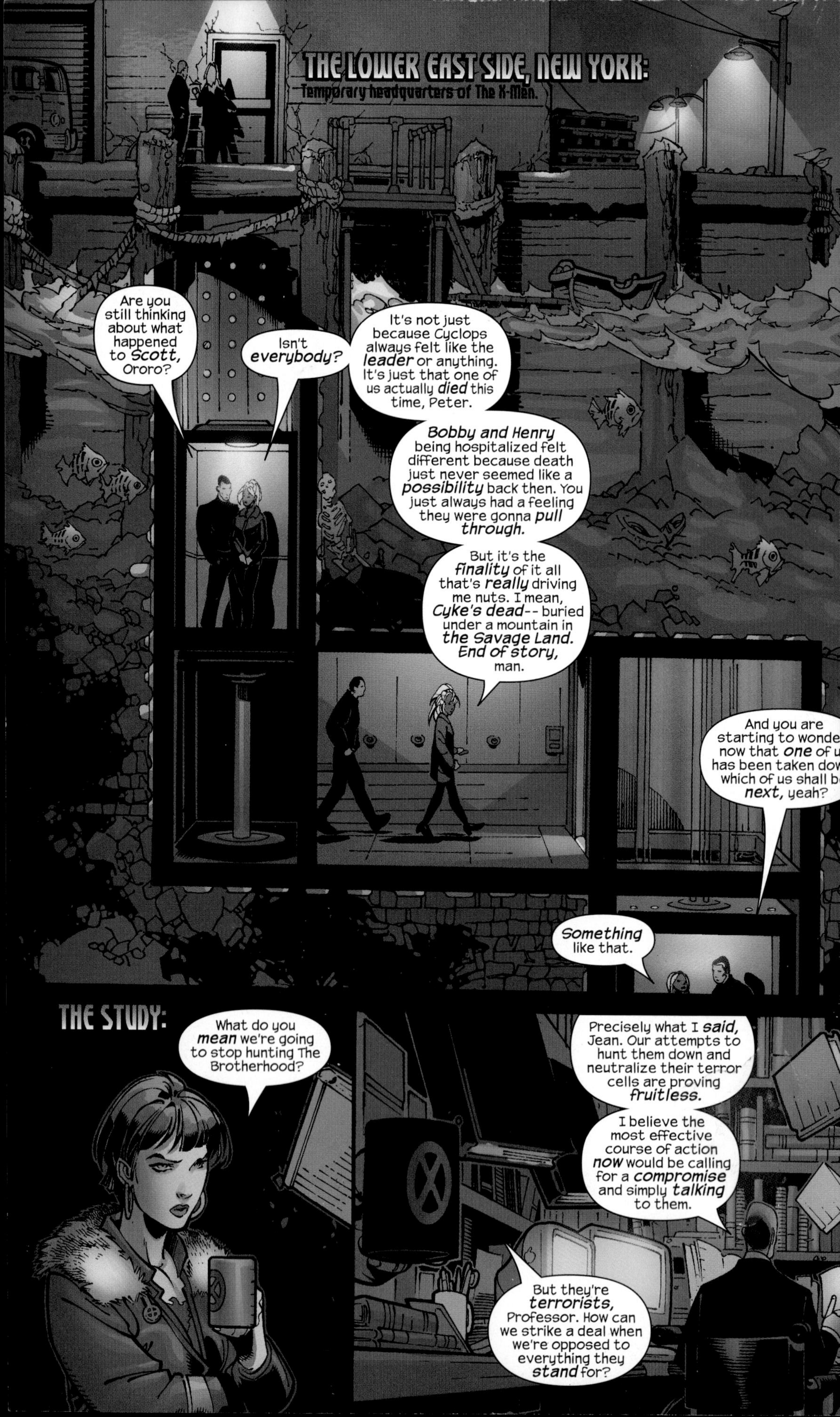
THE LOWER EAST SIDE, NEW YORK:
Temporary headquarters of The X-Men.
Are you still thinking about what happened to Scott, Ororo?
Isn't everybody?
It's not just because Cyclops always felt like the leader or anything. It's just that one of us actually died this time, Peter.
Bobby and Henry being hospitalized felt different because death just never seemed like a possibility back then. You just always had a feeling they were gonna pull through.
But it's the finality of it all that's really driving me nuts. I mean, Cyke's dead-- buried under a mountain in the Savage Land. End of story, man.
And you are starting to wonde now that one of u has been taken dow which of us shall b next, yeah?
Something like that.
THE STUDY:
What do you mean we're going to stop hunting The Brotherhood?
Precisely what I said, Jean. Our attempts to hunt them down and neutralize their terror cells are proving fruitless.
I believe the most effective course of action now would be calling for a compromise and simply talking to them.
But they're terrorists, Professor. How can we strike a deal when we're opposed to everything they stand for?

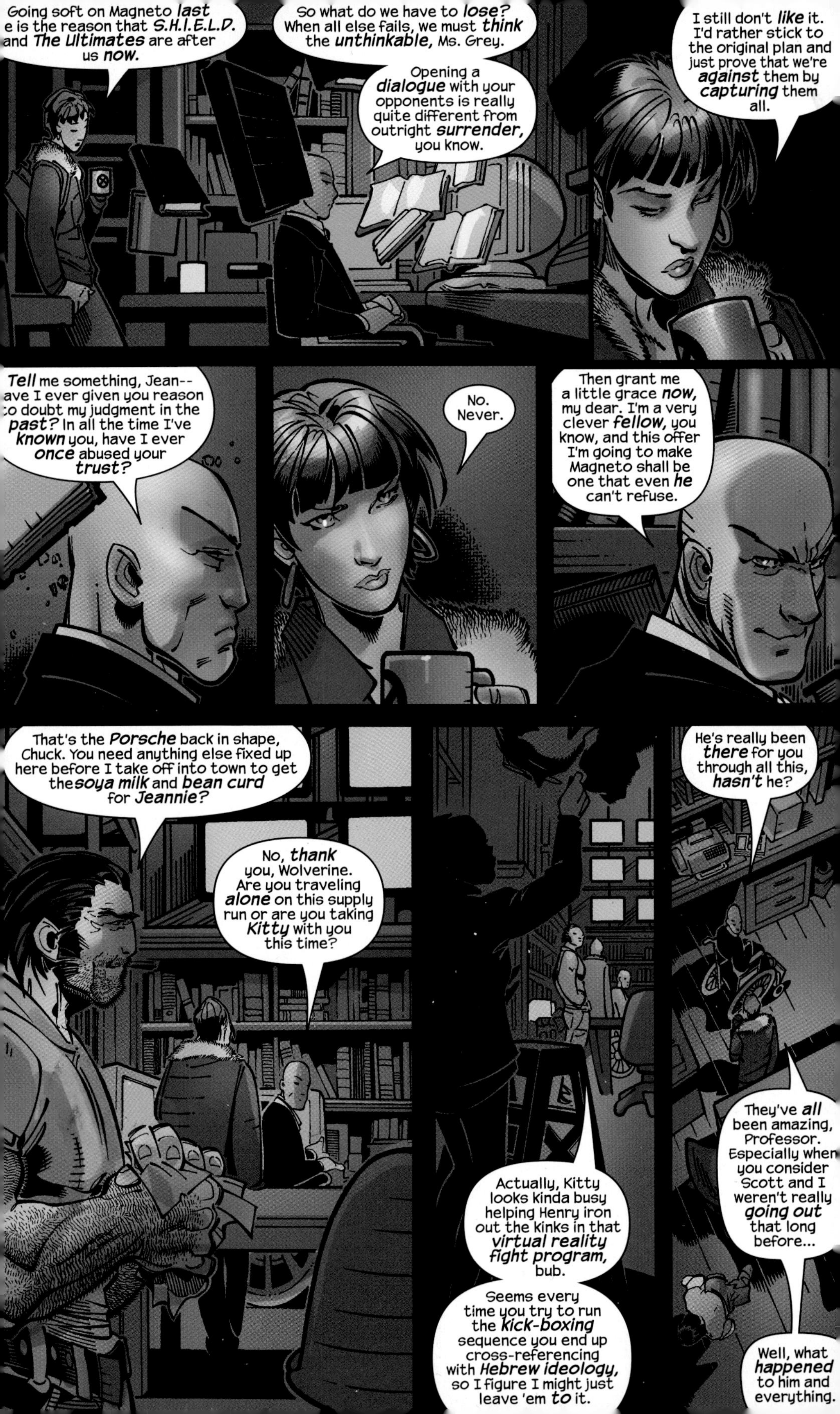
Going soft on Magneto last e is the reason that S.H.I.E.L.D. and The Ultimates are after us now.
So what do we have to lose? When all else fails, we must think the unthinkable, Ms. Grey.
Opening a dialogue with your opponents is really quite different from outright surrender, you know.
I still don't like it. I'd rather stick to the original plan and just prove that we're against them by capturing them all.
Tell me something, Jean-- ave I ever given you reason o doubt my judgment in the past? In all the time I've known you, have I ever once abused your trust?
No. Never.
Then grant me a little grace now, my dear. I'm a very clever fellow, you know, and this offer I'm going to make Magneto shall be one that even he can't refuse.
That's the Porsche back in shape, Chuck. You need anything else fixed up here before I take off into town to get the soya milk and bean curd for Jeannie?
No, thank you, Wolverine. Are you traveling alone on this supply run or are you taking Kitty with you this time?
Actually, Kitty looks kinda busy helping Henry iron out the kinks in that virtual reality fight program, bub.
Seems every time you try to run the kick-boxing sequence you end up cross-referencing with Hebrew ideology, so I figure I might just leave 'em to it.
He's really been there for you through all this, hasn't he?
They've all been amazing, Professor. Especially when you consider Scott and I weren't really going out that long before...
Well, what happened to him and everything.

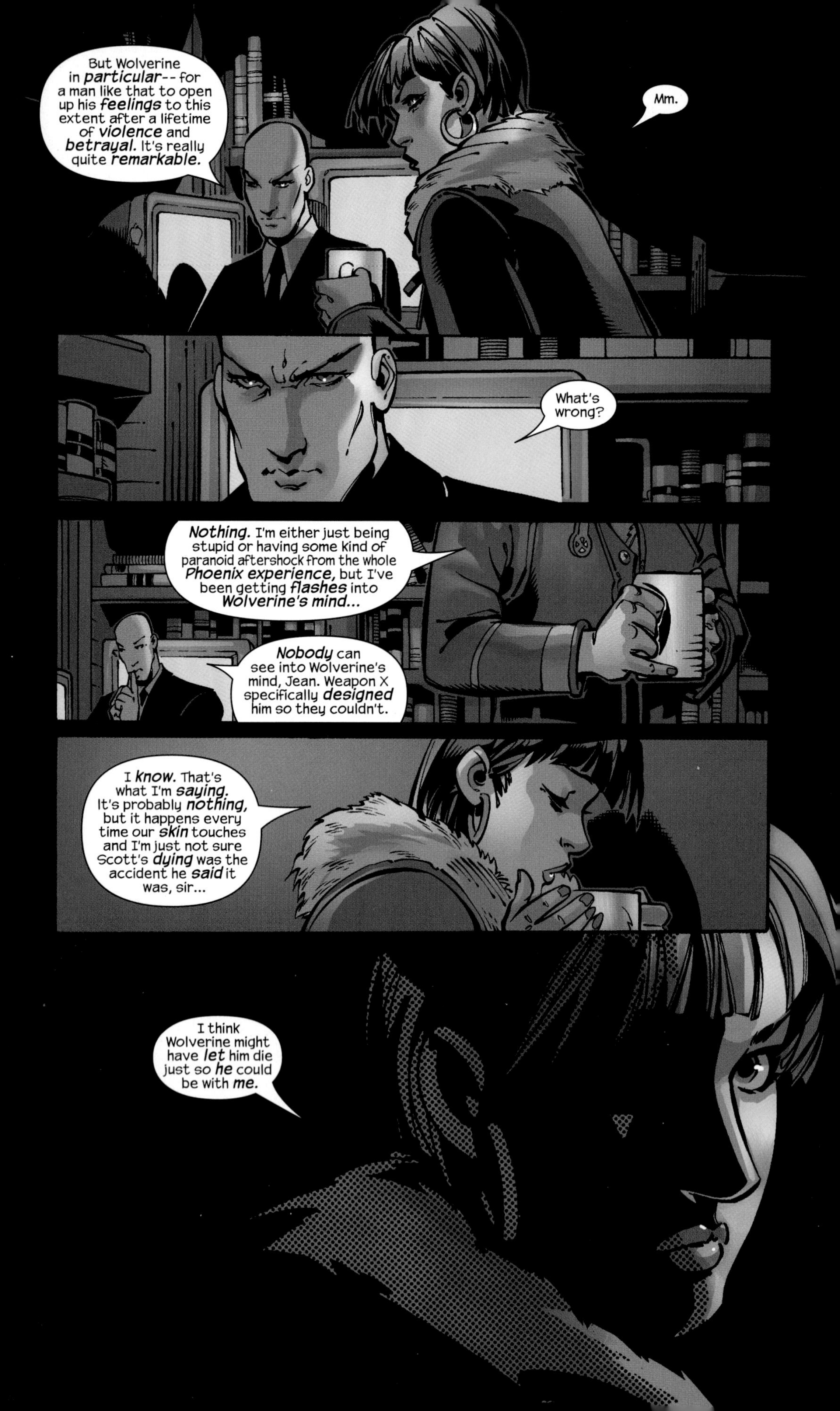

But Wolverine in particular-- for a man like that to open up his feelings to this extent after a lifetime of violence and betrayal. It's really quite remarkable.
Mm.
What's wrong?
Nothing. I'm either just being stupid or having some kind of paranoid aftershock from the whole Phoenix experience, but I've been getting flashes into Wolverine's mind...
Nobody can see into Wolverine's mind, Jean. Weapon X specifically designed him so they couldn't.
I know. That's what I'm saying. It's probably nothing, but it happens every time our skin touches and I'm just not sure Scott's dying was the accident he said it was, sir...
I think Wolverine might have let him die just so he could be with me.

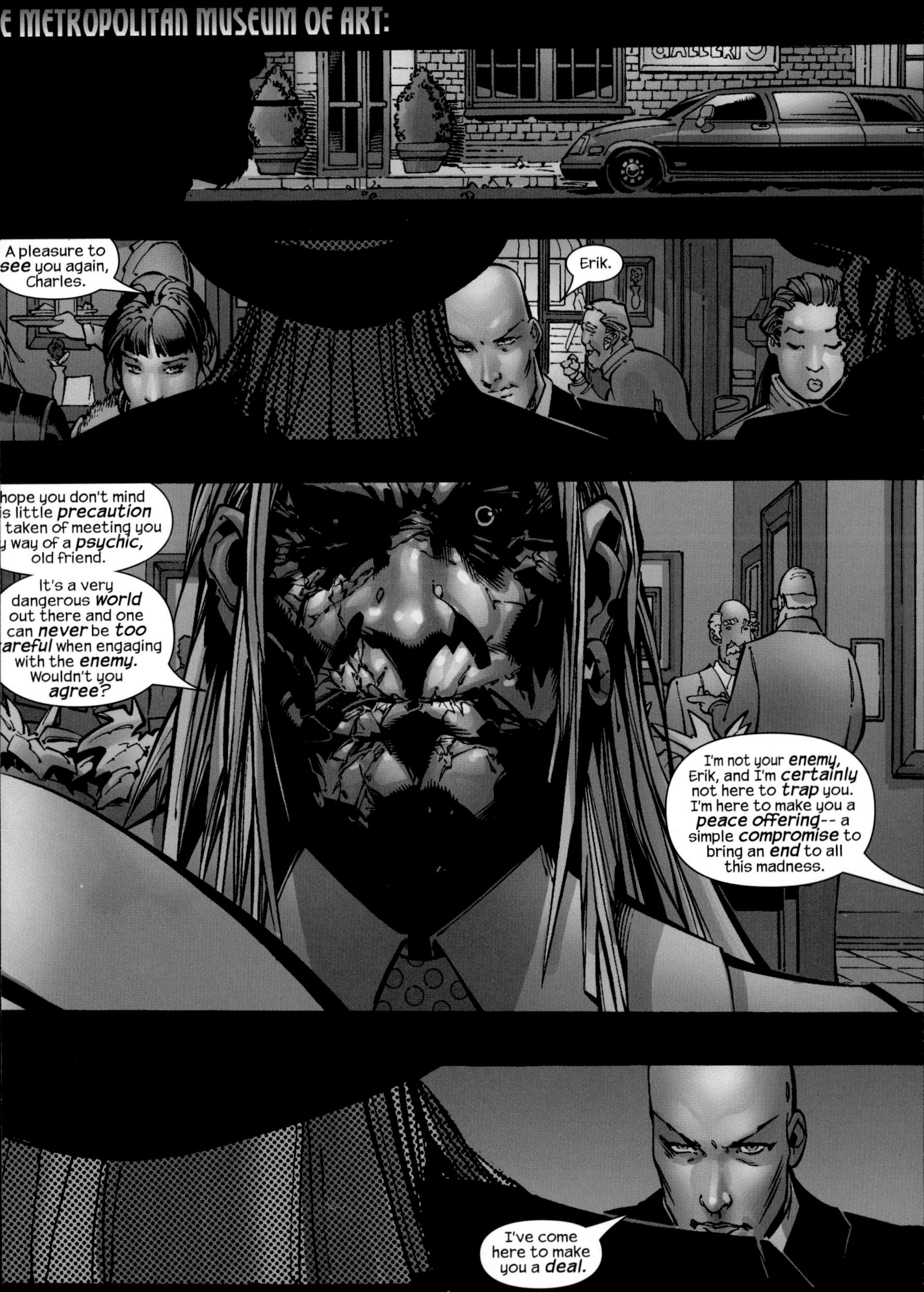

E METROPOLITAN MUSEUM OF ART:
A pleasure to see you again, Charles.
Erik.
hope you don't mind is little precaution taken of meeting you y way of a psychic, old friend.
It's a very dangerous world out there and one can never be too areful when engaging with the enemy. Wouldn't you agree?
I'm not your enemy, Erik, and I'm certainly not here to trap you. I'm here to make you a peace offering-- a simple compromise to bring an end to all this madness.
I've come here to make you a deal.

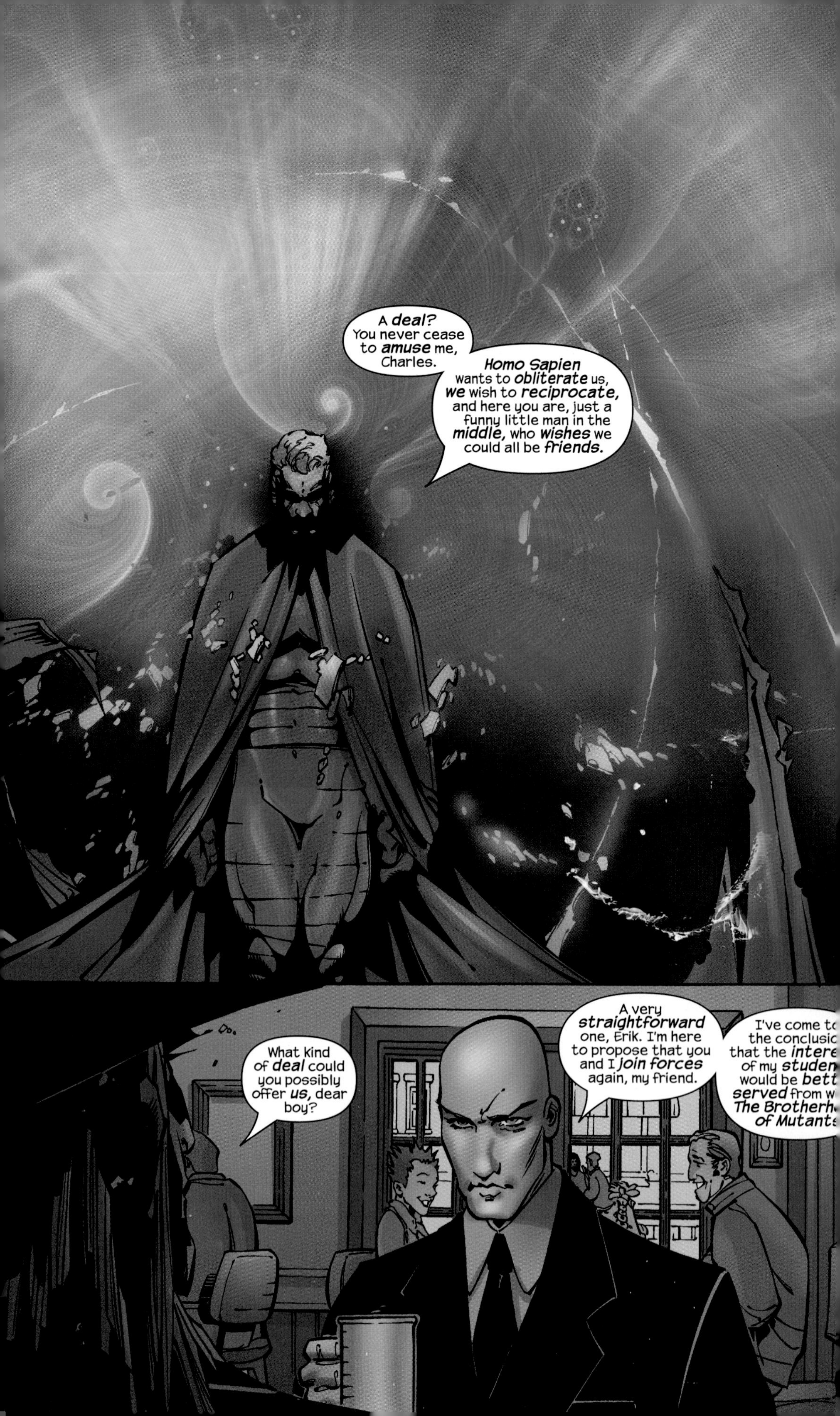
A deal? You never cease to amuse me, Charles.
Homo Sapien wants to obliterate us, we wish to reciprocate, and here you are, just a funny little man in the middle, who wishes we could all be friends.
What kind of deal could you possibly offer us, dear boy?
A very straightforward one, Erik. I'm here to propose that you and I join forces again, my friend.
I've come the that the of my would be served from The of

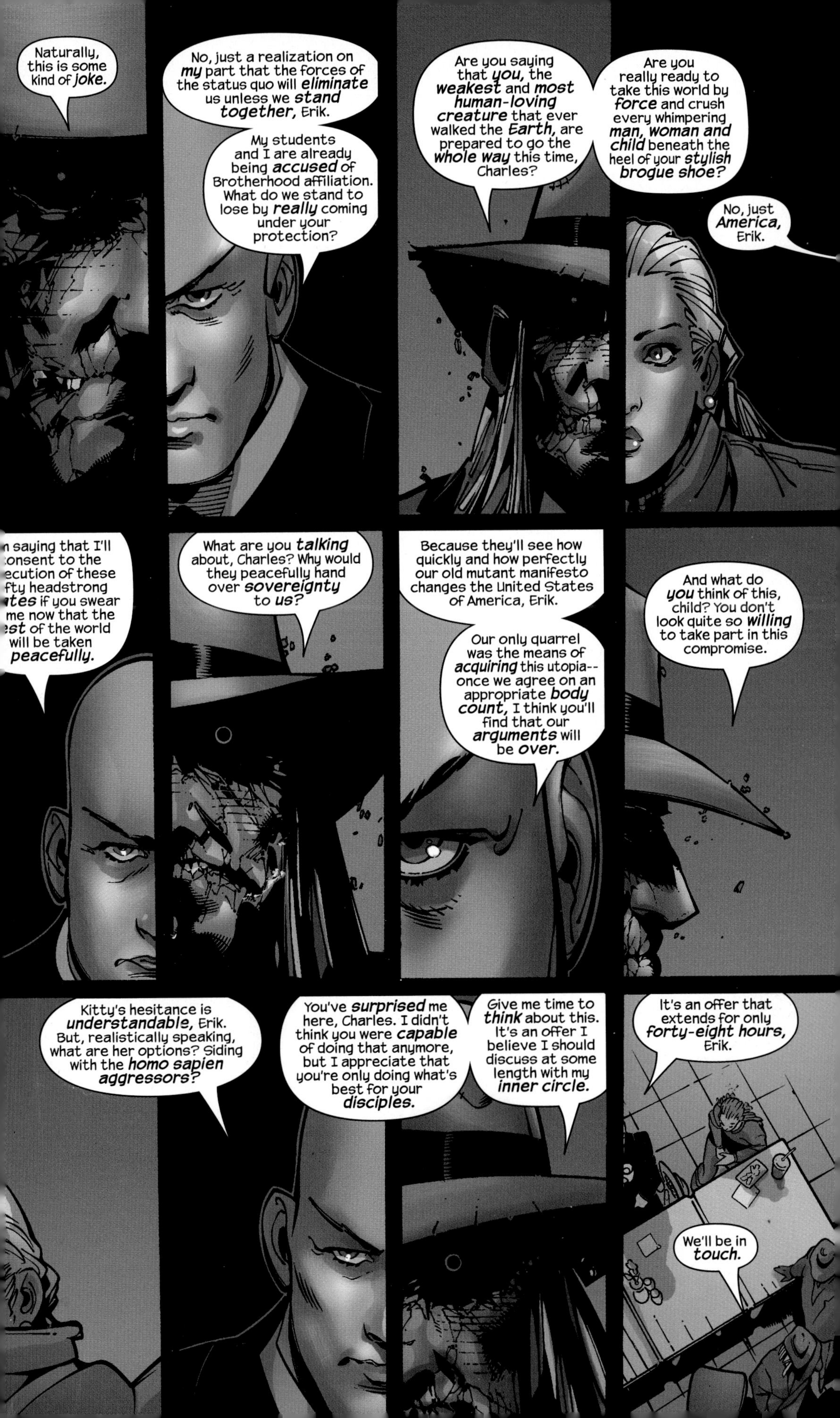

Naturally, this is some kind of joke.
No, just a realization on my part that the forces of the status quo will eliminate us unless we stand together, Erik.
My students and I are already being accused of Brotherhood affiliation. What do we stand to lose by really coming under your protection?
Are you saying that you, the weakest and most human-loving creature that ever walked the Earth, are prepared to go the whole way this time, Charles?
Are you really ready to take this world by force and crush every whimpering man, woman and child beneath the heel of your stylish brogue shoe?
No, just America, Erik.
n saying that I'll onsent to the ecution of these fty headstrong tes if you swear me now that the st of the world will be taken peacefully.
What are you talking about, Charles? Why would they peacefully hand over sovereignty to us?
Because they'll see how quickly and how perfectly our old mutant manifesto changes the United States of America, Erik.
Our only quarrel was the means of acquiring this utopia-- once we agree on an appropriate body count, I think you'll find that our arguments will be over.
And what do you think of this, child? You don't look quite so willing to take part in this compromise.
Kitty's hesitance is understandable, Erik. But, realistically speaking, what are her options? Siding with the homo sapien aggressors?
You've surprised me here, Charles. I didn't think you were capable of doing that anymore, but I appreciate that you're only doing what's best for your disciples.
Give me time to think about this. It's an offer I believe I should discuss at some length with my inner circle.
It's an offer that extends for only forty-eight hours, Erik.
We'll be in touch.

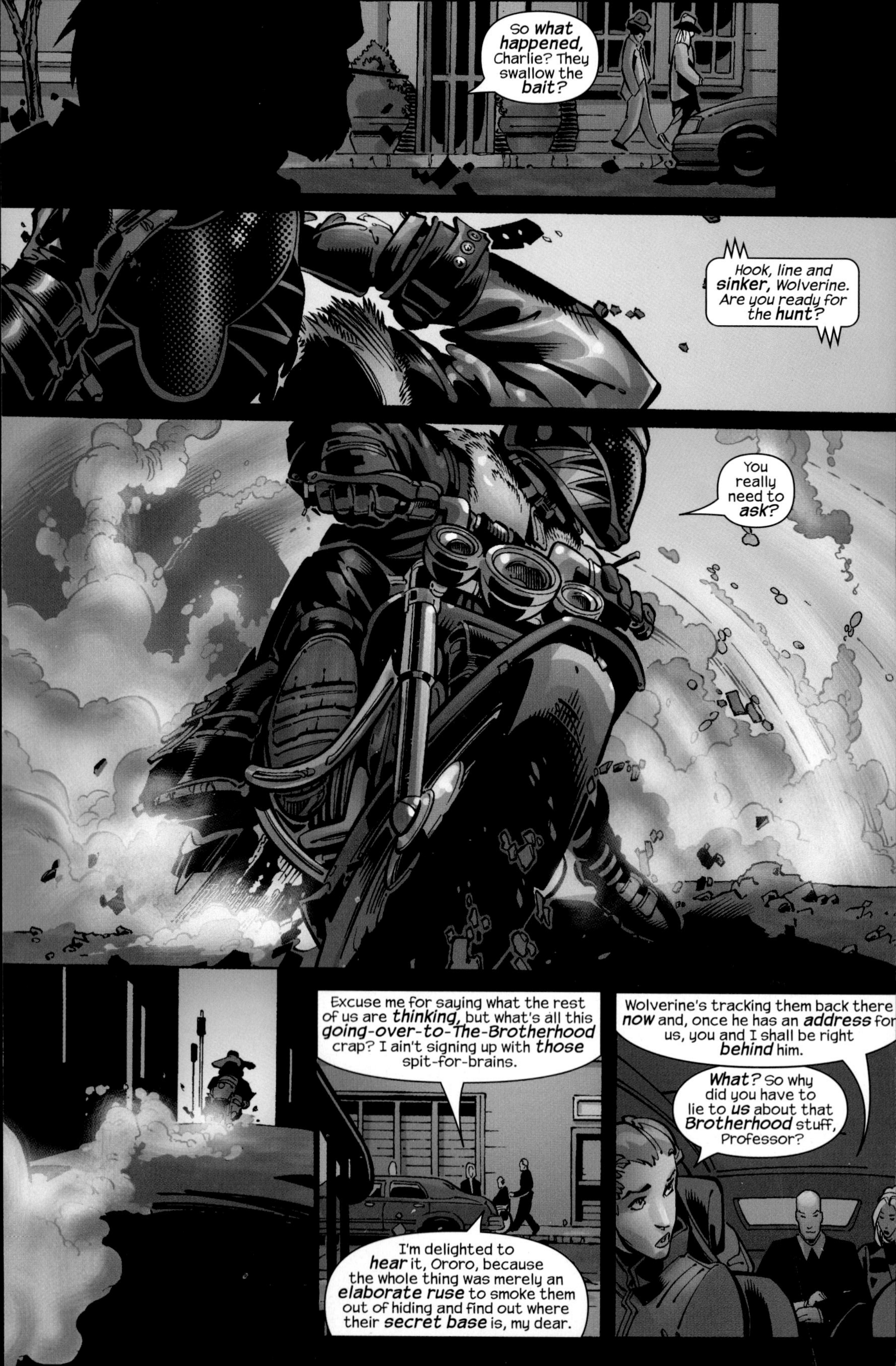
So what happened, Charlie? They swallow the bait?
Hook, line and sinker, Wolverine. Are you ready for the hunt?
You really need to ask?
Excuse me for saying what the rest of us are thinking, but what's all this going-over-to-The-Brotherhood crap? I ain't signing up with those spit-for-brains.
I'm delighted to hear it, Ororo, because the whole thing was merely an elaborate ruse to smoke them out of hiding and find out where their secret base is, my dear.
Wolverine's tracking them back there now and, once he has an address for us, you and I shall be right behind him.
What? So why did you have to lie to us about that Brotherhood stuff, Professor?

...the **telepaths**, right? **Wolverine** might be able to shield his thoughts, but they'd have seen through the rest of us in a **nano-second**.

As usual, you can take your place at the **top** of the **class**, dear Jean. Now let's head back to the safehouse **immediately**...

...your **costumes and vehicles** have already been **prepared**.

So what about this **offer**, Magneto? Charlie Xavier discovered **pragmatism** in his old age and finally seen the **light**?

Don't be **ridiculous**, Linus. Charles is too much of an **egomaniac** to share the **mutant dawn** with anyone, my friend. The whole thing is quite obviously a **trap**.

Where do you think our old friend **Wolverine** was? Clearly, he's ten steps behind our little expedition party and following them back to our **elusive base** at this very **moment**.

No, Charles is **too far gone** to join us now, young man. The **children**, yes, but I'm afraid my partnership with Charles has been **damaged** beyond **repair**.

Still, arranging a **meeting** so he could **follow us home** is actually about three hundred times **craftier** than I'd ever give him **credit** for.

Oh, Charles is a **very** crafty fellow, you know. How he manages to perpetuate this **saint-like reputation** is something I'll **never** understand.

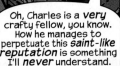

That said, I'm not exactly the most **innocent** creature who ever walked the Earth, as you'll see in a **moment** or two.

What do you **mean**?

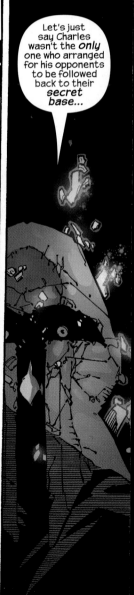

Let's just say Charles wasn't the **only** one who arranged for his opponents to be followed back to their **secret base**...

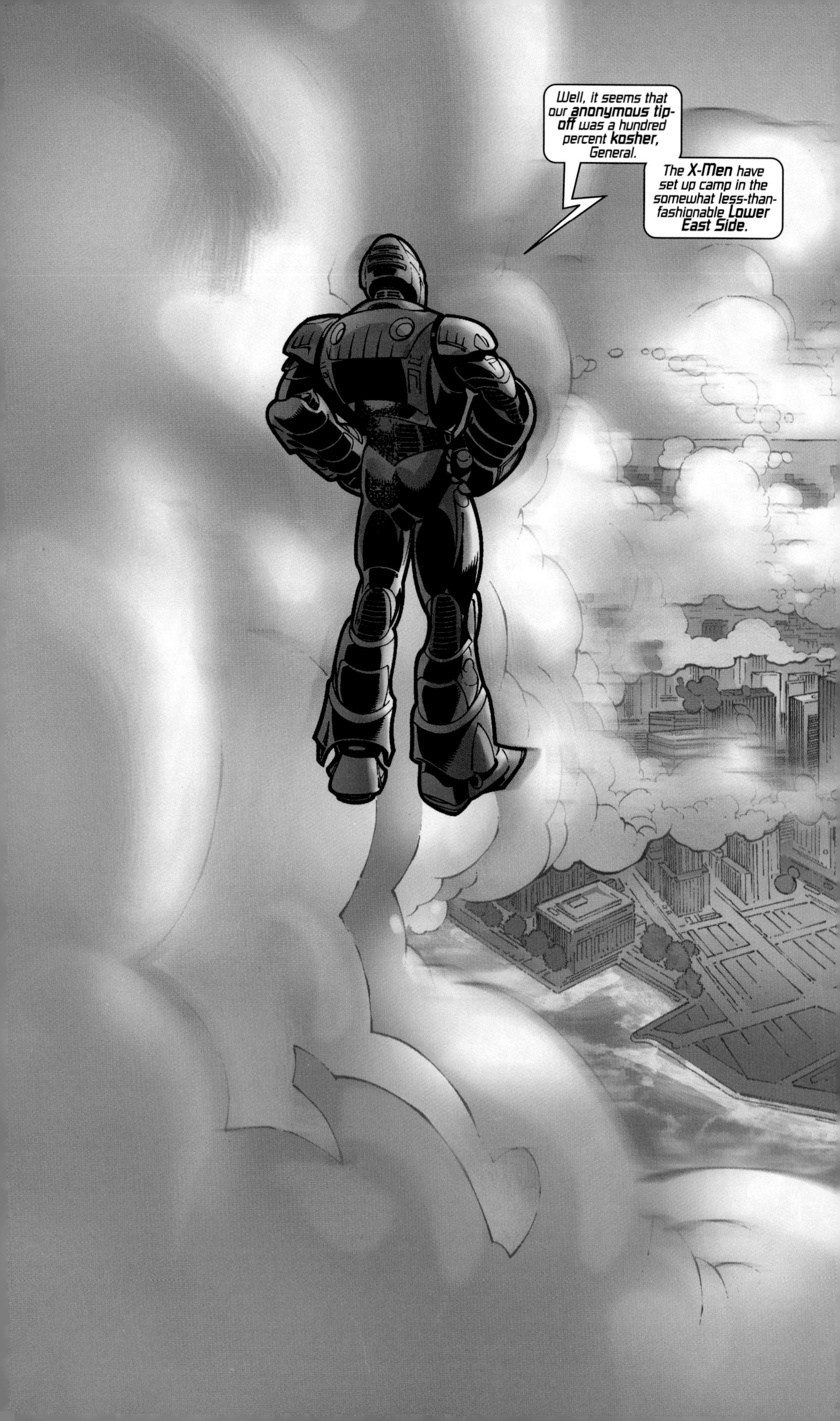
Well, it seems that our anonymous tip-off was a hundred percent kosher, General.
The X-Men have set up camp in the somewhat less-than-fashionable Lower East Side.

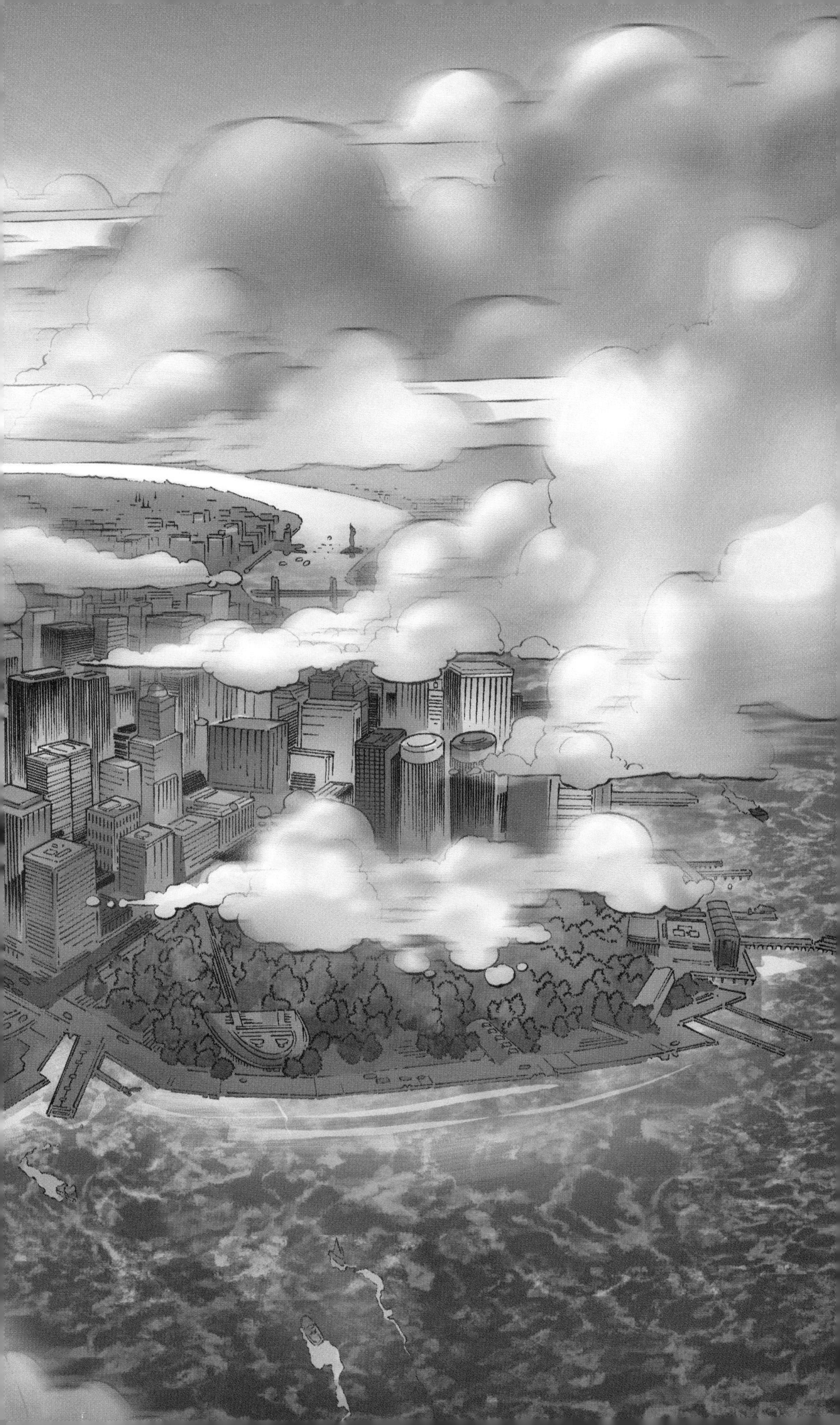

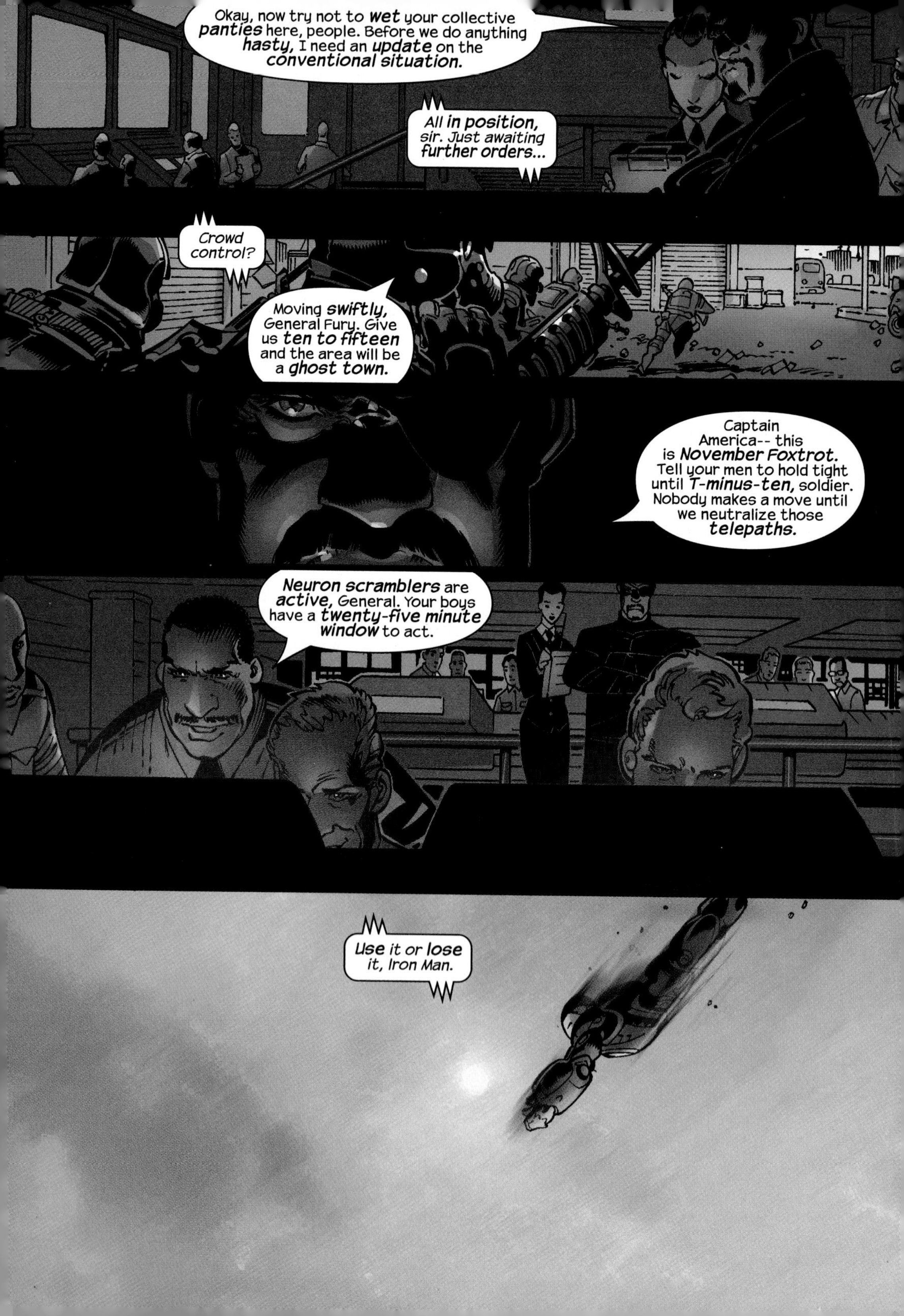

Okay, now try not to wet your collective panties here, people. Before we do anything hasty, I need an update on the conventional situation.
All in position, sir. Just awaiting further orders...
Crowd control?
Moving swiftly, General Fury. Give us ten to fifteen and the area will be a ghost town.
Captain America-- this is November Foxtrot. Tell your men to hold tight until T-minus-ten, soldier. Nobody makes a move until we neutralize those telepaths.
Neuron scramblers are active, General. Your boys have a twenty-five minute window to act.
Use it or lose it, Iron Man.

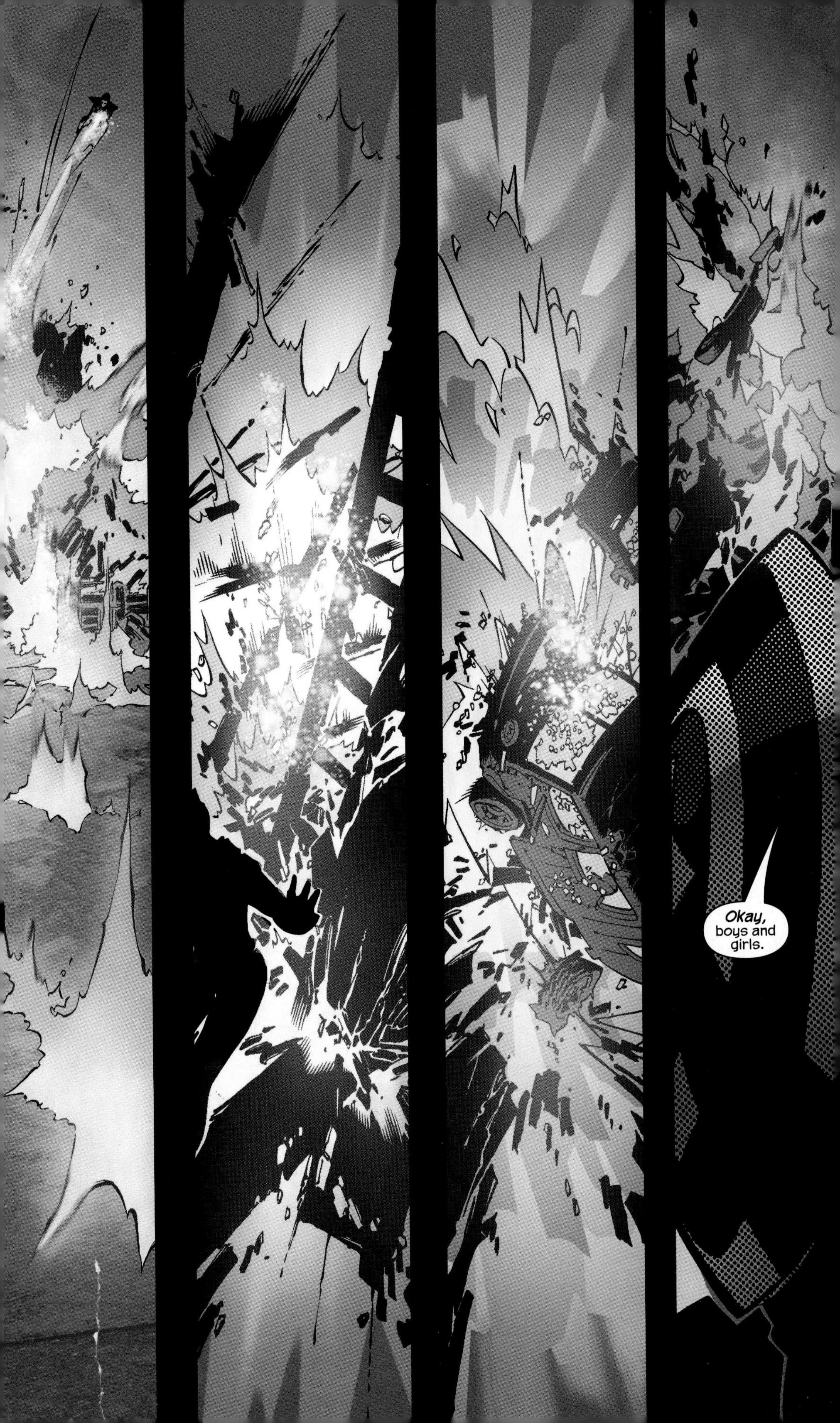
Okay, boys and girls.

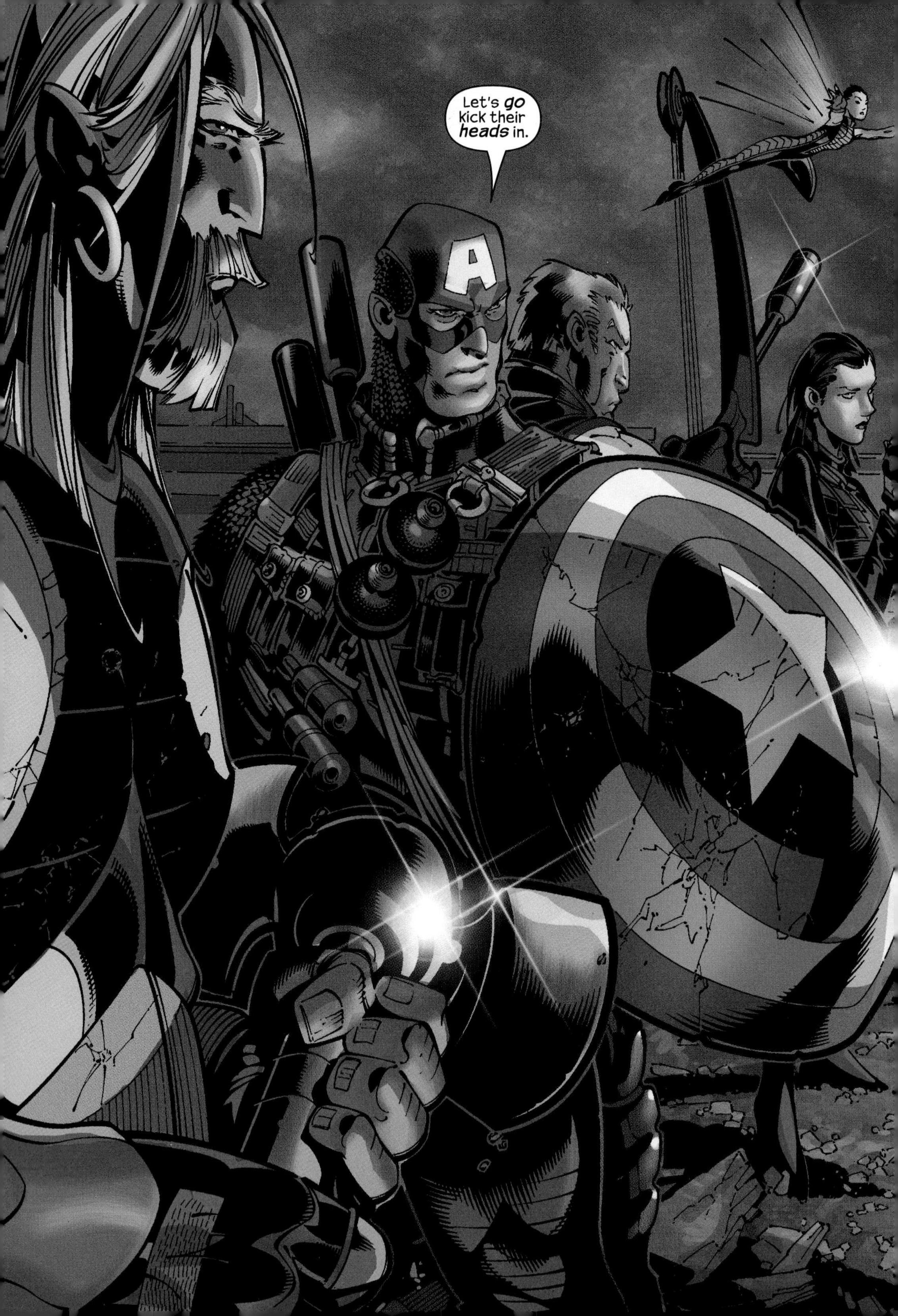
Let's go kick their heads in.

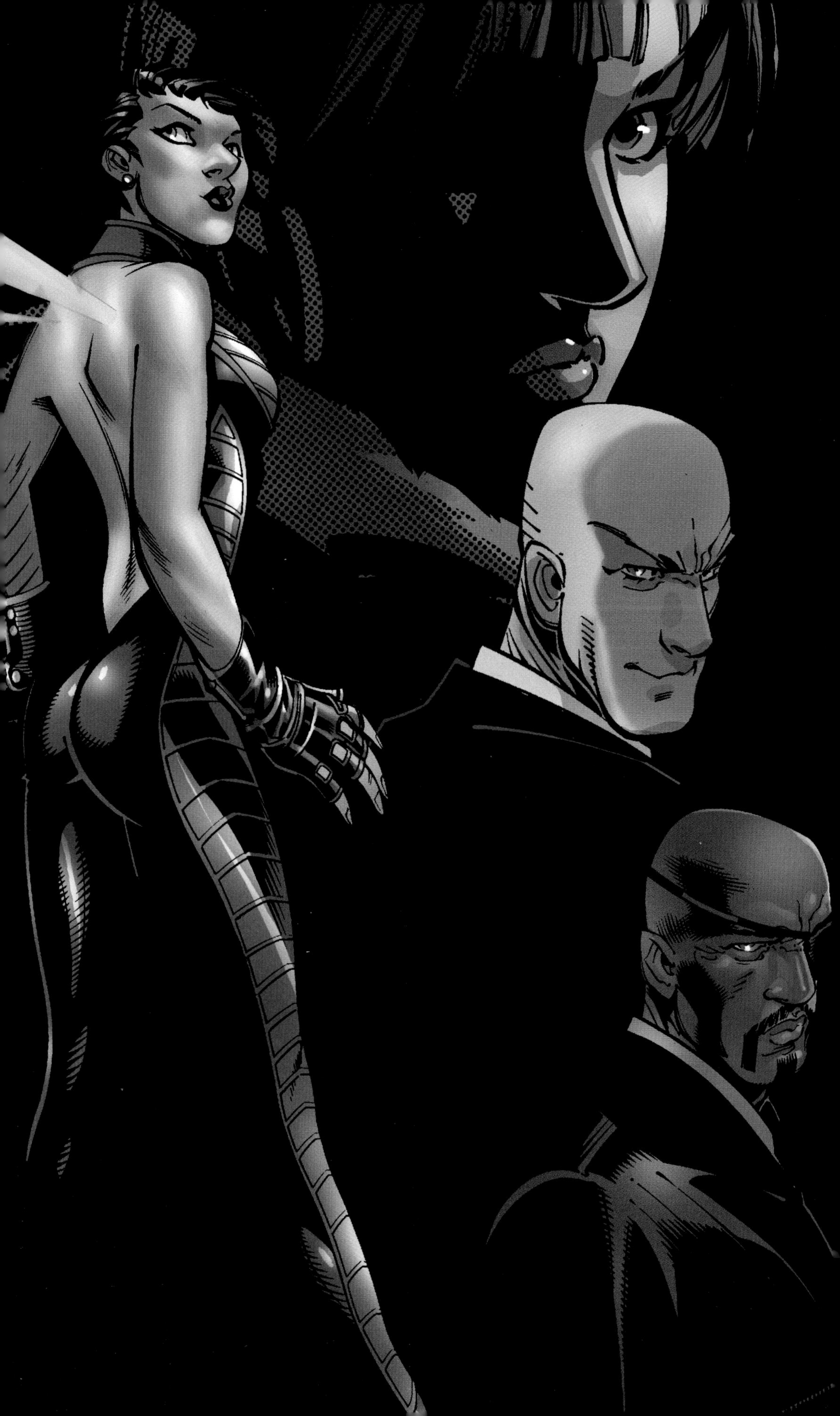

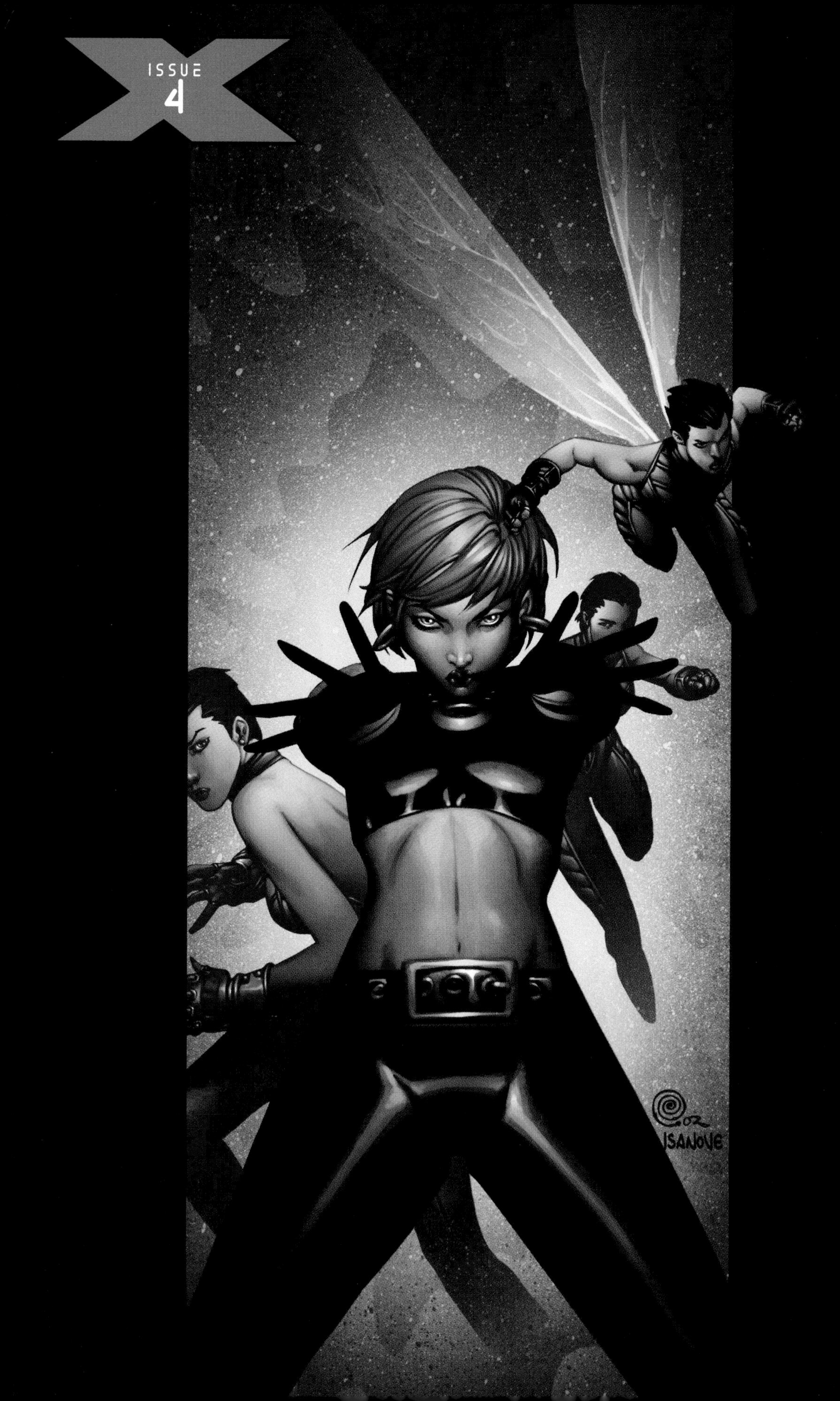
ISSUE
4
ISANOVE

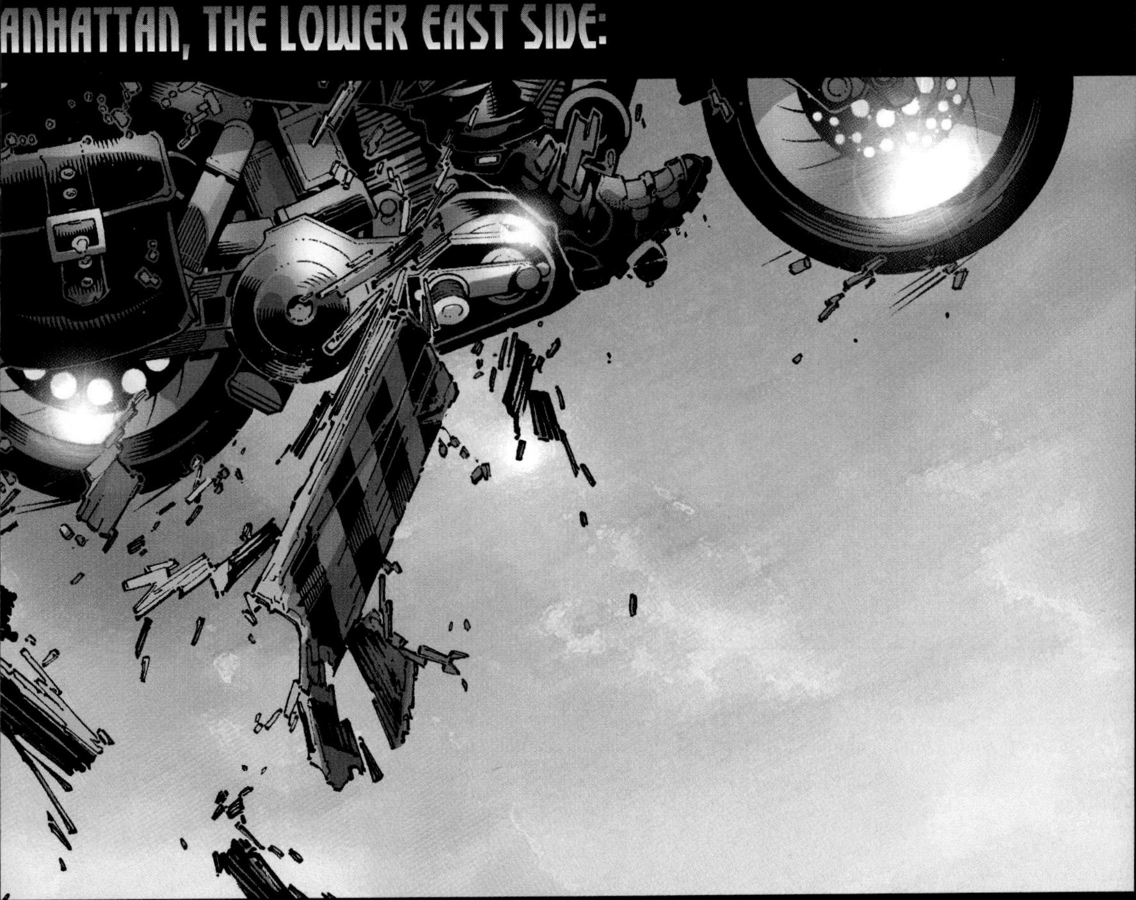
ANHATTAN, THE LOWER EAST SIDE:

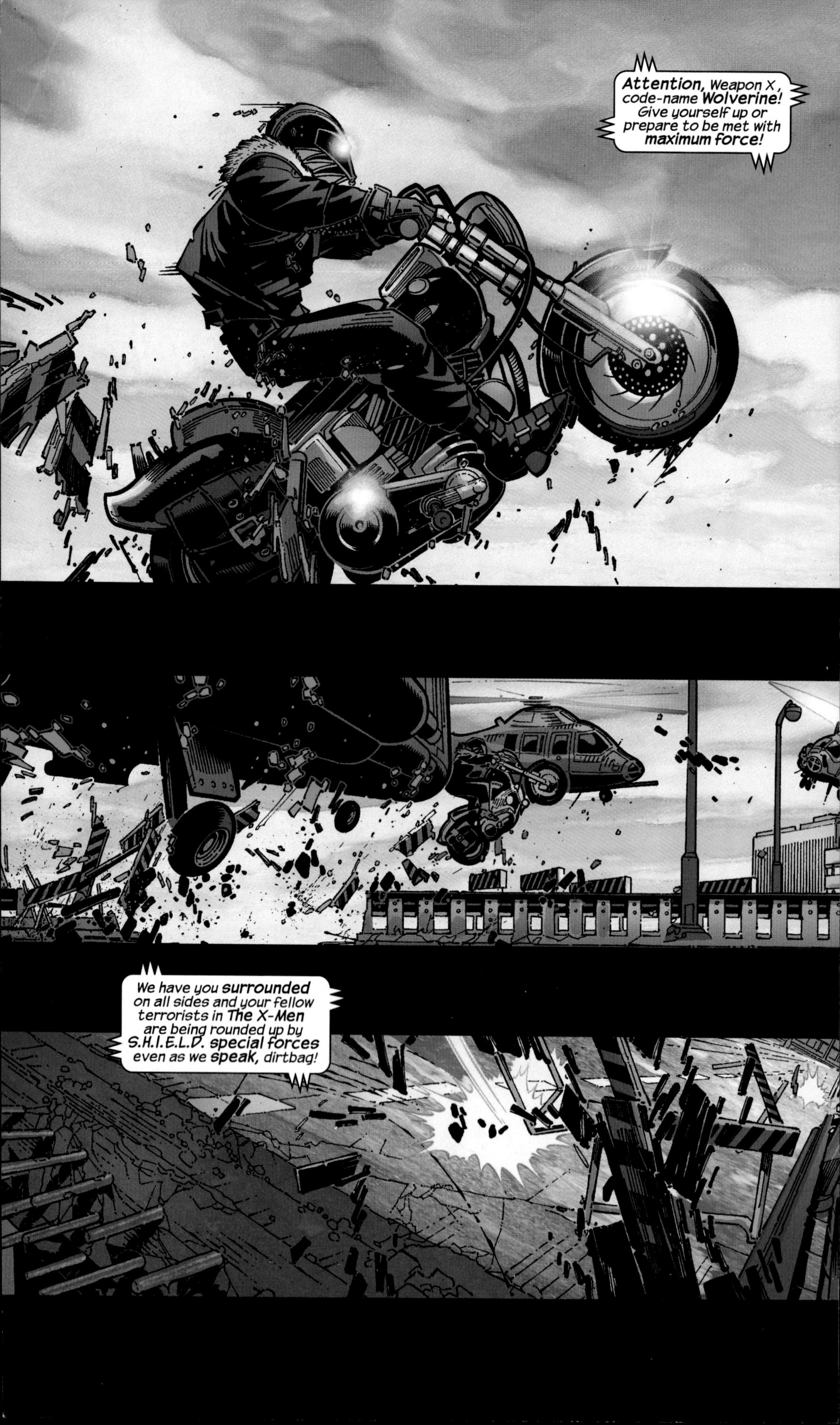
Attention, Weapon X, code-name Wolverine! Give yourself up or prepare to be met with maximum force!
We have you surrounded on all sides and your fellow terrorists in The X-Men are being rounded up by S.H.I.E.L.D. special forces even as we speak, dirtbag!

Escape is not an option!

Rescue is not an option!

Your two remaining choices are a swift arrest and transfer to *Camp X-Factor* down in *Cuba* or a thousand shells from Uncle Sam and a bed-for-one in an *unmarked grave!*

What's it gonna be, freak? What's a tough guy like *you* gonna say to something like *that*, huh?

SNIKT!

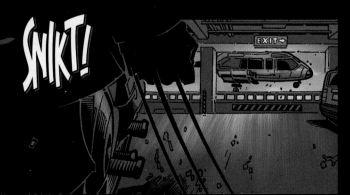

EXIT →

What did he just say?

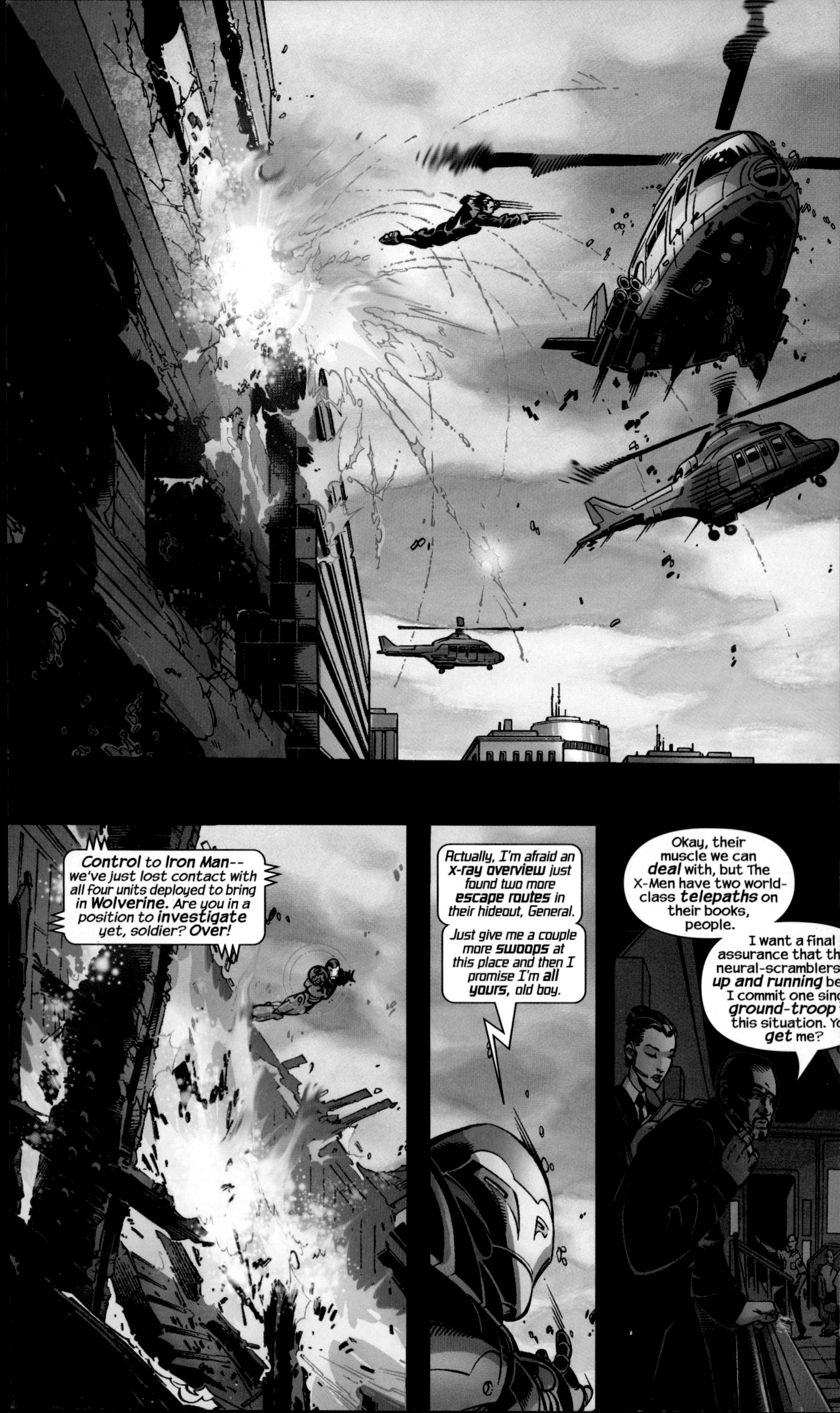

Control to Iron Man-- we've just lost contact with all four units deployed to bring in Wolverine. Are you in a position to investigate yet, soldier? Over!
Actually, I'm afraid an x-ray overview just found two more escape routes in their hideout, General.
Just give me a couple more swoops at this place and then I promise I'm all yours, old boy.
Okay, their muscle we can deal with, but The X-Men have two world-class telepaths on their books, people.
I want a final assurance that th neural-scramblers up and running be I commit one sing ground-troop this situation. Yo get me?

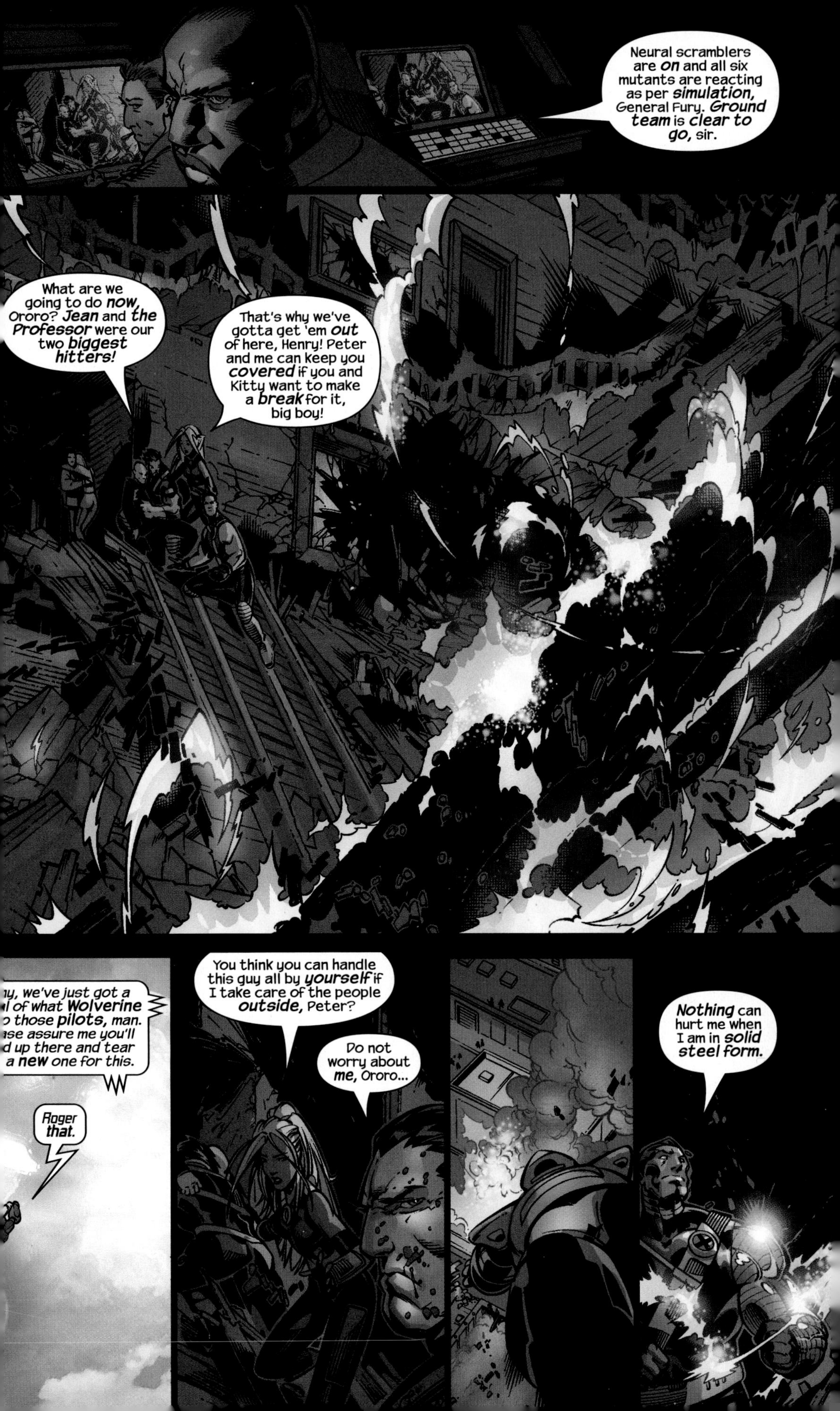
Neural scramblers are on and all six mutants are reacting as per simulation, General Fury. Ground team is clear to go, sir.
What are we going to do now, Ororo? Jean and the Professor were our two biggest hitters!
That's why we've gotta get 'em out of here, Henry! Peter and me can keep you covered if you and Kitty want to make a break for it, big boy!
ay, we've just got a l of what Wolverine o those pilots, man. ase assure me you'll d up there and tear a new one for this.
Roger that.
You think you can handle this guy all by yourself if I take care of the people outside, Peter?
Do not worry about me, Ororo...
Nothing can hurt me when I am in solid steel form.

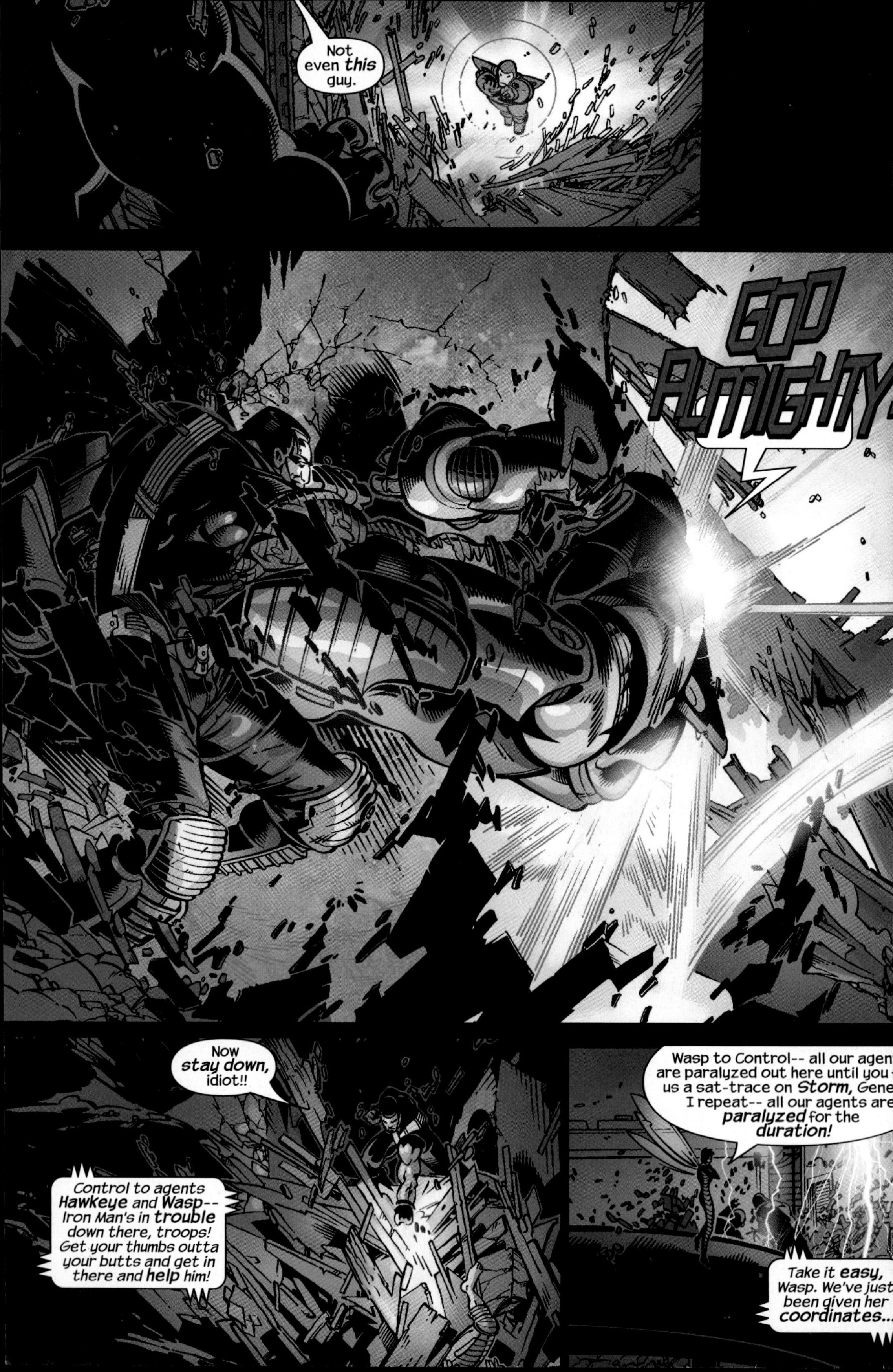
Not even this guy.
GOD ALMIGHTY!
Now stay down, idiot!!
Control to agents Hawkeye and Wasp-- Iron Man's in trouble down there, troops! Get your thumbs outta your butts and get in there and help him!
I repeat-- all our agents are paralyzed for the duration!
Take it easy, Wasp. We've just been given her coordinates...

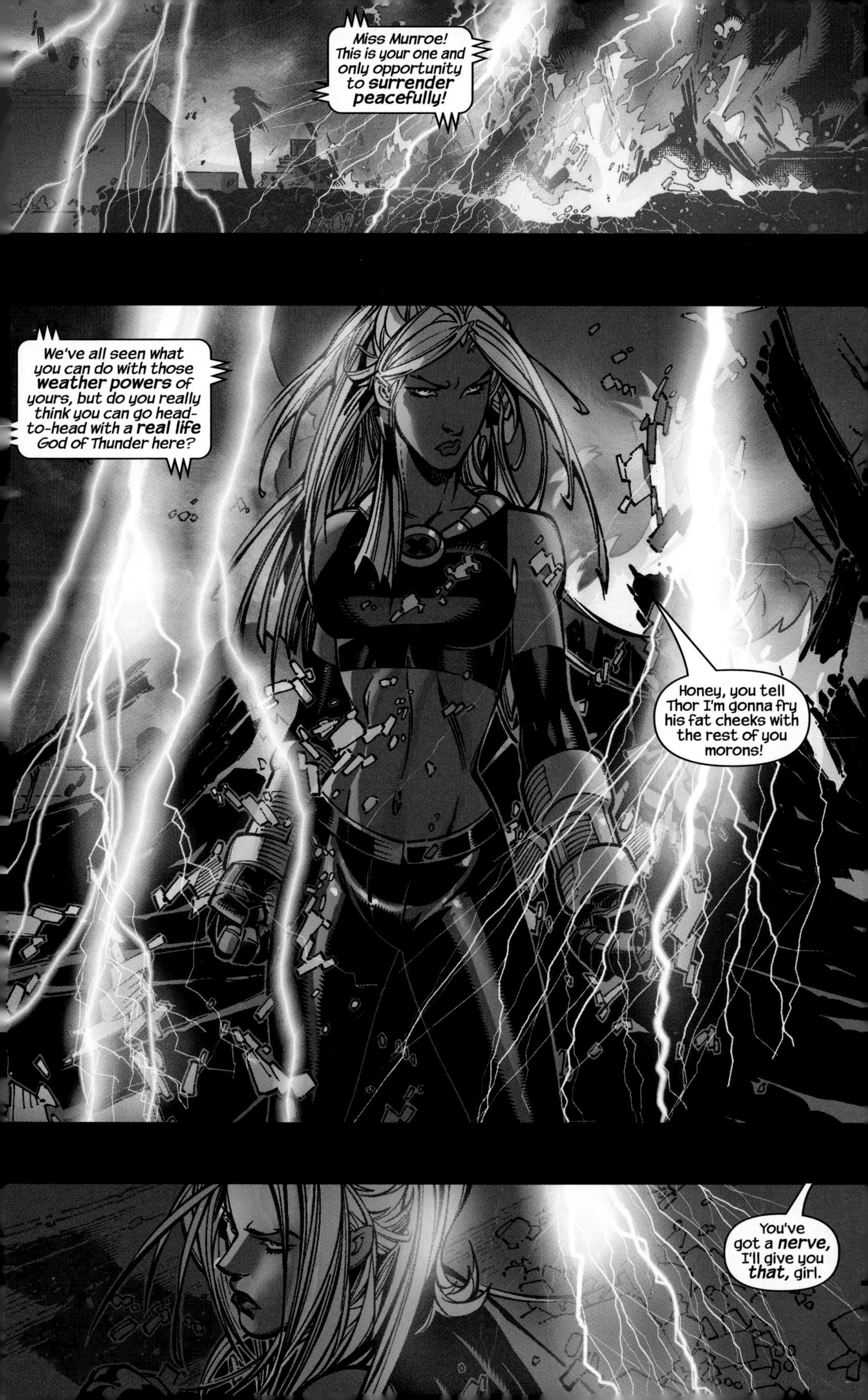
Miss Munroe! This is your one and only opportunity to surrender peacefully!
We've all seen what you can do with those weather powers of yours, but do you really think you can go head-to-head with a real life God of Thunder here?
Honey, you tell Thor I'm gonna fry his fat cheeks with the rest of you morons!
You've got a nerve, I'll give you that, girl.

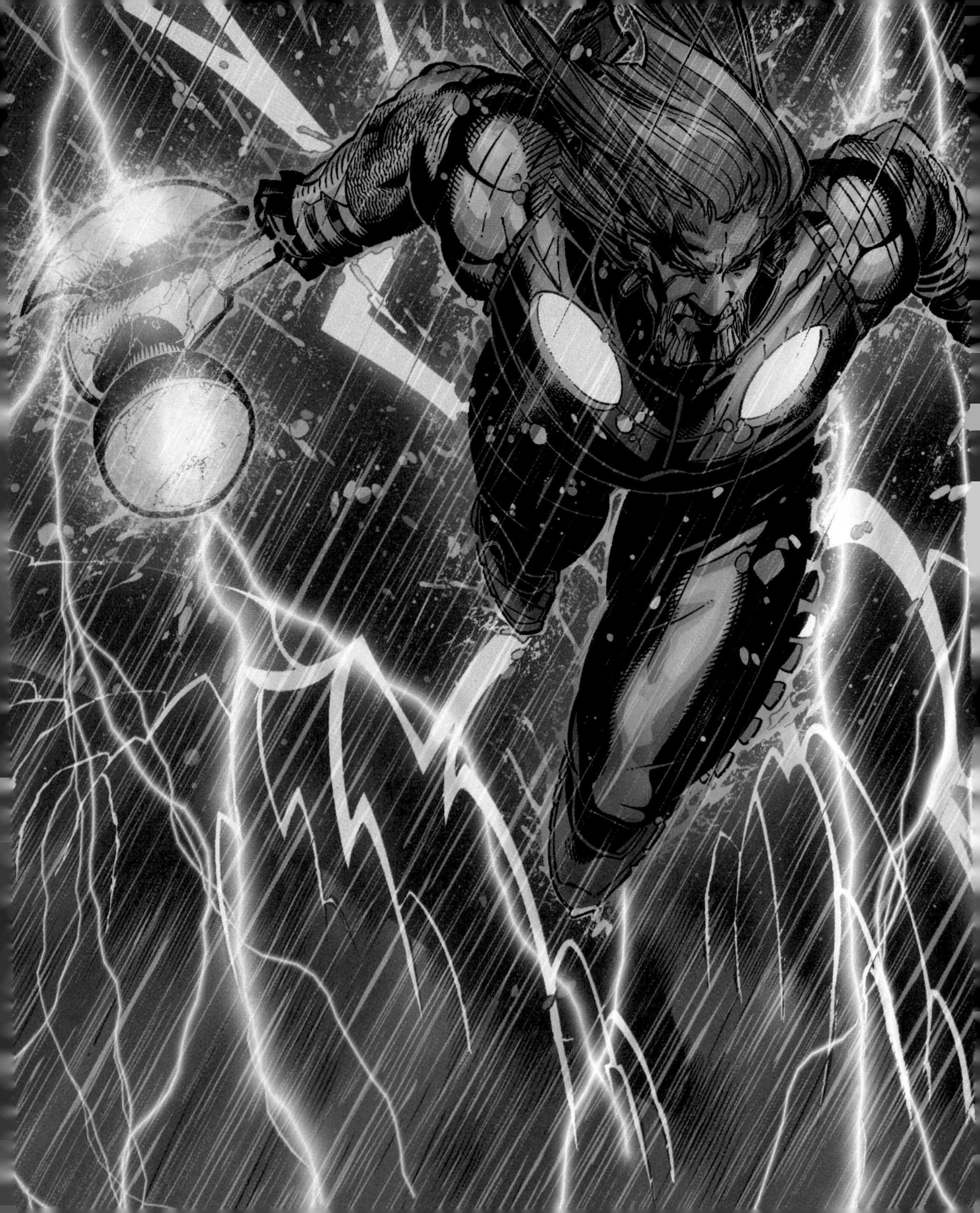

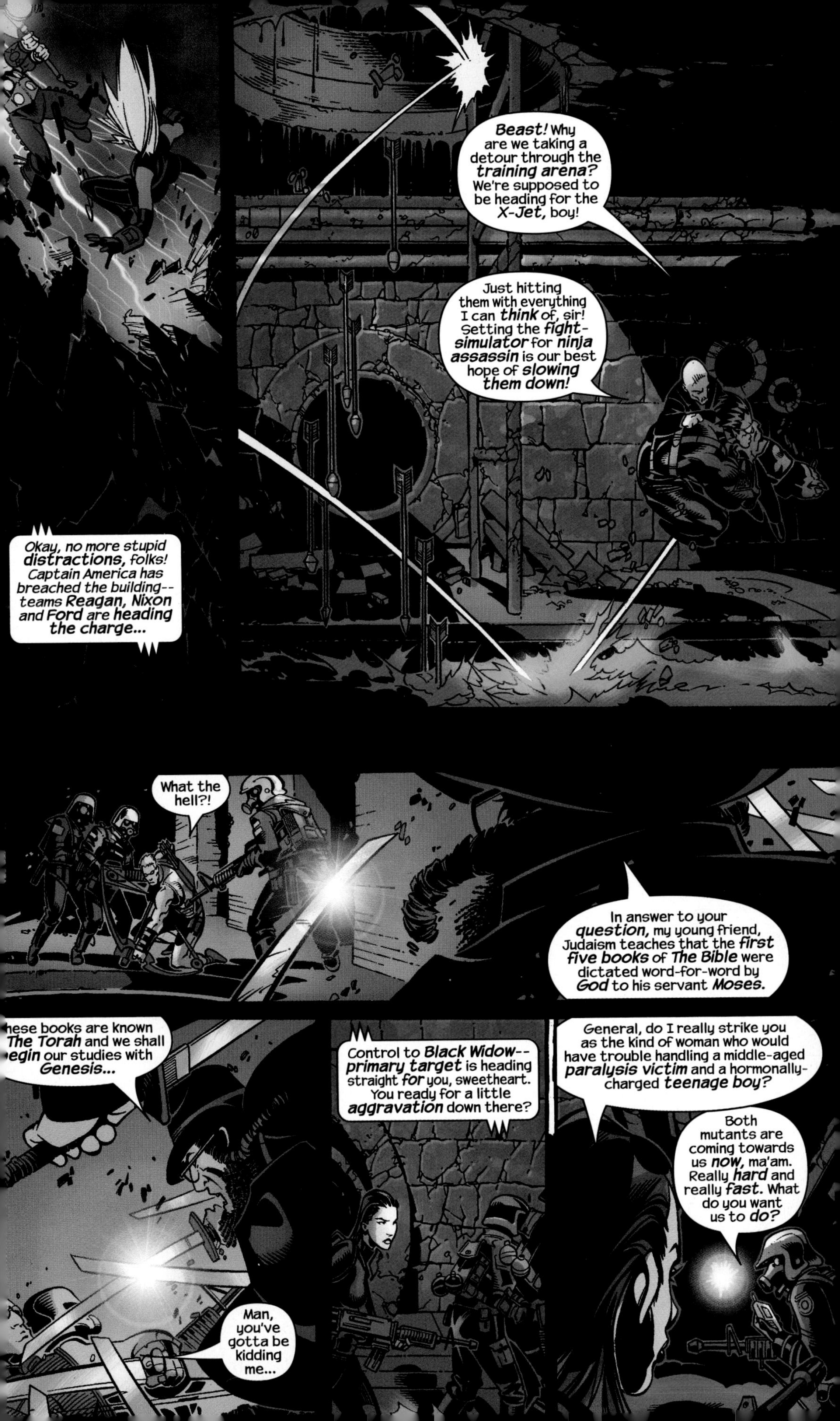

Beast! Why are we taking a detour through the training arena? We're supposed to be heading for the X-Jet, boy!
Just hitting them with everything I can think of, sir! Setting the fight-simulator for ninja assassin is our best hope of slowing them down!
Okay, no more stupid distractions, folks! Captain America has breached the building--teams Reagan, Nixon and Ford are heading the charge...
What the hell?!
In answer to your question, my young friend, Judaism teaches that the first five books of The Bible were dictated word-for-word by God to his servant Moses.
hese books are known The Torah and we shall egin our studies with Genesis...
Man, you've gotta be kidding me...
Control to Black Widow--primary target is heading straight for you, sweetheart. You ready for a little aggravation down there?
General, do I really strike you as the kind of woman who would have trouble handling a middle-aged paralysis victim and a hormonally-charged teenage boy?
Both mutants are coming towards us now, ma'am. Really hard and really fast. What do you want us to do?

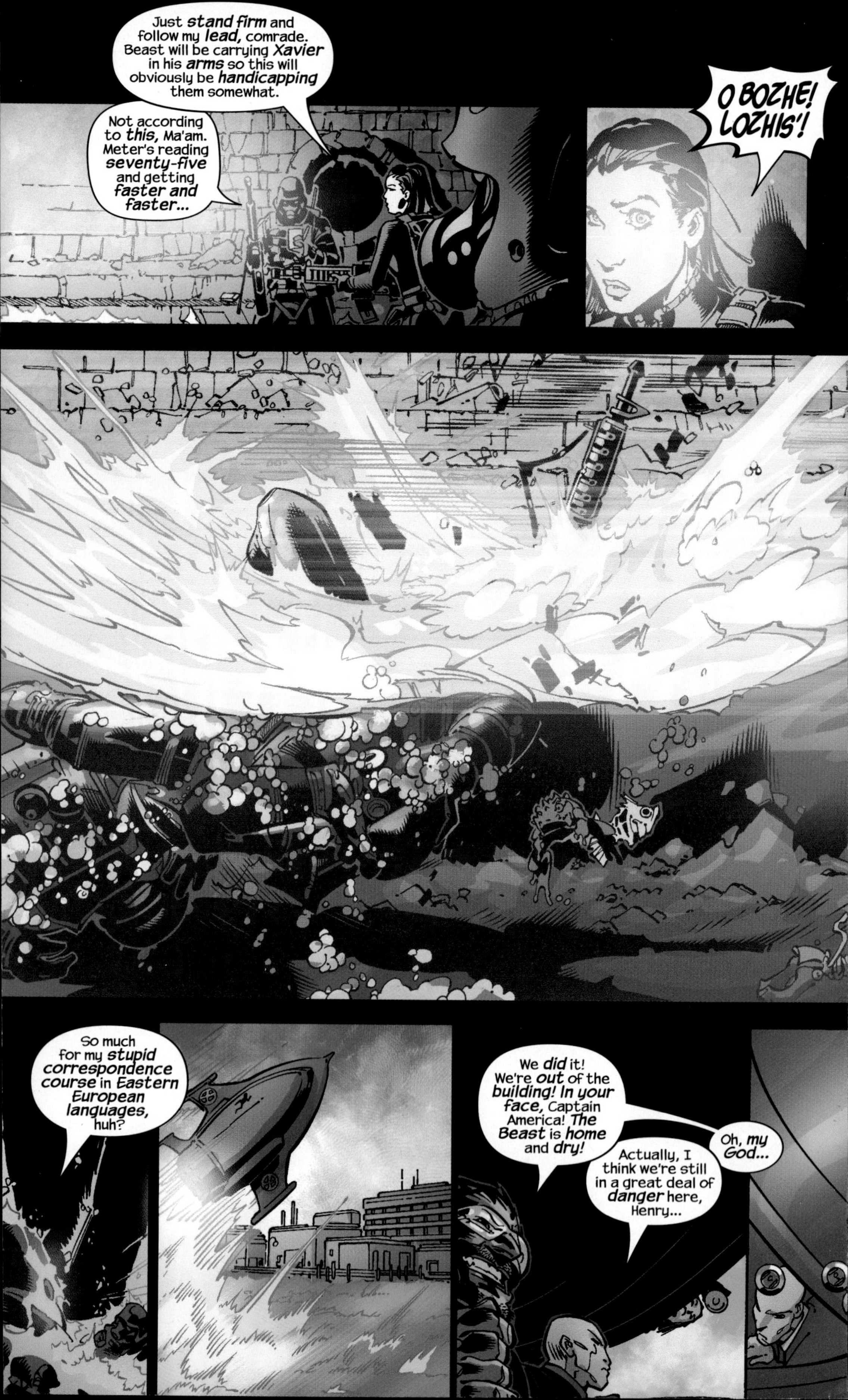
Just stand firm and follow my lead, comrade. Beast will be carrying Xavier in his arms so this will obviously be handicapping them somewhat.
Not according to this, Ma'am. Meter's reading seventy-five and getting faster and faster...
O BOZHE! LOZHIS'!
So much for my stupid correspondence course in Eastern European languages, huh?
We did it! We're out of the building! In your face, Captain America! The Beast is home and dry!
Oh, my God...
Actually, I think we're still in a great deal of danger here, Henry...

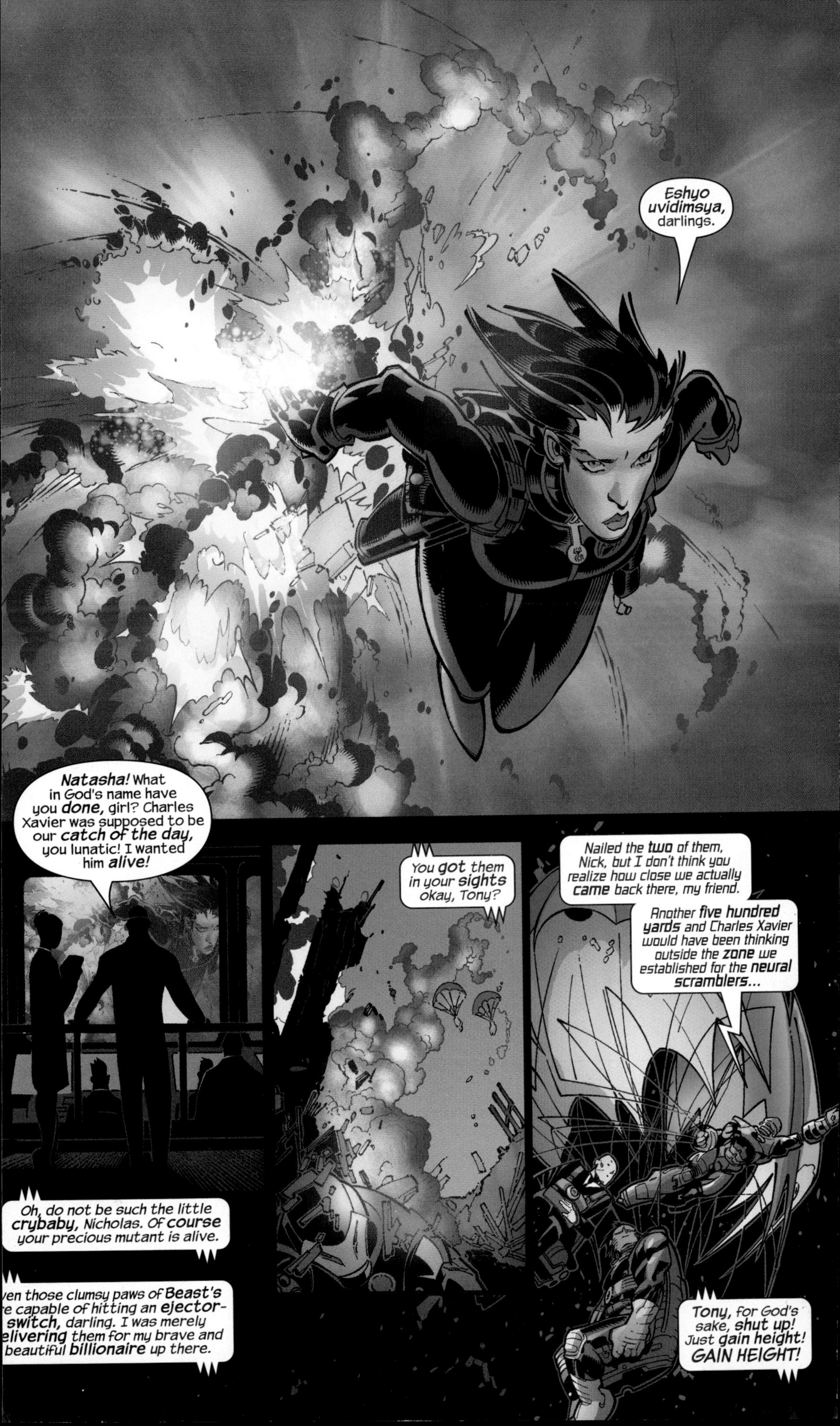
Eshyo uvidimsya, darlings.
Natasha! What in God's name have you done, girl? Charles Xavier was supposed to be our catch of the day, you lunatic! I wanted him alive!
Oh, do not be such the little crybaby, Nicholas. Of course your precious mutant is alive.
ven those clumsy paws of Beast's e capable of hitting an ejector-switch, darling. I was merely elivering them for my brave and beautiful billionaire up there.
You got them in your sights okay, Tony?
Nailed the two of them, Nick, but I don't think you realize how close we actually came back there, my friend.
Another five hundred yards and Charles Xavier would have been thinking outside the zone we established for the neural scramblers...
Tony, for God's sake, shut up! Just gain height! GAIN HEIGHT!

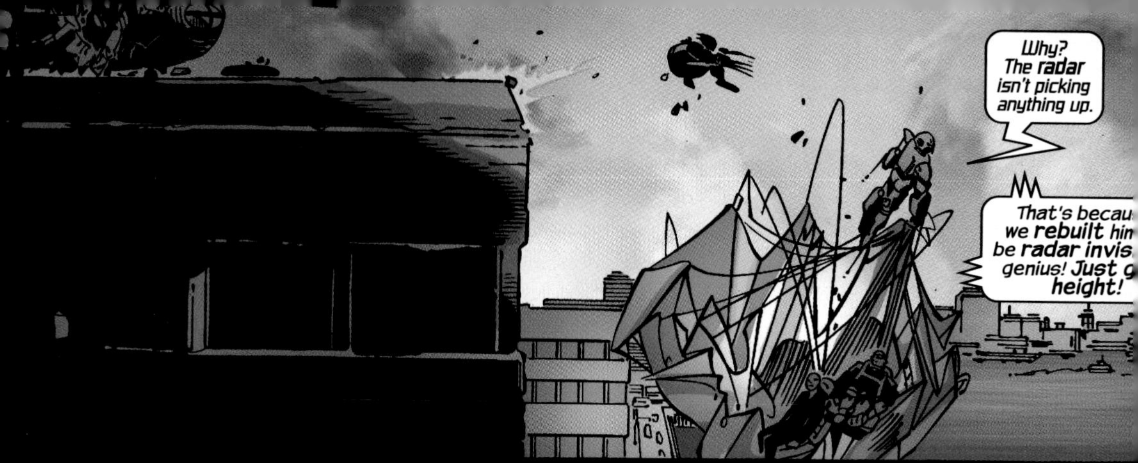

Why? The radar isn't picking anything up.
That's becau
we rebuilt hin
be radar invis
genius! Just g
height!

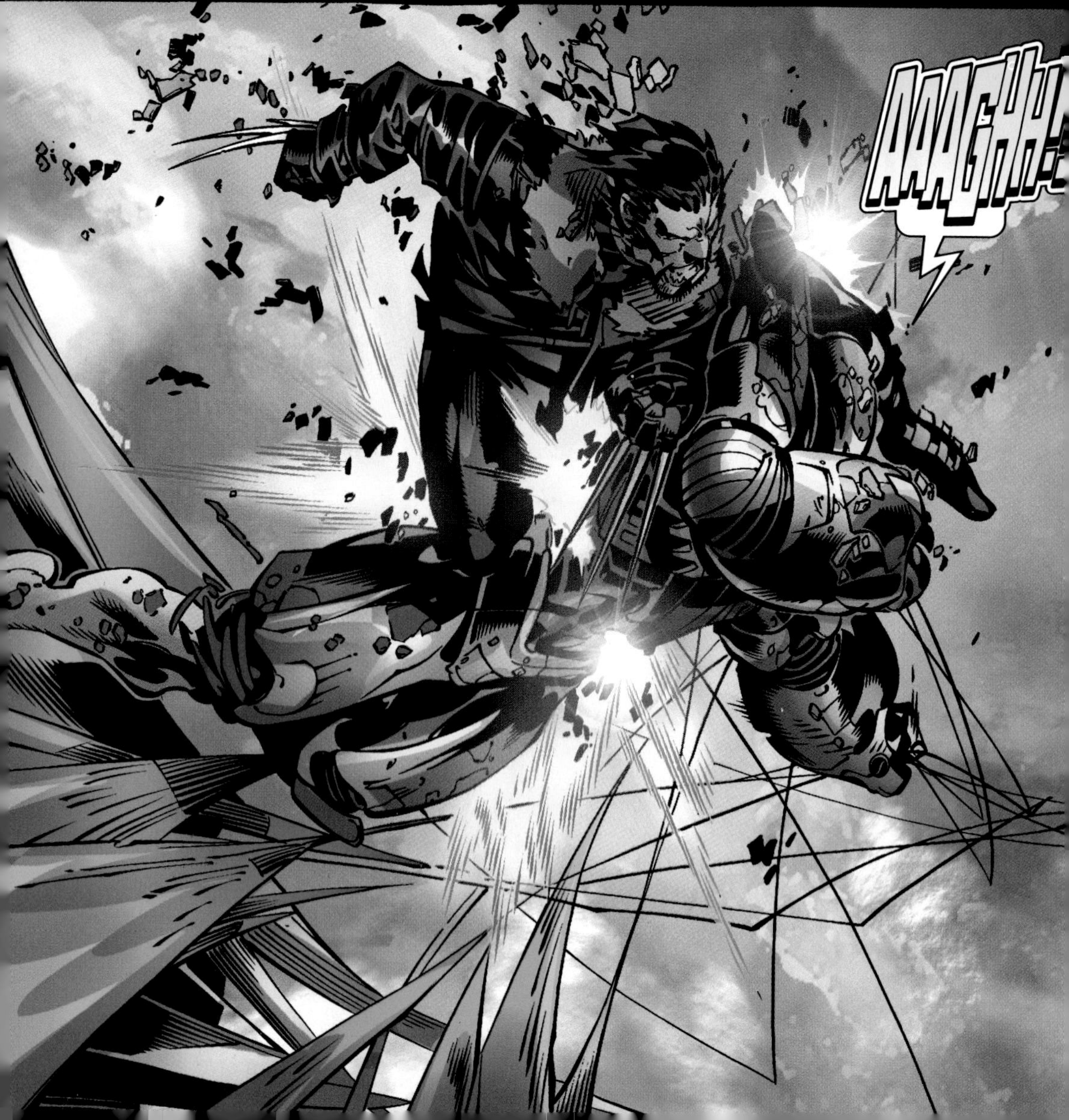

AAAGHH

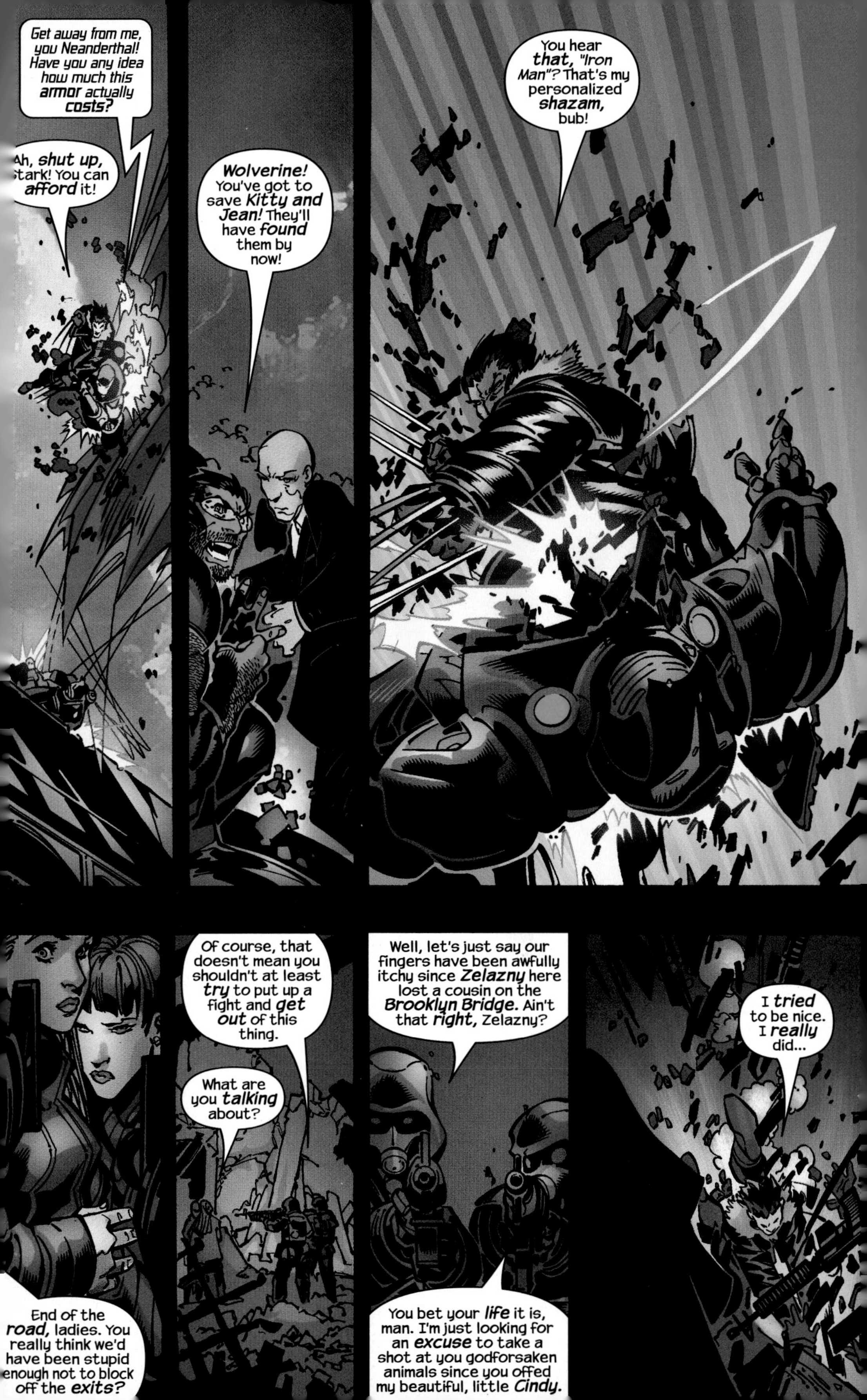
Get away from me, you Neanderthal! Have you any idea how much this armor actually costs?
Ah, shut up, Stark! You can afford it!
Wolverine! You've got to save Kitty and Jean! They'll have found them by now!
You hear that, "Iron Man"? That's my personalized shazam, bub!
End of the road, ladies. You really think we'd have been stupid enough not to block off the exits?
Of course, that doesn't mean you shouldn't at least try to put up a fight and get out of this thing.
What are you talking about?
Well, let's just say our fingers have been awfully itchy since Zelazny here lost a cousin on the Brooklyn Bridge. Ain't that right, Zelazny?
You bet your life it is, man. I'm just looking for an excuse to take a shot at you godforsaken animals since you offed my beautiful, little Cindy.
I tried to be nice. I really did...

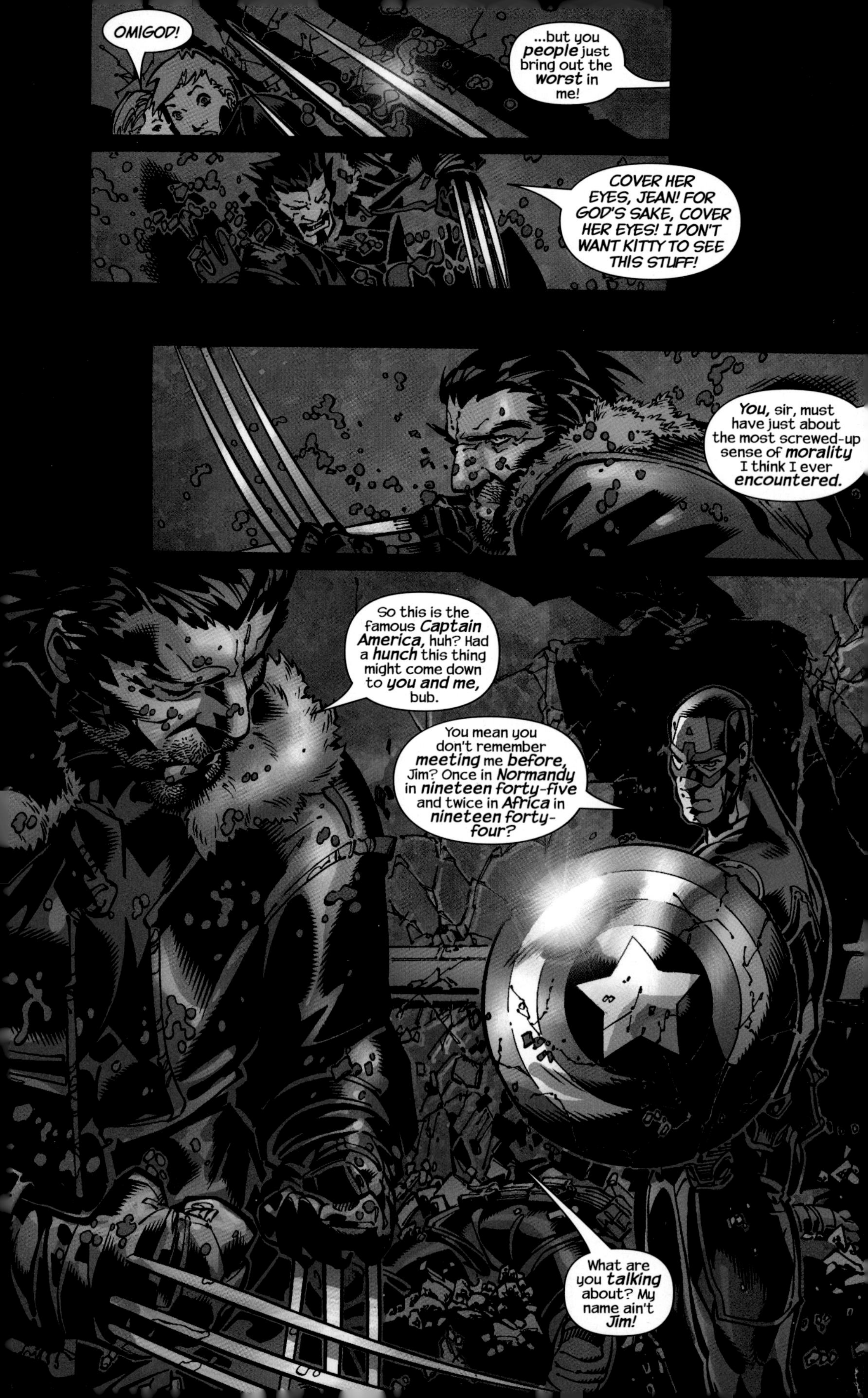

OMIGOD!
...but you people just bring out the worst in me!
COVER HER EYES, JEAN! FOR GOD'S SAKE, COVER HER EYES! I DON'T WANT KITTY TO SEE THIS STUFF!
You, sir, must have just about the most screwed-up sense of morality I think I ever encountered.
So this is the famous Captain America, huh? Had a hunch this thing might come down to you and me, bub.
You mean you don't remember meeting me before, Jim? Once in Normandy in nineteen forty-five and twice in Africa in nineteen forty-four?
What are you talking about? My name ain't Jim!

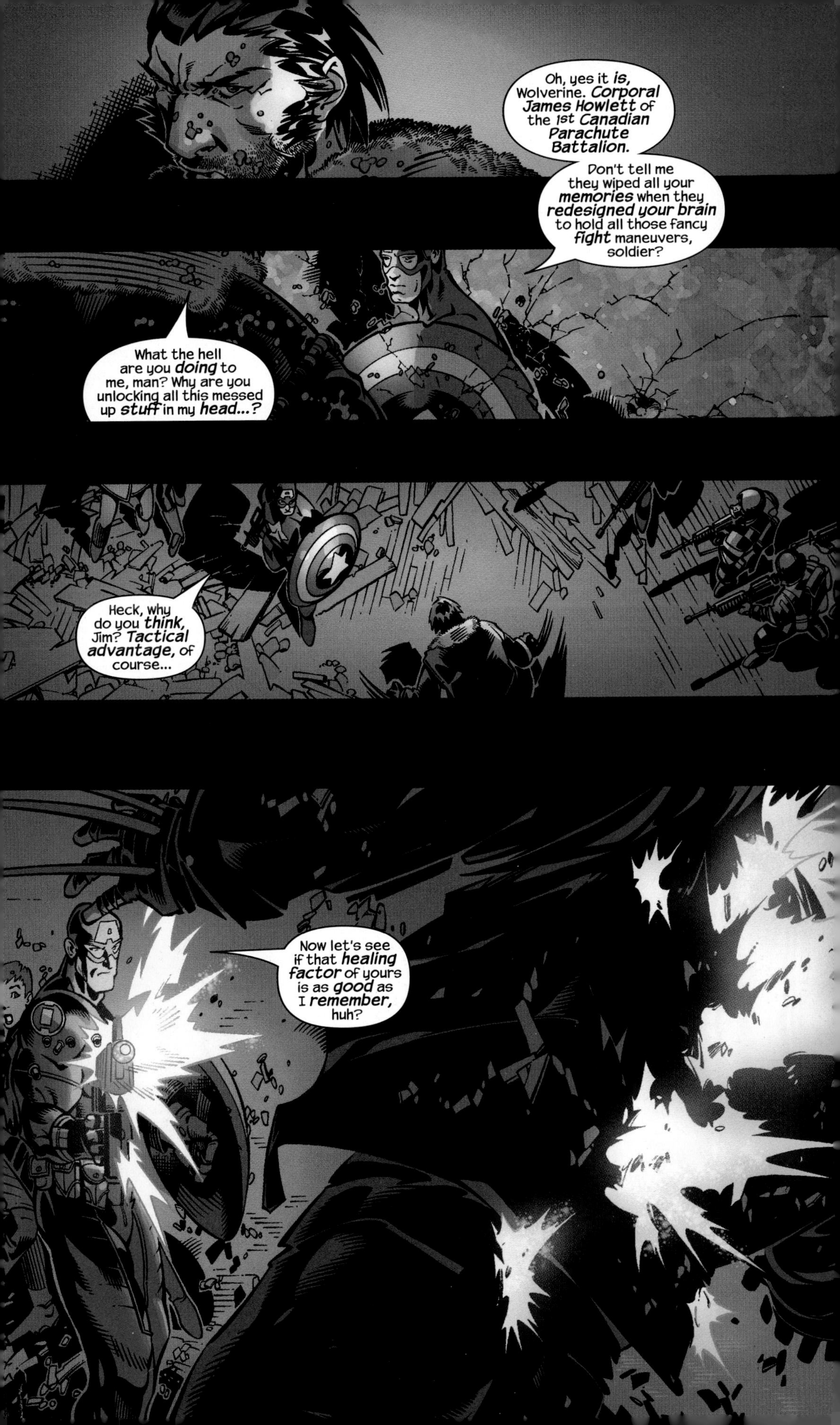
Oh, yes it is, Wolverine. Corporal James Howlett of the 1st Canadian Parachute Battalion.
Don't tell me they wiped all your memories when they redesigned your brain to hold all those fancy fight maneuvers, soldier?
What the hell are you doing to me, man? Why are you unlocking all this messed up stuff in my head...?
Heck, why do you think, Jim? Tactical advantage, of course...
Now let's see if that healing factor of yours is as good as I remember, huh?

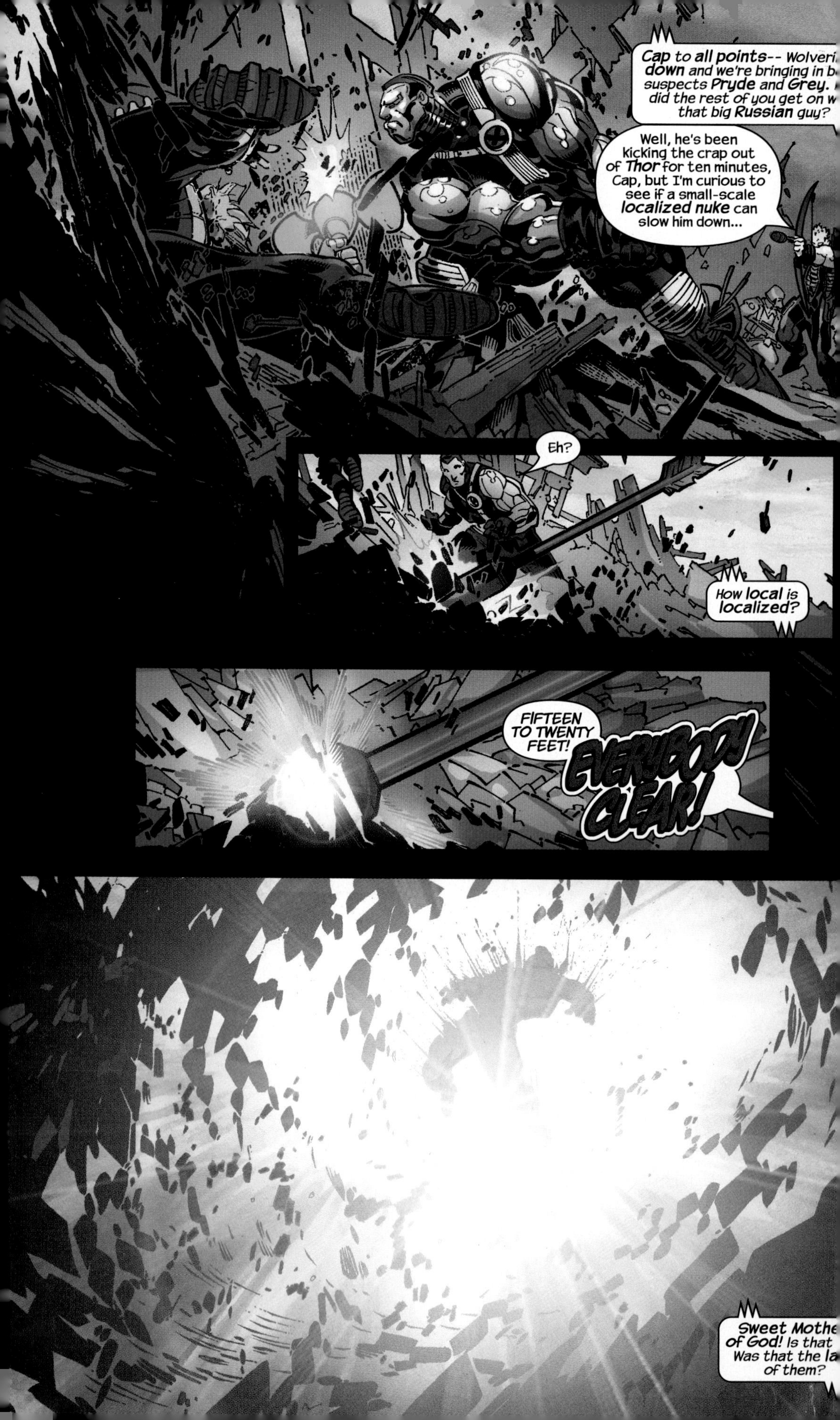

Cap to all points-- Wolveri down and we're bringing in b suspects Pryde and Grey. did the rest of you get on w that big Russian guy?
Well, he's been kicking the crap out of Thor for ten minutes, Cap, but I'm curious to see if a small-scale localized nuke can slow him down...
Eh?
How local is localized?
FIFTEEN TO TWENTY FEET!
EVERYBODY CLEAR!
Sweet Mothe of God! Is that Was that the la of them?

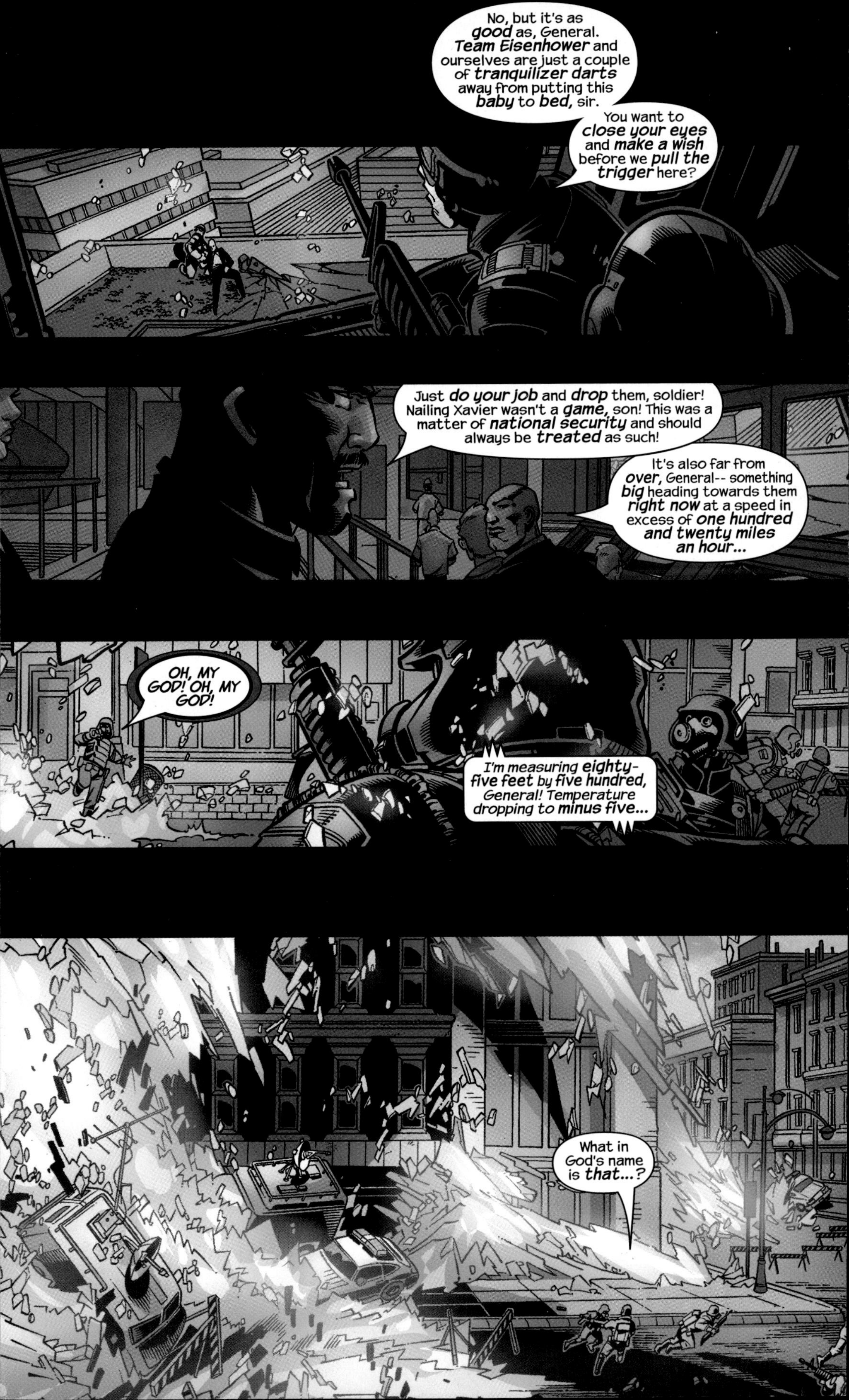

No, but it's as good as, General. Team Eisenhower and ourselves are just a couple of tranquilizer darts away from putting this baby to bed, sir.
You want to close your eyes and make a wish before we pull the trigger here?
Just do your job and drop them, soldier! Nailing Xavier wasn't a game, son! This was a matter of national security and should always be treated as such!
It's also far from over, General-- something big heading towards them right now at a speed in excess of one hundred and twenty miles an hour...
OH, MY GOD! OH, MY GOD!
I'm measuring eighty-five feet by five hundred, General! Temperature dropping to minus five...
What in God's name is that...?

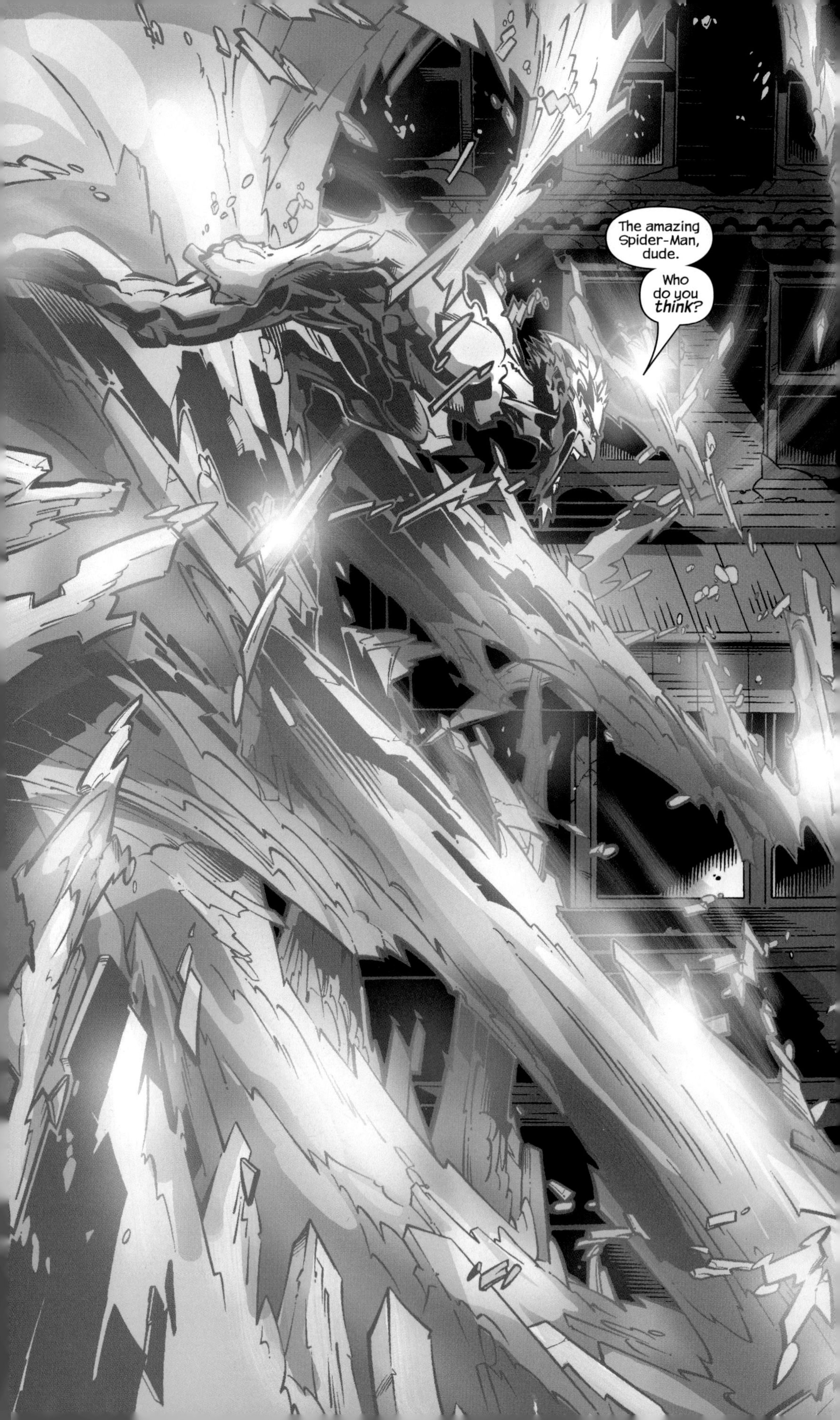
The amazing Spider-Man, dude.
Who do you *think*?

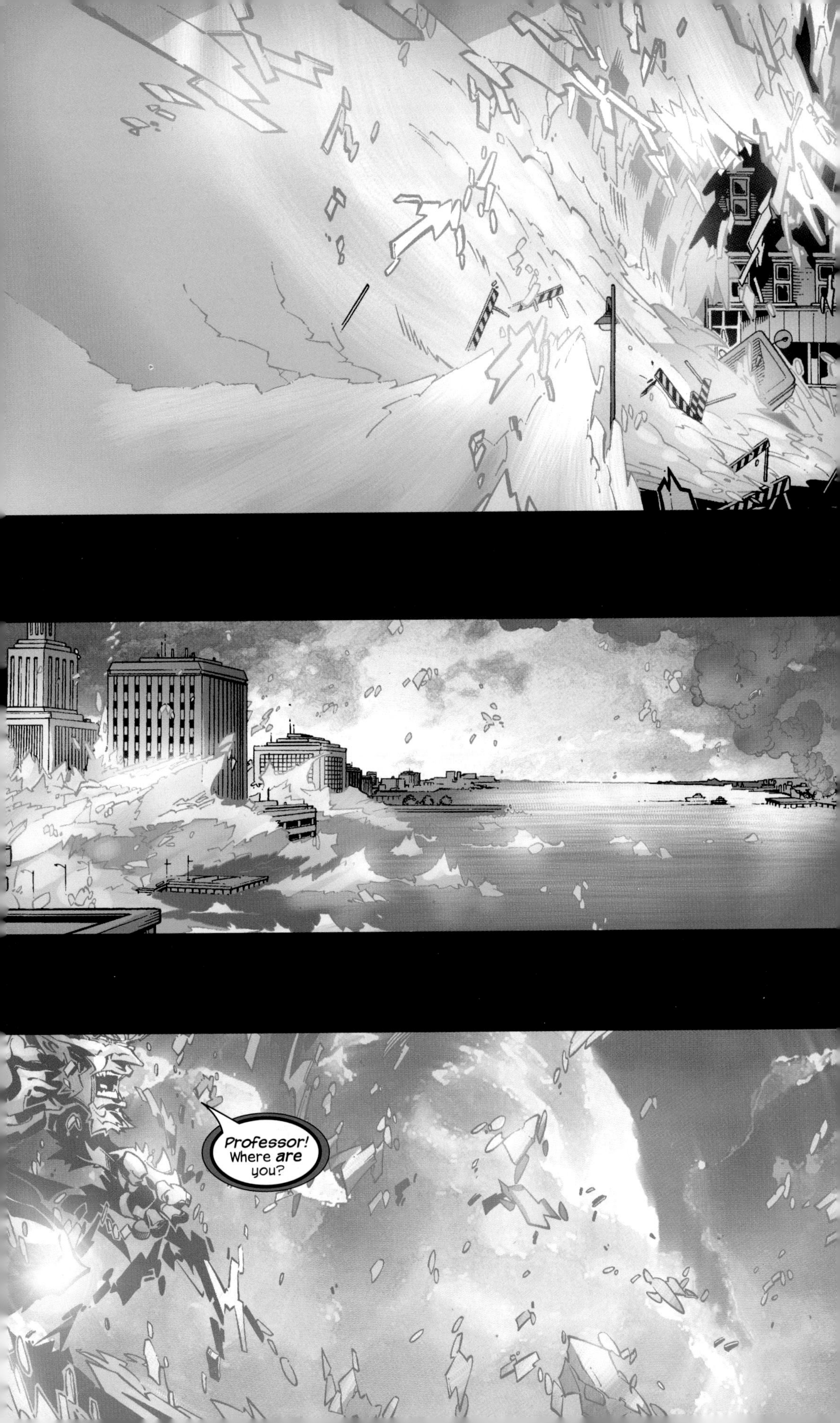
Professor! Where are you?

Technical? What's *happening*?

Beats me, sir. It's like something just switched off *audio* and *video* right across the board.

Professor! Can you *hear* me? Are you *out* there?

Yes, I'm *out* here, Iceman, and you have my thanks for taking out their *neural scramblers*, but I'm afraid there's little time for *catching up*, my X-Men.

As you can see, I've *paralyzed* every *non-mutant mind* within a ten block radius, but they'll breach this soon enough. You must tend to our *injured* and *get out* of here.

But what about *you*, Professor? How are you getting out of here?

My safety is no longer *important*, Jean! All that matters is that *you* escape and your best chance of *doing so* is for me to stay behind!

Now stop *wasting time!* Get Storm and *Wolverine* and *Colossus* out of here before they figure out a way to *close me down*, children!

But how the heck are we supposed to survive out there without *you*, Professor?

JEAN, FOR GOD'S SAKE-- HAVEN'T I TAUGHT YOU ANYTHING ALL THESE MONTHS? JUST CARRY ON WITHOUT ME!

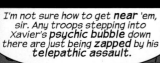

I'm not sure how to get *near* 'em, sir. Any troops stepping into Xavier's *psychic bubble* down there are just being *zapped* by his *telepathic assault*.

Don't *worry* about it, soldier. Lucky for us, I got a *black belt* in thinking ten steps ahead. Ain't that *right*, Mrs. Pym?

Well, at least now I know why you keep your little *secret mutant* on the books.

Target was last seen on a rooftop near *Fifth* and *Market Street*, Wasp. Did you *hear* that? I said Charles Xavier was *last seen* near...

Fifth and *Market!* I *got* him, Nick, but I can't say I'm especially *pleased* with myself about this...

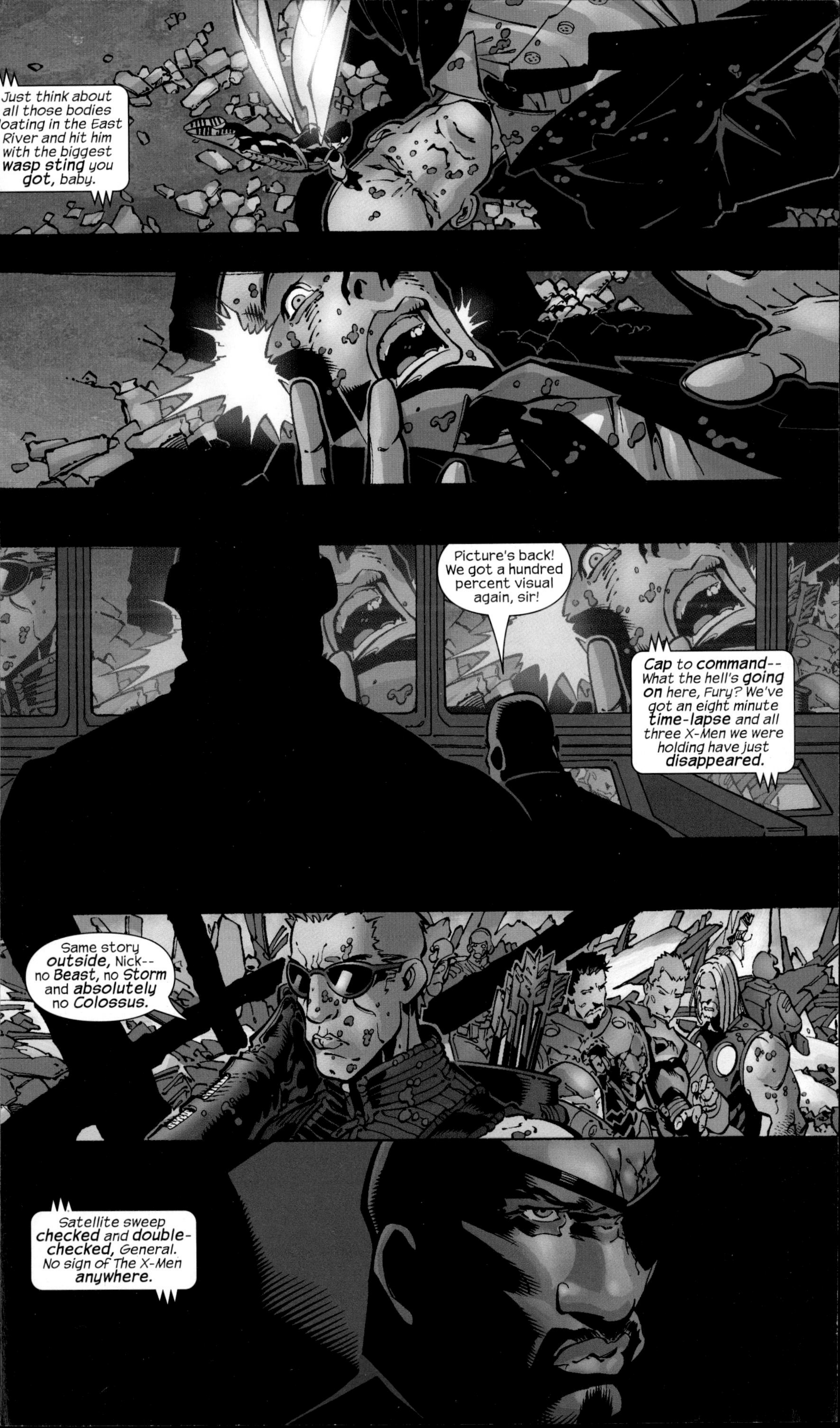

Just think about all those bodies floating in the East River and hit him with the biggest wasp sting you got, baby.
Picture's back! We got a hundred percent visual again, sir!
Cap to command-- What the hell's going on here, Fury? We've got an eight minute time-lapse and all three X-Men we were holding have just disappeared.
Same story outside, Nick-- no Beast, no Storm and absolutely no Colossus.
Satellite sweep checked and double-checked, General. No sign of The X-Men anywhere.

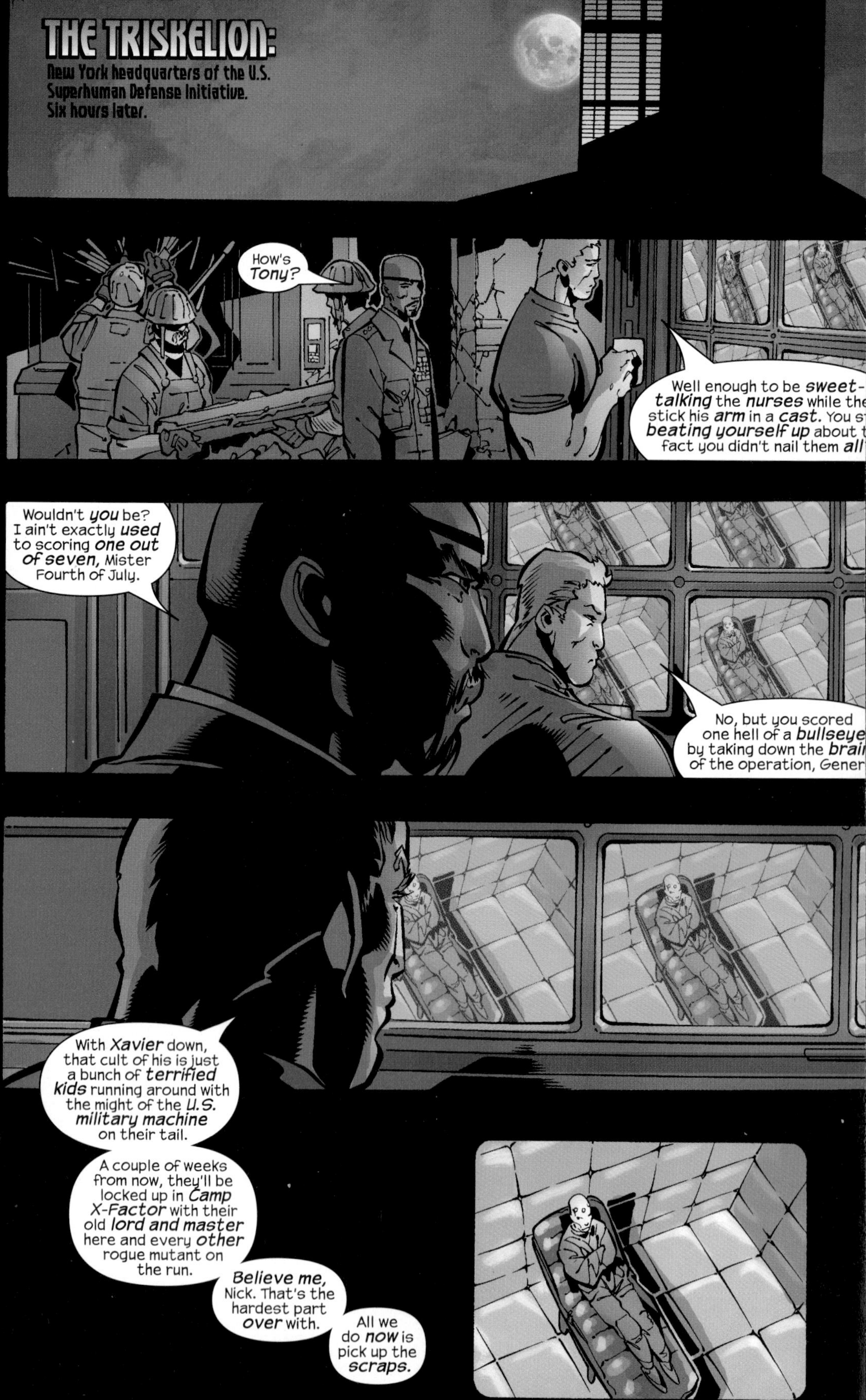
THE TRISKELION:
New York headquarters of the U.S. Superhuman Defense Initiative. Six hours later.
How's Tony?
Well enough to be sweet-talking the nurses while the stick his arm in a cast. You st beating yourself up about t fact you didn't nail them all
Wouldn't you be? I ain't exactly used to scoring one out of seven, Mister Fourth of July.
No, but you scored one hell of a bullseye by taking down the brai of the operation, Gener
With Xavier down, that cult of his is just a bunch of terrified kids running around with the might of the U.S. military machine on their tail.
A couple of weeks from now, they'll be locked up in Camp X-Factor with their old lord and master here and every other rogue mutant on the run.
Believe me, Nick. That's the hardest part over with.
All we do now is pick up the scraps.

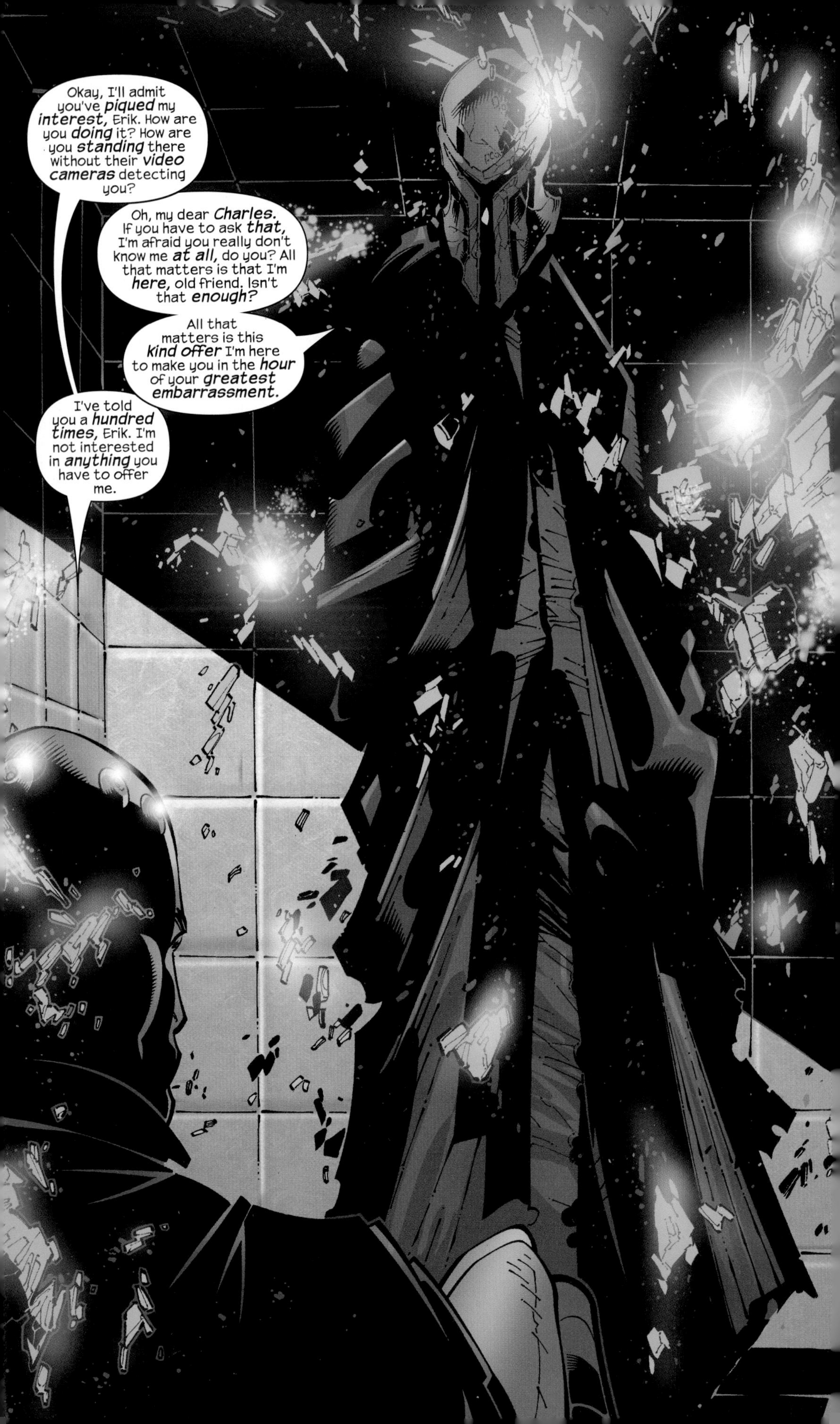
Okay, I'll admit you've piqued my interest, Erik. How are you doing it? How are you standing there without their video cameras detecting you?
Oh, my dear Charles. If you have to ask that, I'm afraid you really don't know me at all, do you? All that matters is that I'm here, old friend. Isn't that enough?
All that matters is this kind offer I'm here to make you in the hour of your greatest embarrassment.
I've told you a hundred times, Erik. I'm not interested in anything you have to offer me.

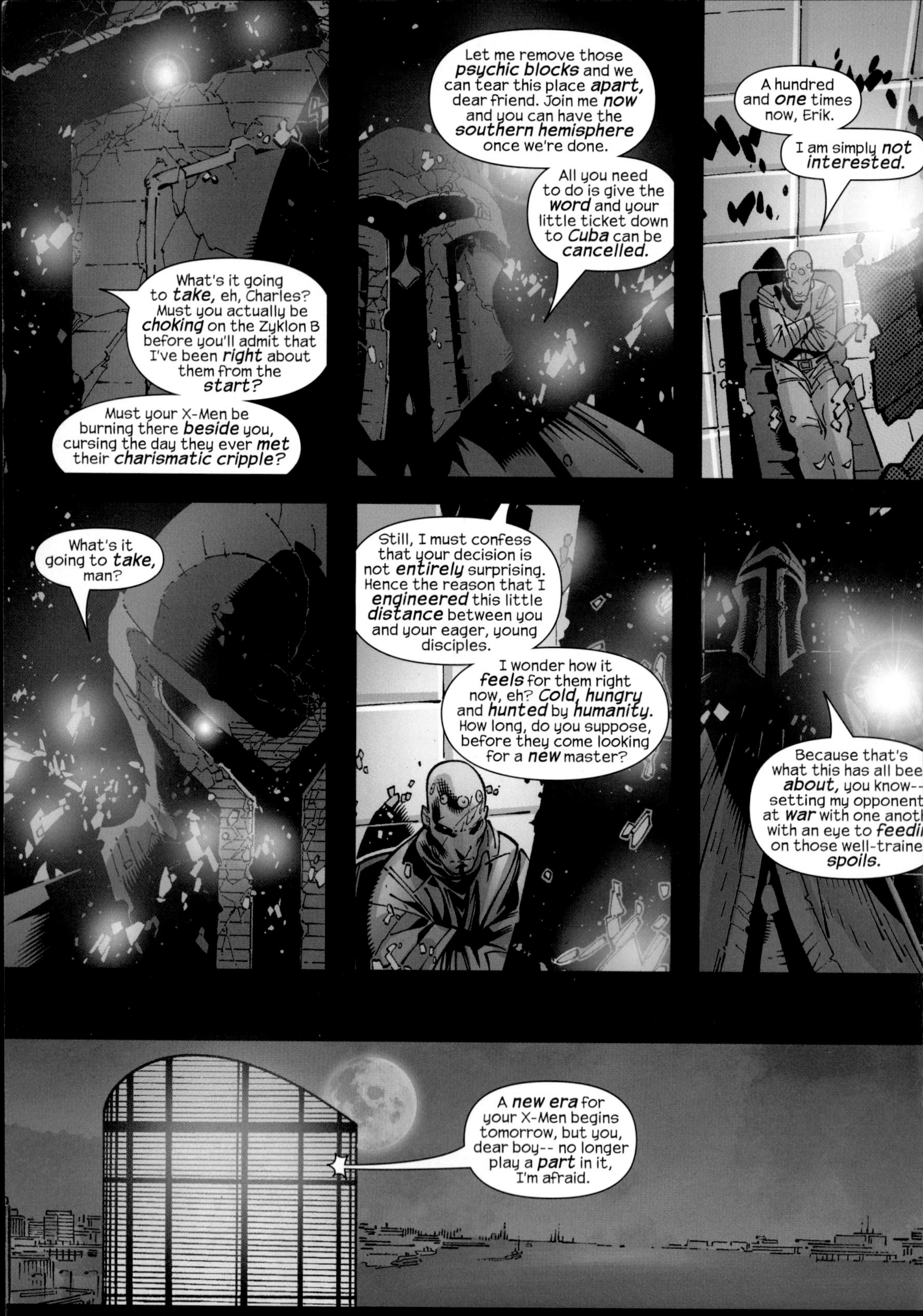
What's it going to take, eh, Charles? Must you actually be choking on the Zyklon B before you'll admit that I've been right about them from the start?
Must your X-Men be burning there beside you, cursing the day they ever met their charismatic cripple?
Let me remove those psychic blocks and we can tear this place apart, dear friend. Join me now and you can have the southern hemisphere once we're done.
All you need to do is give the word and your little ticket down to Cuba can be cancelled.
A hundred and one times now, Erik.
I am simply not interested.
What's it going to take, man?
Still, I must confess that your decision is not entirely surprising. Hence the reason that I engineered this little distance between you and your eager, young disciples.
I wonder how it feels for them right now, eh? Cold, hungry and hunted by humanity. How long, do you suppose, before they come looking for a new master?
Because that's what this has all bee about, you know-- setting my opponent at war with one anoth with an eye to feedi on those well-traine spoils.
A new era for your X-Men begins tomorrow, but you, dear boy-- no longer play a part in it, I'm afraid.

TO BE CONTINUED IN ULTIMATE X-MEN VOL. VI: RETURN OF THE KING

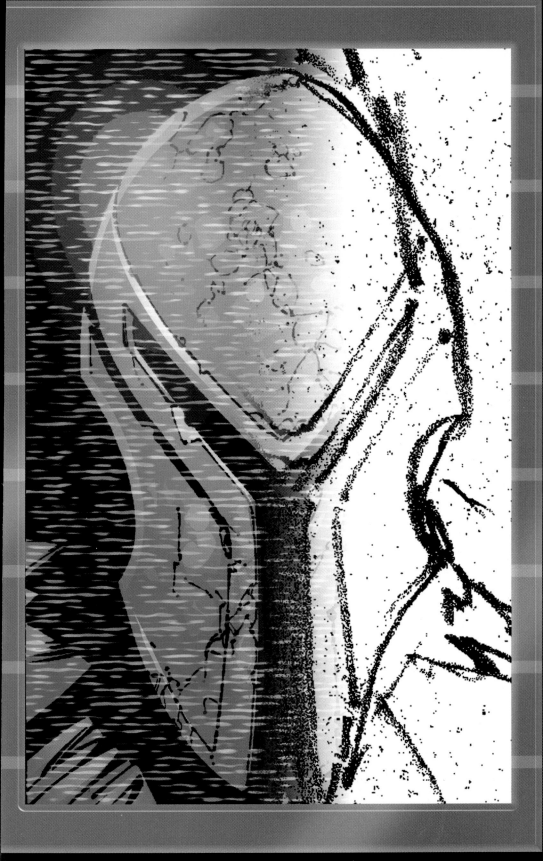

Chris Bachalo
Sketchbook

Magneto

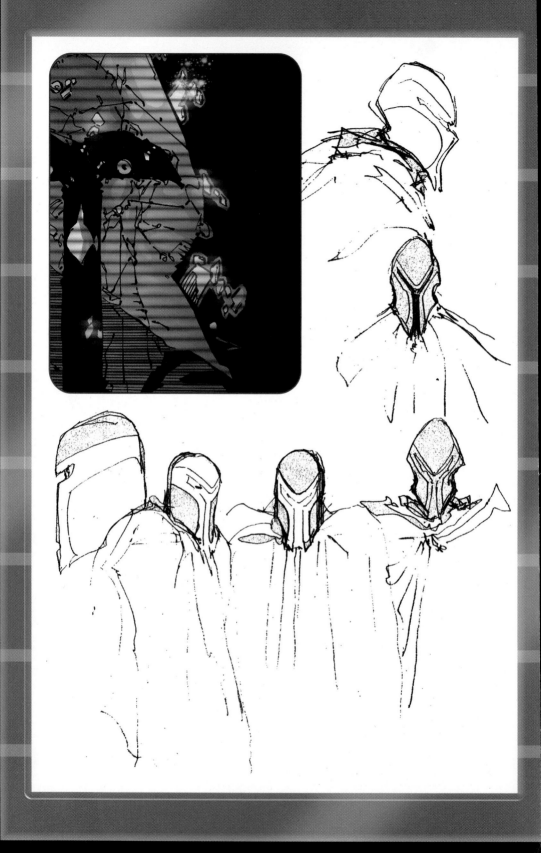

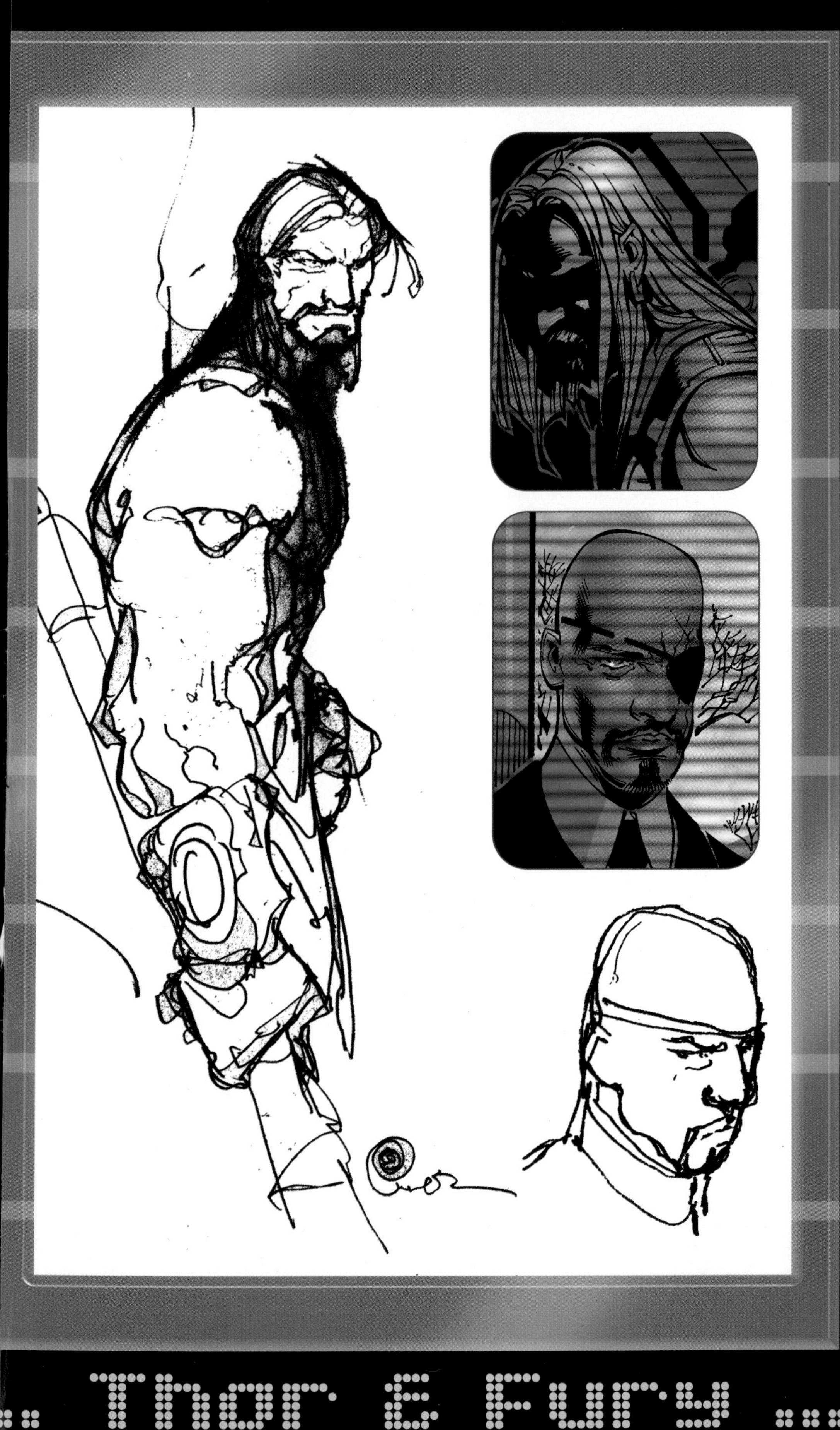

Thor & Fury

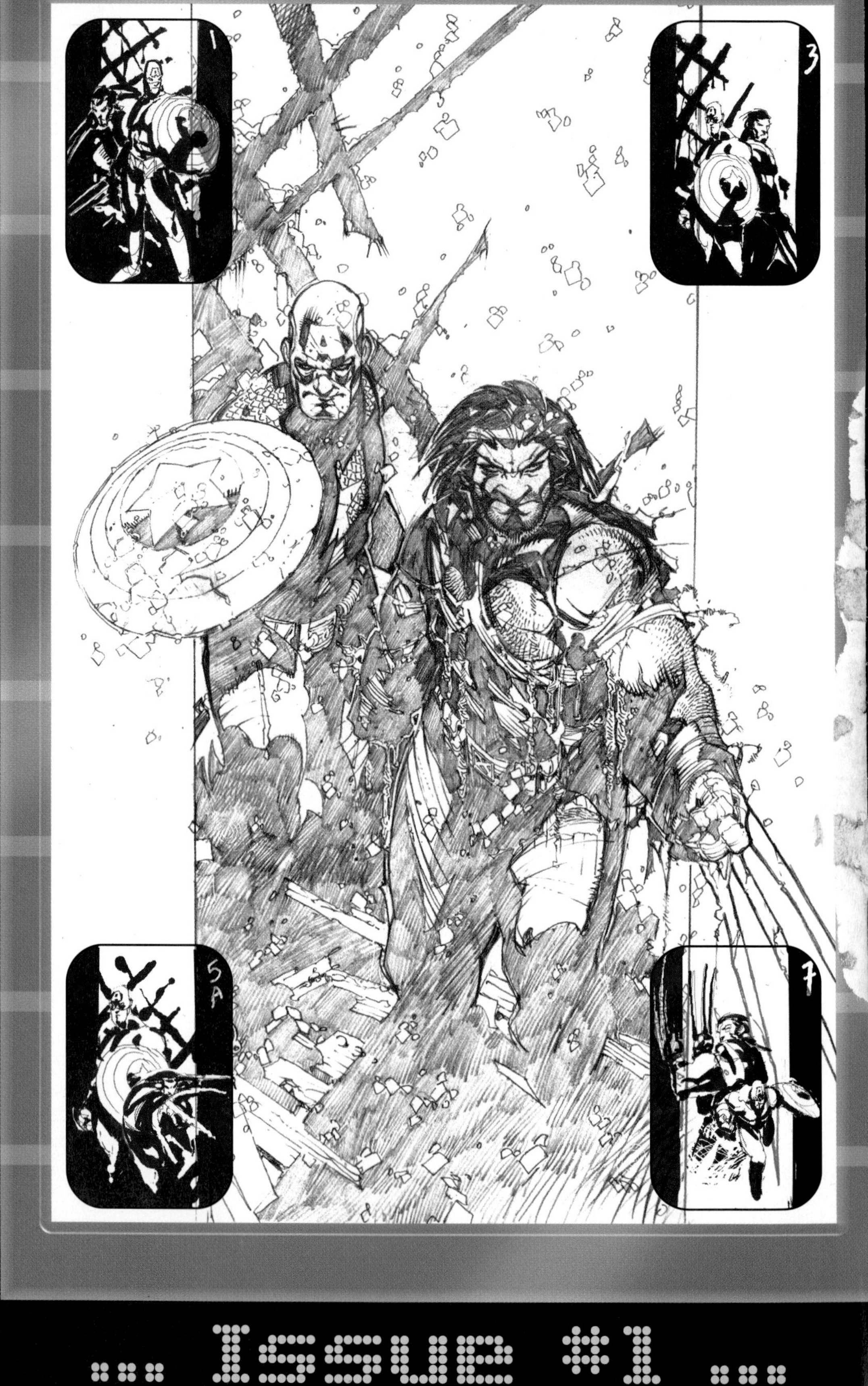
1
3
5A
7

... Issue #1 ...

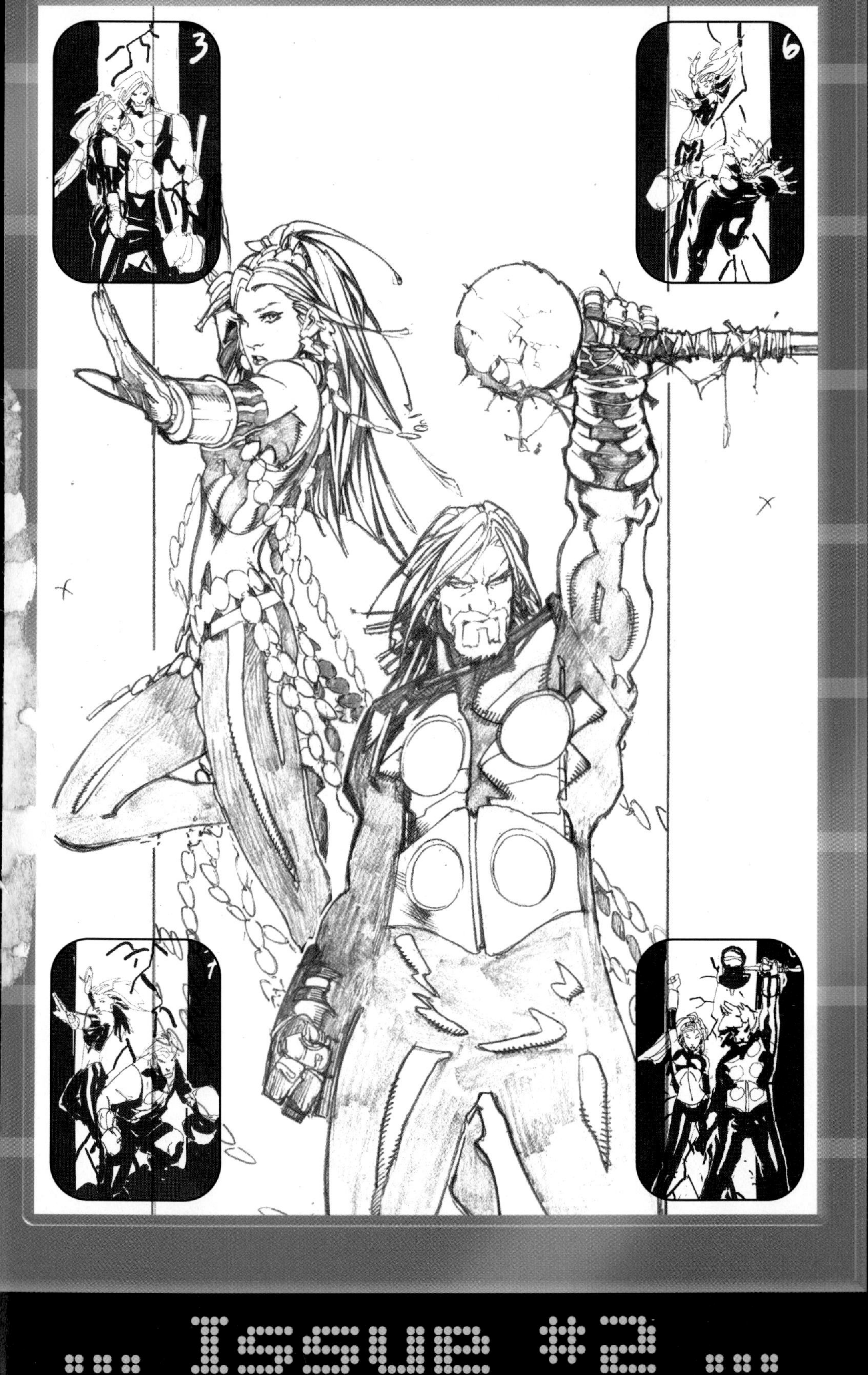
3
6

Issue #2

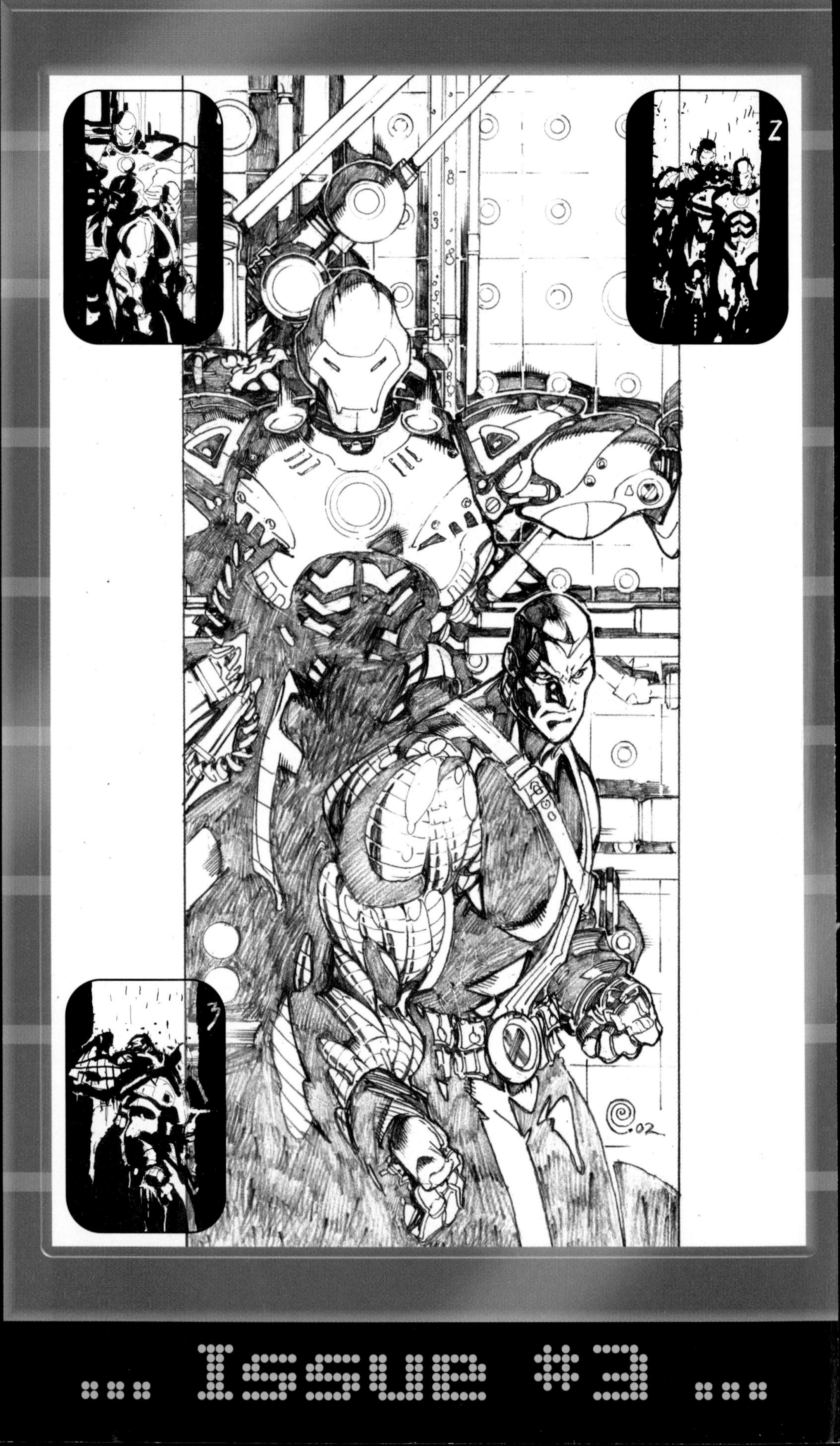

Issue #3

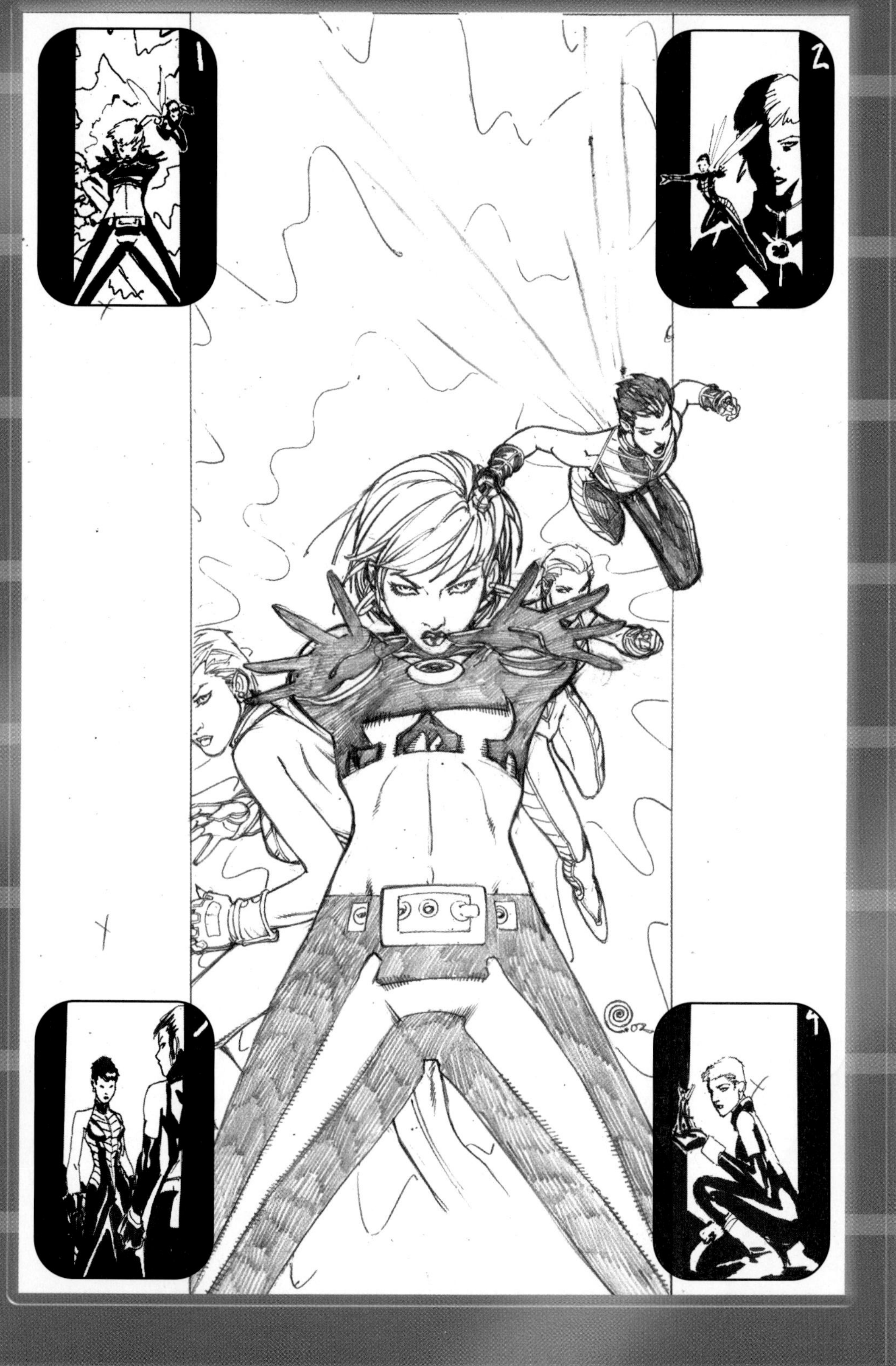

... Issue #4 ...

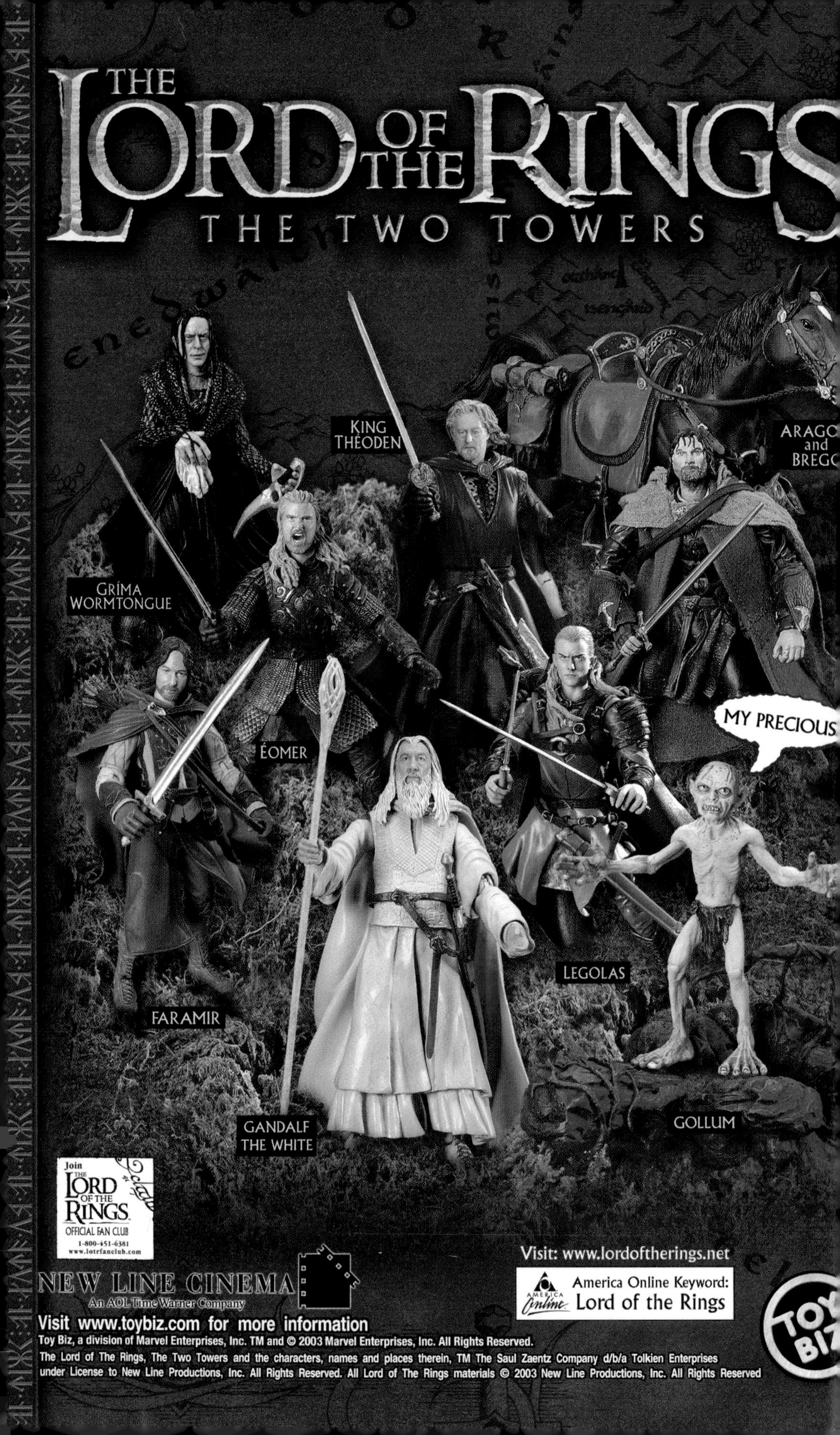
THE LORD OF THE RINGS
THE TWO TOWERS
KING THÉODEN
ARAGO and BREGO
GRÍMA WORMTONGUE
ÉOMER
MY PRECIOUS
FARAMIR
LEGOLAS
GANDALF THE WHITE
GOLLUM
Join THE LORD OF THE RINGS OFFICIAL FAN CLUB
1-800-451-6381
www.lotrfanclub.com
Visit: www.lordoftherings.net
America Online Keyword: Lord of the Rings
NEW LINE CINEMA
An AOL Time Warner Company
Visit www.toybiz.com for more information
Toy Biz, a division of Marvel Enterprises, Inc. TM and © 2003 Marvel Enterprises, Inc. All Rights Reserved.
The Lord of The Rings, The Two Towers and the characters, names and places therein, TM The Saul Zaentz Company d/b/a Tolkien Enterprises under License to New Line Productions, Inc. All Rights Reserved. All Lord of The Rings materials © 2003 New Line Productions, Inc. All Rights Reserved
TOY BIZ

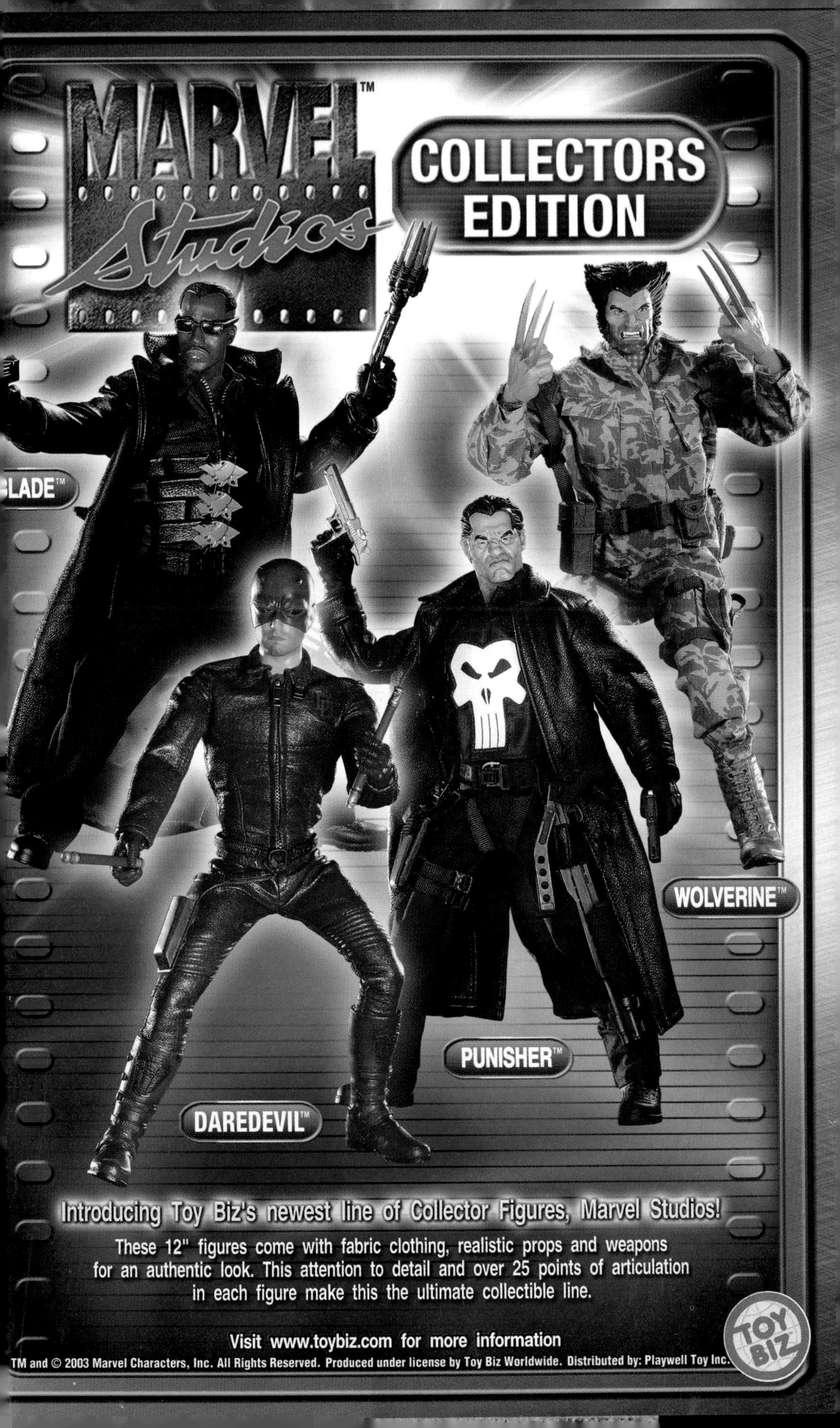

MARVEL™ Studios
COLLECTORS EDITION
LADE™
WOLVERINE™
PUNISHER™
DAREDEVIL™
Introducing Toy Biz's newest line of Collector Figures, Marvel Studios!
These 12" figures come with fabric clothing, realistic props and weapons for an authentic look. This attention to detail and over 25 points of articulation in each figure make this the ultimate collectible line.
Visit www.toybiz.com for more information
TM and © 2003 Marvel Characters, Inc. All Rights Reserved. Produced under license by Toy Biz Worldwide. Distributed by: Playwell Toy Inc.
TOY BIZ

HULK

TWIST 'N SLAM HULK
WITH COLLAPSIBLE BRICK WALL!

RARRGHH

BRUCE BANNER
TRANSFORMING CHAMBER
WITH GAMMA GLOWING ACTION!

RAGE 'N ROAR HULK
WITH REAL WORKING SOUND!

Look for the
entire line of Hulk Movie
action figures and accessories from Toy Biz

3 1191 00727 7957